WJEC/Eduqas **GCSE Drama**

Designing Drama

Lighting, Sound, Set & Costume Design

Sue Shewring

Published in 2021 by Illuminate Publishing Ltd,
PO Box 1160, Cheltenham, Gloucestershire GL50 9RW

Orders: Please visit www.illuminatepublishing.com
or email sales@illuminatepublishing.com

British Library Cataloguing-in-Publication Data

A catalogue record of this book is available from the British Library.

ISBN 978-1-912820-52-8

Printed by Severn, Gloucester

05.21

The publisher's policy is to use papers that are natural, renewable and recyclable products made from wood grown in sustainable forests. The logging and manufacturing processes are expected to conform to the environmental regulations in the country of origin.

Editor: Roanne Charles, abc Editorial
Design and layout and Cover design: EMC Design Ltd
Cover photograph: ton koene / Alamy Stock Photo

Text acknowledgements

Extracts from *Collected Grimm Tales* by Carol Ann Duffy. Published by Faber & Faber. Copyright © Carol Ann Duffy. Reproduced by permission of the author c/o Rogers, Coleridge & White Ltd., 20 Powis Mews, London W11 1JN.

The author would like to thank specialist consultants without whose knowledgable input this book would not have been possible:

 COSTUME   **Fi Carrington**

 **LIGHTING AND SOUND**   **Brent Lees, BCL Lighting Design**   BCL lighting design   facebook.com/BCL-Lighting-Design; Info@bcl-lightingdesign.co.uk

 SET   **Ali McCaw (BA Hons) Theatre Design**

CONTENTS

EVERYTHING BUT THE ACTING

DESIGN IN DRAMA AND THEATRE

This book is about everything that happens on the stage except for the acting!

Designing Drama will help you to costume actors and give them a set to perform on. It will guide you through the process that fills their world with sound and floods the stage with light.

More than that, you will come to understand how the work of the theatre designer brings the world of the stage to life for the most important people in the theatre – the audience.

Whether you are designing sound for a devised piece of drama, or costume for a scripted one, this book offers practical advice and activities to help you develop your knowledge, understanding and creativity.

If you are a performer at heart, this book will help you to master the knowledge and skills needed to write about design in the exam. You will need a good level of knowledge for all the design elements that exam questions could be about. Performance and design work hand in hand to create the harmonious world of the stage. *Designing Drama* will help you to understand how to be part of this creative process from every angle.

HOW TO GET THE MOST FROM THIS BOOK

Practical guides to design roles

These chapters introduce you to each design role and provide practical guidance, advice and activities to help you through the design process. They will give you a good grounding in your chosen design specialism, enabling you to develop your skills, boost your confidence and explore your creativity.

Drama course content

Refer back to the practical chapters as you move on to the chapters that cover design for each assessed component of the course:

- Unit/Component 1: Devising Theatre (Chapter 5)
- Unit/Component 2: Performing Theatre / Performing from a Text (Chapter 6)
- Unit/Component 3: Interpreting Theatre (Chapter 7).

Features of the book

In order to highlight important information, activities and assessment objectives, we have included some special features:

 FOCUS

A note to summarise the main content of the section.

 ASSESSMENT CHECK

Details from the WJEC or Eduqas specification documents to show you which elements of the assessment criteria the guidance and activities will help you to achieve.

 SIGNPOST

These direct you to supporting content from other sections that you are likely to need before you attempt the activities.

TASKS

Activities and exercises to help you learn, practise and develop your design skills.

 DESIGN TIPS

Quick ideas, things to remember and helpful tips from professional theatre design.

 LOOK HERE

A guide to the most suitable sections of support from other chapters.

 This symbol indicates that there is a free download available at www.illuminatepublishing.com. Simply navigate to the product page for this book.

Important technical drama terms are highlighted in blue and collected in a Glossary at the back of the book.

We have also included some sample exam questions and example student-style answers. These will give you an idea of the type of questions that will come up in the exam and how some students might have responded.

In addition, the notes are illustrated by diagrams, sketches, plans and photographs to help you visualise the practical elements of theatre that you can achieve as a Drama designer.

HOW YOU WILL BE ASSESSED

UNITS/COMPONENTS AND ASSESSMENT OBJECTIVES

The three units/components of the WJEC/Eduqas GCSE Drama course are:

1 **Devising Theatre** (assessed by your teacher)

2 **Performing Theatre / Performing from a Text** (assessed by a visiting examiner)

3 **Interpreting Theatre** (written exam).

For these units/components, the assessment objectives, total marks and percentages of the overall GCSE are:

Unit/ Component	Assessment objectives and percentages				Total marks	Overall percentage in GCSE
	AO1: Create and develop ideas to communicate meaning for theatrical performance.	**AO2:** Apply theatrical skills to realise artistic intentions in live performance.	**AO3:** Demonstrate knowledge and understanding of how drama and theatre is developed and performed.	**AO4:** Analyse and evaluate their own work and the work of others.		
Unit/Component 1: Devising Theatre	20%	10%	0	10%	60	40%
Unit/Component 2: Performing Theatre / Performing from a Text	0	20%	0	0	60	20%
Unit/Component 3: Interpreting Theatre	0	0	30%	10%	60	40%

PRACTICAL UNITS/COMPONENTS

You can work practically as a designer for Unit/Component 1 and/or 2, and demonstrate your knowledge and understanding of design in the exam for Unit/Component 3.

Your teacher will assess your work for Unit/Component 1, and external examiners will standardise the marking by looking at examples of videos and portfolios.

For Unit/Component 2, a visiting examiner will assess your work in performance.

Unit/Component 1:
Devising Theatre

As a designer, you will work as part of a group to create, develop and produce an original piece of drama, devised from a stimulus. This is assessed in three parts.

A devised design realisation

This is worth 15 marks and covers AO2. For the choice of the four design roles, you need to produce:

LIGHTING
At least five different lighting states for the performance

SOUND
At least five sound cues for the performance.

SET
One actual set for the performance, including props and appropriate set dressing

COSTUME
Full costumes, hair and make-up for **two different** characters

As part of the supporting evidence, you must also submit:

Lighting: Cue sheets and a lighting plot

Sound: Cue sheets and a sound plot

Set: A set model, a ground plan and photographs of the set

Costume: Final design sketches/photographs of costume, hair and make-up.

The portfolio

Your portfolio should cover your creation and development and your analysis and evaluation of this process. It is assessed against AO1, which is worth 30 marks.

The portfolio must include evidence of your 'research, creation and development of ideas'. This evidence should focus on three stages:

- How your ideas have been researched, created and developed in response to the stimulus
- How ideas from the chosen practitioner/genre have been incorporated in the piece to communicate meaning
- How ideas have been developed, amended and refined during the development of the devised piece.

For each stage, you need to provide approximately 250 words, along with illustrative material. This could include:

- sketches
- photographs
- ground plans
- diagrams
- storyboards
- mood boards
- sections of script
- digital media, including brief recordings of sections of a rehearsal or other material, such as sound clips.

You can produce your portfolio as:

- a blog
- an audio-visual recording
- an audio commentary on the illustrative material.

You will also write an evaluation of your final design in performance. It is worth 15 marks for AO4. You will have 90 minutes, under supervision, and can have two sides of A4 bullet-point notes with you.

As well as identifying your chosen stimulus and practitioner or genre, there will be three sections to your evaluation. You are required to **analyse** and **evaluate**:

1 the realisation of your design in the final performance

2 how your own design skills contributed to the effectiveness of the performance

3 your individual contribution to the performance, including how well you fulfilled your initial aims and objectives (referring to your stimulus and practitioner/genre).

Unit/Component 2:
Performing Theatre / Performing from a Text

In your group, you will interpret a playscript. You will prepare and perform **two key extracts** from the text. Your teacher can guide and support you; a visiting examiner will assess you.

This component covers AO2 and is worth 60 marks.

Practical design requirements
For the choice of the four design roles, you need to produce:

👆 **Lighting:** At least **four** different lighting states

🎵 **Sound:** At least **four** different sound **cues**

🔨 **Set: One** set, which is dressed and includes props

👕 **Costume: One** full costume with hair and make-up.

Artistic intentions
You must also produce a written explanation of approximately 150 words that outlines:

- how you intended to **interpret** the scenes

- how the text was edited to create the final performance.

THE WRITTEN EXAM

Unit/Component 3: Interpreting Theatre
There is a written exam at the end of the course that lasts 1 hour 30 minutes.

Section A: Set text

This assesses AO3 and is worth 45 marks.

As part of Section A, you will be asked to describe and justify how you would use given design elements in a performance of your chosen set text. These design-based questions are worth 18 marks.

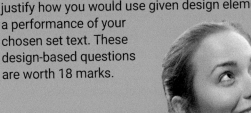

Section B: Live theatre review

This assesses AO4 and is worth 15 marks.

Section B gives you the choice of writing about an element of performance or a given element of design from a live theatre production you have seen.

You will reflect on your experience as an audience member. This will include analysis and evaluation of production style and how a design element was used to create meaning.

FOCUS

- How design elements enhance theatre.
- A brief guide to the design process.

UNDERSTANDING DESIGN IN DRAMA AND THEATRE

THEATRE DESIGN

The focus of this book is design: the theatrical elements of set, costume, lighting and sound. Often known as stagecraft, design covers all the creative, non-performing aspects of staging a theatrical production for an audience.

As a student of Drama, you might have experienced the thrill that comes from putting on a costume or feeling the lights come up on you at the beginning of a scene. While actors wearing simple black outfits can create powerful drama on their own, the integration of performance and theatrical design generally lifts the experience to another, higher, level.

Working in design

Theatre design has evolved over the centuries, and the roles of the designers are as necessary in today's professional theatre as those of director and actor. If theatre design and the technical elements of lighting, sound, costume or set excite you – and you don't mind the travelling that is often involved – careers in the backstage elements of theatre are certainly to be found.

Many colleges, universities and drama schools have courses for designers and technicians that you could investigate to follow on from your Drama courses in school. In addition, the skills required for theatre lighting, costume, make-up and sound apply equally well to the music, television, film and festival industries. These are interesting careers with potentially more employment opportunities compared with acting for example.

> **Fi Carrington, a freelance wardrobe supervisor and costume designer, says:**
>
> *I trained on a theatre costume design course and now do some teaching on a degree course. Most of the students don't have too much difficulty getting freelance work in theatre, film and television.*

The role of design in drama

The role of a theatre designer involves working with a director and other designers to produce workable design ideas for a drama production. There is usually an element of research to be done in relation to the script and historical **periods** and contexts, for example. The designer and director will eventually agree final, budgeted designs and then begin the creation of these in terms of:

- making costumes and sets
- setting plans for rigging, operating and cueing lighting and sounds.

Adaptations to these final designs might be needed as the performance grows closer and issues crop up during rehearsals.

The design process: rehearsal and performance

The technical rehearsal

An important moment in the design process is the technical rehearsal. Here, the performers 'walk' through a complete performance during which they will need to stop, re-perform and skip sections of the play as design details are finalised. This is known as working **cue to cue**, meaning that each sound and lighting cue is covered and repeated as necessary. This happens until the designers and technicians are confident that the production can run smoothly and maintain the desired artistic intentions. Set and costume changes will also be run through.

Technical rehearsals are notoriously long and taxing for all those involved, but no professional or amateur production can be satisfactorily achieved without one – or sometimes two!

Dress rehearsals

The dress rehearsal is a designer's opportunity to test their design in real time. Lighting and sound designers can practise operating their designs following the script. This means that they can prepare for and then activate their plotted cues. Meanwhile, costume and set designers will often sit in the auditorium with the director, taking notes on what has and hasn't worked well, so that problems can be addressed before the first performance.

Work during the performance

Once a show or run, if there are multiple performances, is underway, there is still work to be done. Costumes have to be cleaned and maintained (although this is done by wardrobe maintenance or dressers in professional theatre). Similarly, sets (including props and set dressings) and technical equipment need to be checked and maintained.

Stage management

In charge of this whole process is the **stage manager**, who co-ordinates all the backstage and technical elements during rehearsals and performances. The stage manager works closely with designers and technicians as well as performers, controlling the production. If you continue your involvement in theatre after your course, stage management is a very important role that could interest you.

Practical design and the exam

Practical components and the written exam are closely related!

- Try to see all your practical work in Components 1 and 2 as preparation for the written exam, where you will have opportunities to use your developing knowledge and skills.
- Even if you are working as a performer for one or both of the practical components, be aware of the design work and opportunities for all the design elements: lighting, costume, sound and set.

TASK I.1

In your next practical drama lesson, where an improvisation or piece of scripted performance is shown, decide on the following in your group:

- What costumes would enhance your performance?
- How could set be used to add meaning and interest to the performance?
- How might you use coloured stage lighting or spotlights to help focus the audience?
- Can you plan one sound cue to emphasise a significant moment in the performance?

The proscenium arch gives a picture-frame effect above and on each side of an end-on stage.

STAGE SPACE AND SPATIAL RELATIONSHIPS

All types of theatre designers need to create their designs with close regard to the relationship between acting areas and audience. This relationship will partly depend on how a stage or performance area is arranged.

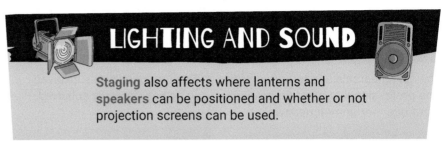

LIGHTING AND SOUND

Staging also affects where lanterns and **speakers** can be positioned and whether or not projection screens can be used.

SET

The **stage configuration** is critically important as it affects the type and size of scenery that can be placed in and behind the acting areas.

COSTUME

Varying amount of detail is required, depending on the proximity of the actors to the audience.

Stage configurations

You need to be aware of the different types of stage configurations and the advantages they offer and difficulties they present for theatre designers.

Proscenium arch stage

Possible advantages

- Typically Victorian staging: highly appropriate for classical or period plays in a traditional style. Musicals are often staged on prosceniums.
- Creates an intimate acting area.
- Usually includes a small apron area in front of the curtain that can be used for performance during scene changes.
- Gives the audience a sense of peeking into another world.
- Audience seating and/or the stage is often **raked** to improve sightlines.
- Backdrops, projections and large pieces of scenery work well.
- Straightforward in terms of lighting and sound design.
- Detail in costume and set is not crucial as the audience is at a distance.
- Footlights work well and offer additional lighting angles.

Potential problems

- Sightlines are problematic as the side panels of the arch might obscure parts of the stage for some of the audience.
- Pillared seating areas can also reduce visibility for the audience.
- If the stage is raked, anything on wheels must be wedged or have brakes.
- Many auditoriums have raised circles, which means that some of the audience is distant and almost above the acting area.

- Small props are not always easy to see because of the distance between the acting area and the back of the **stalls** or circle.
- Often involves seating part of the audience in raised circles, which means some viewers are a long way from and almost above the acting area while the front row of the stalls is very close. Sound and lighting must be carefully balanced to compensate for this.

LOOK HERE

See page 204 for a diagram showing positions on stage.

End-on stage

Possible advantages

- A neutral stage configuration that lends itself to a range of periods and styles.
- Similar to proscenium arch in that a distinct and separate world can be created.
- Backdrops, projections and large pieces of scenery work well.
- Straightforward in terms of lighting and sound design.

Potential problems

- The distance between the back of the audience and the acting area can be lengthy.
- If the stage is raked, anything with wheels will need to be wedged or have brakes.
- If seating is not raked, sightlines can be a problem.
- Details in costumes and small props might not be seen clearly.

Thrust stage

Possible advantages

- The large apron provides an acting area close to the audience, which helps the audience to feel involved.
- Props and costumes can be detailed.
- The main stage can incorporate large pieces of scenery, projection and backdrops.
- Useful for using different levels, as many thrust aprons include a step.

Potential problems

- Sightlines can be very complex. Audience members on the side banks of seating, for example, will struggle to see action on their side of the main stage.
- No scenery or tall pieces of furniture can be placed on the apron.
- Side-lighting the apron can be problematic as the audience could be dazzled: steep angles are needed.

An end-on stage in a small auditorium.

Timothy Mackabee's award-winning design for *The Odd Couple* at Dallas Theatre Center.

The Railway Children at King's Cross Theatre.

The New Vic Theatre, Newcastle-under-Lyme.

The Dukes Lancaster promenade performance of
A Midsummer Night's Dream, with Andy Serkis as Lysander.
This took place in a local park. Locations included woodland,
lawns and next to (and even on) a lake.

Traverse stage

Possible advantages

- The acting area is close to the audience, creating a more intimate relationship.
- Props and costumes can be detailed.
- The two ends of the acting area can incorporate large pieces of scenery, projections and backdrops, creating different 'worlds' or locations.

Potential problems

- No scenery or large pieces of furniture can be placed on the traverse itself.
- Side lighting can be problematic as the audience can get dazzled: steep angles are needed.
- Costumes need to be detailed at the back too.
- Having audience members directly opposite each other can be distracting.

Theatre in the round

Possible advantages

- The acting area is closer to the audience, which helps the audience to feel involved.
- This configuration allows directors and designers to use the space imaginatively.
- Having performers enter and exit through the corner aisles (close to the audience) can be exciting.
- Props and costumes can be detailed.

Potential problems

- No scenery or large pieces of furniture can be used.
- Lighting is problematic as the audience can be dazzled: steep angles are needed.
- Costumes need to be detailed at the back too.

Promenade theatre

This type of staging is unique. It involves the audience walking (a promenade) from one location to another with the actors. Locations are often outdoors, or in large buildings such as warehouses.

Possible advantages

- Very exciting for both audience and performers.
- Creates an atmosphere of 'we're all in this together'.
- Suits productions with outdoor locations.

Potential problems

- The weather!
- Challenging for all design options.
- Considerable health and safety risks.

PRACTICAL GUIDE TO LIGHTING DESIGN

Chapter

1

FOCUS

- The purpose and power of stage lighting.
- The technical and creative skills in lighting design.

ASSESSMENT CHECK

This section will help you to understand how you can:

- use visual elements to create mood, atmosphere and style
- communicate intention and create impact for an audience.

INTRODUCTION TO LIGHTING DESIGN

The purpose of stage lighting

At the moment when the house lights go down in the theatre, the lighting designer introduces the audience to the world of the performance. It is as though the audience holds its collective breath ready to enter that world. The first lights that illuminate the stage can create a magical moment. If the lighting design is not right, however, the cast might struggle to grab and keep the audience's attention, and other design elements might not combine well.

Stage lighting can be described as having four main functions:

VISIBILITY
Audience members need to be able to see the actors and the set.

FOCUS
Lighting draws attention to specific areas of the stage.

MOOD
The uses of colour and **intensity** (brightness) have a powerful **atmospheric** affect. These choices can also link to a play's themes and meanings.

LOCATION/SETTING
Similarly, colour choices, intensity and effects (such as a wash or a spotlight) can create a sense of time and place for the audience.

This lighting design is by Nic Farman (with a set by Lily Arnold) for Hornchurch Queens Theatre. It is suitably mysterious and sinister, arousing the audience's curiosity and setting an atmospheric scene for *The Invisible Man*.

TASK 1.1

In a darkened room, experiment with the effects of torchlight. Choose an object in the room and investigate:

- how visible you can make it using a different number of beams
- what size and shape of shadow you can produce
- the different effects produced by front, back and side lighting
- how you can change the atmosphere by using fewer or more torches
- how the **intensity** changes when you move closer or further away.

The power of lighting

A significant difference between lighting a room in your house and lighting the stage is that you should have a blank 'canvas'. Another is that you have considerably more choice of varied and exciting effects. The thinking that determines where you put your desk light and which lightshade you choose is intensified in the role of stage lighting designer as you can use different heights, colours, shapes, shadows and **fades**. You could move suddenly or gradually from one **lighting state** to another and build or reduce intensity of light as the scene demands.

The importance of lighting design

You will find that, as lighting designer, you have a unique power to influence the focus and mood of the audience. You can 'create' sunlight or moonlight, fires and lightning. You can be really creative and your work is an extremely important contribution to a harmonious world for the audience.

Lighting styles

Different genres, styles and forms of performance call for different types of lighting. Bertolt Brecht, for example, often **flooded** the stage with harsh white light. He wanted the audience to be constantly aware that they were watching a play rather than real life. For the same reason, he would keep **lanterns** in full view and sometimes leave the house lights on too.

On the other hand, Konstantin Stanislavski developed a style of theatre that sought realism in every aspect. He used lighting to focus the audience on, for example, an item of set. In today's theatre, **backlighting**, and projections of, for example, clouds would add atmosphere and realism.

DESIGN TIP

The best designers and operators are so skilful that the audience is not consciously aware of the stage lights at all. Unless the designers specifically want them to be...!

TASK 1.2

Watch some different styles and genres of film and/or television. (Here are a couple of example scenes where lighting makes a powerful impact.) Pay particular attention to the lighting effects.

Use the following chart to record what you notice about the effects created. Include, for example, the use of colours and intensity and the mood of the scene.

Title	Genre	Special effects	Time of day / season of the year / weather	How atmosphere is produced and impact it has
Chicago	Musical comedy/ drama	Overhead **spotlight** picks out the character and creates a halo effect on her blonde hair. She is the star!	Stage conditions – general coverage of blue light on the stage creates a cool effect; the character stands out.	Blue lights in the background with possible use of fog machine help the main character to 'shine'.
Star Wars: The Empire Strikes Back				

How can I design lighting as part of this course?

You can opt for lighting design in either or both of the practical sections of the course. If you choose to work as lighting designer in Unit/Component 1, you will work in a small group and help to develop the piece, but your specific responsibility will be to create a lighting design for the performance.

Unit/Component 2 is similar, but you will work with a script.

Unit/Component 3 is the written exam. Working practically with lighting will give you the knowledge and understanding to write confidently about lighting in your set text or a performance you have seen.

TYPES OF
STAGE LANTERN

Your school or college might have these types of lighting fixture. Each has its own particular purpose.

FOCUS

The different types of lantern and their variety of uses.

✓ ASSESSMENT CHECK

Learning some of the technicalities of stage lanterns works towards AO3. You will also show that you can select appropriate equipment and determine its position in order to realise the intended design.

NOTE

Stage lights are called **lanterns** or **lighting fixtures** because **bulbs** are known as **lights** (or **lamps**).

FLOOD

These are basic lanterns, generally with an open or glass front, which produce a wide flood of light. Think floodlit sports events.

Useful for: Lighting large areas of the stage or back cloths: generating a 'flood' of light.

Limitation: The beams' size or shape cannot be controlled.

NB: Where you place and direct these lights is very important as the light will 'spill' everywhere it points.

FRESNEL

Pronounced 'freh-nell', these lanterns have a lens at the front with a 'stepped ring' finish to it.

Useful for: Lighting large or small areas of the stage.

Benefits: The steps on the lens make the light even, making it easy to blend the **focus** of one light to the next.

Several fresnels focused onto several areas can light the whole stage evenly (giving general cover).

By moving the lamp closer to or further away from the lens, you can control the size of the beam.

Barn doors (shutters that fit onto the front of the lantern) can control the spread of the beam.

BIRDIES

Birdies are very small lanterns (as small as 12cm). Tiny par cans are the most frequently used type of birdie.

Benefit: Surprisingly bright, they are ideal for hiding on stage or using on the stage edge as footlights.

PAR CANS

These beam lights (lens-less lanterns) get their name from the lamp inside. The lantern itself is simply a **'can'** in which the **par** lamp is contained. The PAR (Parabolic Aluminised Reflector) is a sealed beam unit consisting of a lamp, reflector and lens in one.

Useful for: Producing a very bright beam, something like a cross between a floodlight and a Fresnel.

Benefits: These lights are excellent for highlighting an area or using with colour filters or gels to produce the bright colourful beams often seen at pop and rock concerts.

Limitation: The only way to change the beam size is either to move the whole fixture, or to physically change the lamp to narrow, medium or wide.

PROFILE SPOT

These versatile lanterns are longer and thinner than floods and spotlights. They also have levers half way down, which are the shutters that control the size and shape of the beam.

Useful for: A soft- or hard-edged beam, produced by moving the lens (not the lamp as in fresnels) forwards or backwards. **Profile** lights with hard edges can create a typical 'spotlight' beam. Alternatively, several profiles focused with a soft edge can overlap for general cover. Profile spots are the type of lantern used to project images with **gobos**.

Benefits: The beam control is generally narrower and more controllable than a fresnel, so a profile spotlight can be further away, while still remaining bright, without 'spilling' light into unwanted areas. The built-in shutters of a profile spotlight mean that barn doors are not needed. They are used to shield areas of the stage that you don't want to light. They can also shape the beam to create a square of light or to focus a tight beam on a particular object or performer.

Follow spot

Follow spots are modified profiles mounted on a tripod and operated manually to track an individual as they move around the stage. You will have seen them used in events such as ice skating.

Gobo

A gobo is a very thin steel plate with a cut-out pattern that fixes over a lens. It is used to project a **silhouette** of images such as trees or windows. The images produced are mainly two-dimensional. The colour is dictated by the colour **filter** or **gel** put in front of the lens. They can produce stunning effects.

LED LANTERN

Many schools are now using theatre lanterns with an **LED** source. The most common is probably an LED par can, but there are now LED floods, profiles and fresnels.

Useful for: The light inside is most commonly made up of red, green and blue LEDs which can be selected or combined to create a variety of colours.

Benefits: LED lights use less power, generate less heat and save on the cost of replacing bulbs and buying colour filters or gels.

Limitations: They can be expensive, and controlling their **colour palette** requires computer software.

AUTOMATED MOVING LANTERNS

Often seen at concerts and large-scale events, moving lanterns are very versatile. They are generally manufactured as profile spots or fresnels.

Benefit: The focus, beam size, gobo and colour are controlled by the software on a **lighting desk** or **console**. The desks usually have libraries of different light fixtures, which enables relatively easy programming and operation, and adds versatility and complexity to a design.

Limitations: They are expensive and require a computerised lighting desk.

UNDERSTANDING YOUR LIGHTING RESOURCES

FOCUS

Organising your equipment and resources.

ASSESSMENT CHECK

Knowing the equipment you have and how to use it helps you to make good decisions during the development process. This works towards AO2: 'Apply theatrical skills to realise artistic intentions in live performance.'

DESIGN TIP

If you are not familiar with some of the equipment, learn about it before you start any major design work. Don't be frustrated if this takes time. And don't be afraid to ask for help.

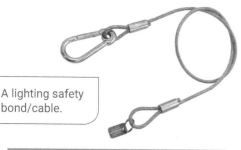

A lighting safety bond/cable.

TASK 1.4

Sketch a simple diagram to show the position, type and angle of rigged lights relative to the stage. Identify gels, gobos and barn doors that are in place. (An example lighting plot is given on page 31.)

What lighting equipment is available?

It is essential to know what resources are available, so you can create a practical design. Typical lighting equipment includes:

- lanterns (as we saw on the previous pages)
- colour gels and gobos
- a lighting desk (a manual **board**, or computer software)
- a lighting **rig** or lighting stands
- a **dimmer** (unless your school uses only LED lights).

Don't be put off if your school or college does not have lots of lighting equipment. As long as you have at least two different types of lantern and a way of controlling them, you can light an acting area.

Ask your teacher if you can run an audit of the available lanterns. This could mean looking up into the rigging and identifying the numbers of different types of lantern, or checking in the storeroom. The following tasks will also help you to document and rig your production.

Identifying what lighting fixtures you have and what works best where will avoid having to move lanterns to a completely different area of the rig.

TASK 1.3

1. Make notes on the operating equipment you have and any queries about it. (Some examples have been given to start you off.)

Lighting desk	Lighting rig/ stands	Dimmer	Lantern accessories
Manual or **digital**?	• Number of sockets on the rig? • Number and types of stand or boom?	Position and type of **dimmer rack**?	• Gobos • Barn doors • Gels • **Safety bonds** (There must be one for each lantern you rig!)

2. Identify the lanterns available in school (including quantities). Note down ideas on how you might use them in your design, for example:

Type	How many?	Key features and uses
Fresnels		• Soft-edged beam. • Best used close to the stage. • Barn doors can alter shape and size of beam. • Gobos and colour gels can be added.
Profile spots		• Powerful enough to use further from the stage.
LEDs		
Par cans		
Automated moving lanterns		

Taking care of your lanterns

Lanterns need to be kept clean. Dusty lanterns give off a burning smell and dirty lenses are less effective at transmitting light. If you can clean your lanterns (de-rigged and unplugged, of course) it is important to:

- use a window cleaning product and soft cloths for lenses, avoiding smears
- wipe the metal body with a damp cloth
- avoid touching halogen lamps because fingerprints cause hot spots that quickly degrade the lamp. If a lamp is accidentally touched it should be cleaned with methylated spirit or isopropyl alcohol.

Controlling your lighting

Every lighting system is controlled by a desk, which can be manual (with or without a computer facility) or a software programme. It does not matter what type of desk you have as long as you can use it confidently.

Online manuals are available for many modern desks and software programmes along with tutorials. This is very useful research, particularly when your teacher and performers are busy.

TASK 1.5

1 Find time to develop your knowledge and skill with the lighting desk. See if you can achieve:
   - a **snap** between two lighting states (for example DSL and USR)
   - a **cross-fade** between two lighting states
   - fading up a lighting state at a **pace** that feels right for the start of a performance and fading out for the ending
   - a sequence that brings a sense of excitement (This might involve moving between a number of states at a high pace. Would you end the sequence with a snap to **blackout** or a fade?)
   - an effect that adds tension. (Could you end with a snap to blackout?)

2 Switch everything off carefully.

Human resources

You should supervise the rigging, focusing, programming and operating of the design as appropriate. This means that you need to be centrally involved in these aspects of the design, but, for health and safety reasons, you almost certainly will not be rigging and focusing lanterns yourself. So, you will need help!

TASK 1.6

As soon as possible, meet the person with the knowledge, clearance and time to be involved. Find out:
- what they are prepared to do
- what their availability is
- how much notice they need to rig and focus the lanterns.

NOTE

Your site supervisor or a technician is likely to be responsible for the electrical maintenance of school equipment and you should never be involved in that aspect of upkeep. If you have any concerns about the safety of a piece of electrical equipment, such as exposed or loose wiring, report this immediately to your teacher.

 DESIGN TIP

You must never distract the actors during rehearsal. Ideally, arrange a time slot during rehearsal times in which you can experiment without disturbing the cast.

 DESIGN TIP

Be appreciative and flexible with your human resources. They will already be busy!

ASSESSMENT CHECK

This section will help you to demonstrate your knowledge and understanding of how theatre is developed and performed (AO3).

ANGLES, COLOUR AND INTENSITY

Light in the real world

Daylight

Theatre lighting frequently seeks to re-create natural lighting, so begin your design thinking in the real world.

During daylight hours our light source is the Sun. The time of day affects the angle at which the Sun's light hits the Earth. The season and the weather (amount of cloud cover) affect the intensity (brightness) of the sunlight.

TASK 1.7

1 Assuming you are in a room with at least one window, and it is daytime, turn off any artificial lights. Look around you for a minute and note the following:
   - How many sides of the room have portals (windows/doors)?
   - Where can you see bright light? Where does it come from?
   - Where are the shadows? What shape and length are they? Why?
   - How deep (dark) are the shadows?
   - Does the atmosphere vary in the room because of the light? How?
2 Draw a sketch of the room, representing areas of light and shade.

Night-time

When the Sun sets, the Moon and stars create significantly less natural light, so we use artificial light.

TASK 1.8

Thinking about inside and outside:
1 Write down three sources of artificial light.
2 Use them to write two or three sentences about how artificial light has different affects from natural light. An angle-poise lamp, for example, creates a small area of intense white light, whereas a candle creates a dim, flickering warm light.

Think about angle, colour, intensity and atmosphere when comparing natural and artificial light.

DESIGN TIP

Be aware that light bounces off surfaces – particularly light-coloured and shiny ones.

Naturalistic
(real-world) lighting on stage

Light in the real world is usually the starting point for stage lighting. (You might explore non-naturalistic effects later.)

As the lighting designer, you have a number of tools with which to control light on the stage:

* the number of stage lanterns
* the types of lantern (see pages 18–19)
* where lanterns are positioned (angle and distance)

* the shape of beam produced
* the intensity of the beam projected
* The colour of the beam.

Key lights

There is always a **key light** in the real world. It might be natural sunlight coming through a window, or moonlight, or the artificial light of a desk lamp, for example. A lighting designer will always be aware of the key light and will generally reproduce it on stage with a lantern or group that is more intense than the others. If the light is supposed to be coming from inside the room through artificial lighting, you could show the source of this light, such as a bedside lamp.

Angles

The angle of lighting to suggest sunlight, for example, is also very important. If it was early morning sunlight, would you want your 'sunlight' to come from a steep angle or a shallow one? (How high is the Sun in the early morning?) Side lights at different heights can create the same effect.

Natural light

The key to natural lighting is to re-create the quality that comes with different times of day and weather conditions. There are several shades of warm, straw-coloured gels available that suggest sunlight. You could use cooler blue colours for an overcast day, and paler blues for moonlight.

Lighting in *The Wider Earth* creates ripples, waves and sparkles as well as the naturalistic blue of under the sea.

TASK 1.9

Create a mini world and light it artificially to create the senses of sunlight and moonlight.

1 Use cardboard to create a small scene which includes a cut-out window.
2 Use torches (perhaps on a mini tripod) to experiment with lighting the scene.
3 Try coloured gels to create different times of day and night. You could also consider different weather conditions.

 DESIGN TIP

Stage lanterns are very bright. It is crucial that they do not shine onto the audience and dazzle them.

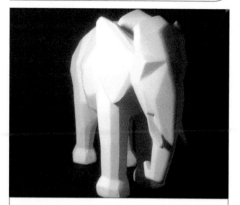

Front-lit, from straight ahead.

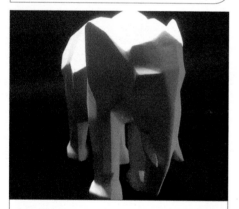

Lit by one light from the front at one side.

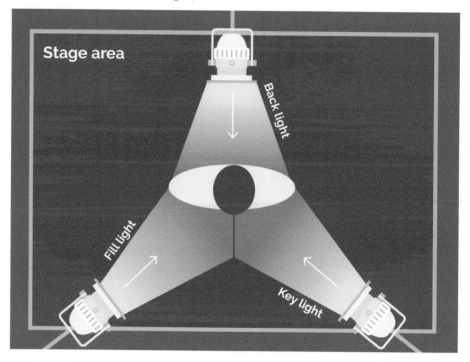

Back-lit.

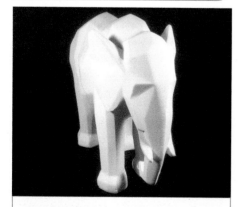

All three lights used equally.

Three-point lighting

Three-point lighting is widely accepted as an ideal starting point for naturalistic lighting. Light coming form only one angle would produce unwanted shadows. So, a second lantern is placed at a 45-degree angle to balance this. In addition, if you only light from the front, the effect is rather flat. To solve this, back light would give a naturalistic, 3D effect.

One of your three lights is the key light. This is likely to be a light that comes from the front, as is the **fill light**, which reduces shadow.

Stage area

Back light

Fill light

Key light

Colour

Colour is one of the most important keys to adding mood and atmosphere to stage lighting. You can see this above, in the explanation of how different colours are used to imitate sunlight and moonlight.

Technical points

White light is produced when a lantern does not have a coloured gel (filter) in front of the lens. In LED lights, white light is produced when all four colours are equally balanced. White light is the brightest light.

Introducing colour is a crucial part of any lighting design. With LED lanterns, you can programme each lighting cue to a specific colour by altering the balance between primary colours (red, green and blue). This versatility means each lantern can project a different colour for every cue if necessary.

Traditional (often older) lanterns use filters or gels to add colour to the beam. Unlike LEDs, each lantern can only be used to project one colour within a single performance. Gels are specially made sheets of thin, transparent, heat-resistant plastic. They are available in a wide range of colours, and can often be bought as a set. Sheets can be cut to fit gel holders that slide into or onto the front of the lantern.

Creative notes

White light is very bright and quite harsh and hard. Simply changing the intensity of the beam is very limiting. To produce more natural or atmospheric effects, you need to add colour.

The following suggestions are starting points for naturalistic lighting.

- Straw gels give a natural sunlight effect.
- Yellows and oranges create a warm, happy atmosphere.
- Pale blue adds a moonlit quality.
- Blues generally create colder and sadder moods.
- Lavenders and lilacs are neutral colours and work well in balancing other colours for a subtle effect.

As a general rule, it is best to use paler colours out front and darker colours from the sides or back of the stage.

Intensity (brightness)

Along with colour, changing the intensity of light is a powerful creator of atmosphere.

The lighting desk gives you as designer control over how bright the beam is (think of household dimmer switches).

Individual lanterns can be made brighter or dimmer using the controls on the lighting desk or board. It is usual to start at 70 per cent and then move up or down to create the effect you want. Be aware that taking the brightness below 20 per cent is likely to give too dim a beam. Coloured filters will also affect the power of a lantern's beam, with darker colours creating a significantly dimmer light.

DESIGN TIP

Always remember to consider coloured lighting alongside set and costume to avoid disrupting the desired overall effect.

LOOK HERE

You will find more information about colour in 'Special effects in lighting' on the following pages.

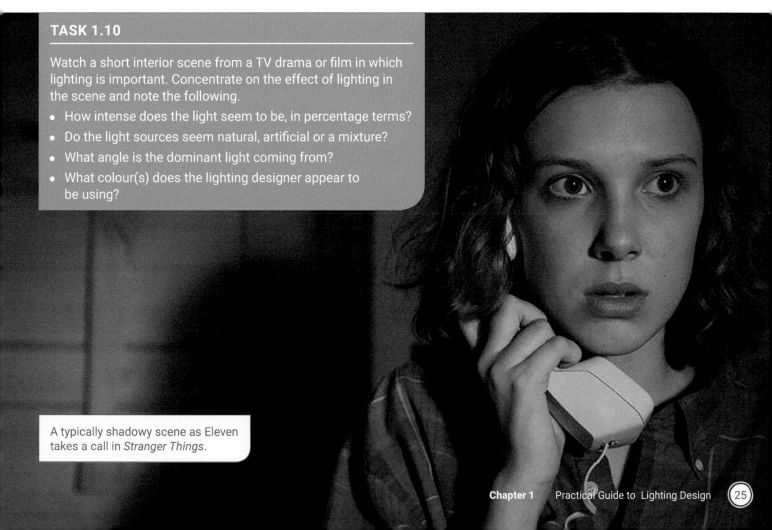

TASK 1.10

Watch a short interior scene from a TV drama or film in which lighting is important. Concentrate on the effect of lighting in the scene and note the following.

- How intense does the light seem to be, in percentage terms?
- Do the light sources seem natural, artificial or a mixture?
- What angle is the dominant light coming from?
- What colour(s) does the lighting designer appear to be using?

A typically shadowy scene as Eleven takes a call in *Stranger Things*.

ASSESSMENT CHECK

This section will help you towards AO1: 'Create and develop ideas to communicate meaning for theatrical performance.'

SPECIAL EFFECTS IN LIGHTING

What are special effects?

All theatre lighting has a powerful effect. It can be difficult to separate special effects (or specials) from other lighting states and there are no strict rules. Generally speaking, special effects (FX or SFX) are those that have a very specific, short-term purpose in a theatre performance.

The Rocky Horror Picture Show at the Winnipesaukee Playhouse combines performer spotlights and LED lanterns with the naturalistic lighting (such as the chandeliers) from the room created by the set. (Lighting design by Matthew Guminski.)

In the scene above, for example, overhead spotlights create four distinct areas. They have the effect of isolating each performer. If this lighting effect was only used once or twice during a production, it would probably be 'special'. If it was used frequently, however, it would be the production's typical spot lighting state.

DESIGN TIP

Modern LED lights are a good option for lighting designers. They are very useful for practical effects. You could, for example, adapt a bicycle headlight, adhesive cupboard lights or the flashing lights designed for pet collars!

TASK 1.11

1 In the script or devised piece you are currently involved in, identify a moment that might be enhanced by a special effect. (This could be a **practical effect**, or one involving a spotlight that uses a particular angle, colour or gobo.)

2 What effect do you want the special effect to have on the audience? How could you create the effect?

3 If possible, test your ideas. How does the special effect influence meaning, mood, style or characterisation?

4 Take a photograph and make notes to remind yourself of what you have achieved.

Practical special effects

These effects are closely linked to the performers, who generally operate or wear them. Examples include:

- a camp-fire flame made of a battery-operated red light, switched on by an actor
- an 'oil' lamp with a flickering LED candle in it, again operated by the actor
- a light on a costume or at the end of a fairy wand.

Using key lights with special effects lighting

In the illustration below, a key light is used alongside the practical special effect of a camp fire to complete the illusion. The key light illuminates the face of the performer because the practical effect is not bright enough. A key light like this could be positioned at the front of the stage or at a low level in the wings to shine up onto the actor's face.

In this production of *Harry Potter and the Cursed Child*, the actors have practical battery lights on their wands, which they can turn on and off themselves.

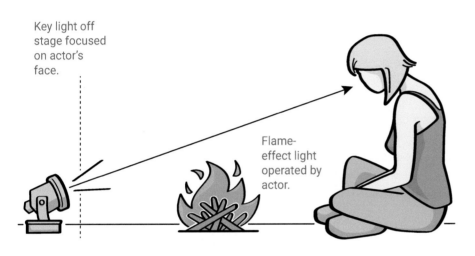

Key light off stage focused on actor's face.

Flame-effect light operated by actor.

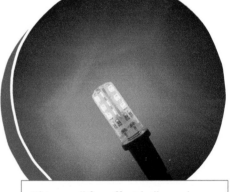

This small fire-effect bulb can be used to simulate orange flames and embers with a flicker-effect control.

The opposite of key lighting is fill light, which is often softer. It could be another, less bright, light source, or it could come from general light reflected off surrounding walls, for example.

Naturalistic special effects

Naturalistic effects reproduce particular lighting that you might find in real life, and that the characters in their world would be able to see. Examples include:

- a lightning strike, which can be produced by quickly flashing a white floodlight. (This would be enhanced by an accompanying sound effect!)
- a disco effect, which could be created with LED lanterns or by manually flashing red, blue and green filtered spotlights. (Of course, it is also possible to use an automated moving lantern or a mirror/disco ball.)

Non-naturalistic special effects

These are the weird and wonderful, supernatural types of effect and could include, for example:

- the use of red and green filters combined with a fog machine to suggest an alien planet
- a slowly pulsing red spotlight focused on a character who is being aggressively questioned.

This production of *The Tempest* uses red, green and blue lighting together with an eerie set design and translucent costume to present the other-worldly nature of the island.

FOCUS

The critical skill of how to move from one lighting cue to the next.

ASSESSMENT CHECK

This design skill is included in AO2: 'Apply theatrical skills to realise artistic intentions in live performance.'

DESIGN TIP

A seven-second cross-fade would be a good place to start your experiments.

LIGHTING TRANSITIONS

What is a lighting transition?

In your own home, you simply switch a light on or off: you move from darkness to light and vice versa at the flick of a switch. You might have some rooms with dimmer switches, allowing you to gradually increase or decrease the light's brightness.

In the theatre, in a more sophisticated way, a lighting designer can use the lighting desk to control the speed at which each lantern is made dimmer or brighter. This is known as a **transition**.

Types of transition

Snap
As the name suggests, a snap transition is a sudden movement of lights from on to off or vice versa.

Cross-snap
The sudden movement from one lighting state to another.

Fade
In lighting terms, this means making the lights gradually brighter and dimmer with a high degree of control.

Cross-fade
The gradual movement from one lighting state to another. This is achieved by simultaneously dimming one lighting state and brightening another until one is fully down and the other is fully up.

Choosing which type of transition to use

The more gradually you fade or cross-fade, the less aware the audience will be of the transition. This creates a calmer atmosphere. At the end of a performance, you might fade the lights to **blackout** over about five seconds to give the audience time to recognise that the performance is over. A slow fade to black also gives the audience time to reflect on what they have just seen.

On the other hand, a snap or cross-snap transition has a startling effect. It might jolt the audience and make a sharp contrast to the previous scene.

TASK 1.12

Harold Pinter's play *The Caretaker* includes a long speech in which a man reveals his life story. It is not a happy one. This is the stage direction:

> During Aston's speech the room grows darker. By the close of the speech only Aston can be seen clearly. Davies and all the others objects are in the shadow. The fade down of the light must be as gradual, as protracted [drawn out] and as unobtrusive as possible.

The stage darkens around Daniel Mays as Aston in *The Caretaker* at The Old Vic.

Work with a partner to discuss:
- Why was this detailed stage direction about lighting given?
- What effect might it have on the audience?

RESEARCH FOR LIGHTING

Assessing additional lighting needs

As you progress with your lighting design, you will identify what additional resources you need, if any. In addition to basic equipment such as lanterns and safety bonds, you might find that you need, for example:

- gel sheets in specific colours
- gobos
- filter and/or gobo holders for lanterns
- small LED lights to use as part of a special effect.

Budget

Once you have an idea of the costs of these items, present this to your teacher. If your teacher agrees that these things should be bought, you will be given a small budget. Once this has also been agreed in your group's design meetings, you need to stick to it.

Finding the best deal

It is well worth shopping around for the best-value products. The internet will be the place for much of what you are looking for. Local pound shops and charity shops, however, might be a cheaper source of some practical effect components, such as bicycle lights.

Alternatively, you might be able to borrow or hire items like gobos and their holders from a local theatre. If so, make sure that their accessories fit your equipment.

> Battery-operated bicycle safety lights can be useful in special effects.

TASK 1.13

Find good sources – in terms of choice, availability and stock – of:
- a colour filter (gel) sheet
- a B-sized gobo of a window
- a replacement lamp (bulb) for a 1kw fresnel.

FOCUS
Finding and costing additional items to complete your lighting designs.

ASSESSMENT CHECK
This research and decision-making shows that you can create and develop ideas to communicate meaning for theatrical performance (AO1).

> A gobo over a precisely directed light can have a striking effect.

DESIGN TIP
Make sure you know exactly what you need before you begin shopping.

FOCUS

Examples and guidance to help you prepare the diagrams and charts you need.

ASSESSMENT CHECK

If you design lighting for Unit/Component 1, this section will help you to produce the necessary documents.

SIGNPOST

Complete Task 1.3 on page 20 first to check what resources you have. There is no point creating a lighting design for 28 lanterns if you only have access to 18!

LOOK HERE

There is guidance on compiling and using a cue sheet on pages 32–33.

If you are devising, go through the stages in 'Lighting Design for the Devised Piece', beginning on page 128.

LOOK HERE

A detailed example of a lighting cue sheet for *Hansel and Gretel* is available on the *Designing Drama* product page at illuminatepublishing.com.

HOW TO DOCUMENT YOUR LIGHTING DESIGN

What documents should I produce?

You need to create a detailed **cue sheet**, **lighting plot** (rigging diagram) and schedule (list of all the equipment you have used).

These diagrams and charts can look complicated, but the advice on these pages will help you to complete excellent documents.

Why should I create these documents?

Plans and cue sheets provide lighting technicians with plans to follow. Even if a designer were to do all the technical work themselves, they could not carry in their heads all the information needed to rig and operate. Lighting charts and plans serve the same purpose as ground plans and model boxes do for set designers.

The documents you draw up will help you practically as well as going in your portfolio and being shown to the visiting examiner.

The lighting plot and schedule provide details of the lanterns and their accessories, along with a plan of where they are rigged. The plan should include a key that explains any symbols used in it.

The cue sheet contains details of every lighting change. It contains all the information needed to operate the lighting in performance.

The equipment and its location

You can only group and rig your lanterns once you know what lighting states and effects are required and where. So, you will already have marked your lighting ideas on the script. You might even have an early cue sheet.

If you are working on a devised piece, you will be becoming clear about all the lighting states and special effects that you are setting out to achieve.

As you get closer to rigging, you will need to produce finished versions of the following documents.

TASK 1.14

Practise drawing up each document as you go along with your design, so that you are confident by the time you are working on the production.

The lighting schedule

You can organise details of all the lanterns, gobos, barn doors and so on in any way you want.

Types and quantities of lanterns

A simple list like the one below is fine.

Lighting schedule: *Hansel and Gretel*	
Type of lantern	**Quantity**
Fresnel	11
Par can	2
Profile spotlight	11

Accessories

Here is an example of a **colour count** (using Lee brand filters). It records the different gels used, the size of the colour frames they fit into and how many gels of each you will need. In other words, how many lanterns each colour is going to be used in.

Show	Hansel and Gretel		
Venue	Main Hall		
Colour code	**Name**	**Type (of frame)**	**Count (number of gels required)**
L020	Medium Amber	7.5" colour frame	1
L117	Steel Blue	10" colour frame	2
L132	Medium Blue	7.5" colour frame	2
L201	Full CT Blue	7.5" colour frame	2
L203	¼ CT Blue	7.5" colour frame	8
L770	Burnt Yellow	7.5" colour frame	3

The lighting plot

This document (a detailed example is given below) can contain a great deal of information. The most important is the type of lantern and where it is to be positioned on the rig.

The key to the plot

This tells the reader what the symbols and numbers on the lighting plot mean. Yours could be simpler than this one, on the left, which also shows some different lantern types.

DESIGN TIP

You could create a similar document to a colour count to give details of gobos used.

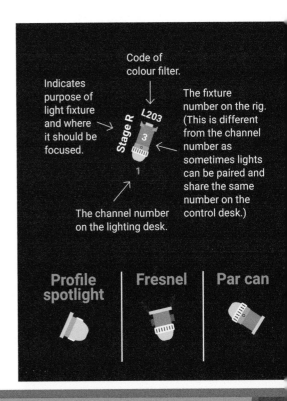

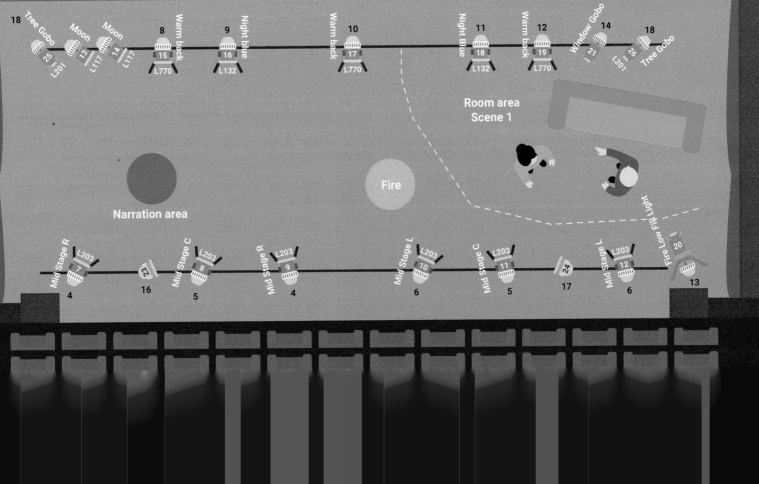

- The stage at which your lighting design really comes together.
- Creating a lighting cue sheet, which is essential for running a show's lighting and required for assessment.

ASSESSMENT CHECK

Achieving the important goal of the cue sheet means that you have all the information needed to use your theatrical skills to realise artistic intentions.

You can also use your cue sheet to analyse and evaluate your own work (AO4).

LOOK HERE

Check how you might use transitions by revisiting page 28.

DESIGN TIP

Remember the requirements that your design should indicate at least **five** lighting states in Unit/Component 1, and at least **four** in Unit/ Component 2.

PLOTTING THE LIGHTING DESIGN

Fixing your cues

In this book, we are using the term **plotting** to mean the act of setting the lighting for every part of the production. The cue sheet should record details of every lighting cue decided. If you have lighting software, record each cue digitally, as you go along.

You will need to make several decisions for each cue, including:

- which lanterns are used
- how bright they should be
- what colours (if any) are needed
- whether any special effects are required
- the type and length of transitions.

Conditions for successful plotting

- Enlist a helper! If you can, invite a younger student who is already involved or interested in lighting to be your assistant – they will be learning too. Your assistant can walk around the acting area so that you can see the effect of your work clearly.

- Choose a quiet time. There is no point trying to plot during a rehearsal or when people need the main (house) lights on.

- Collect everything you need, including:

  - the annotated script or scene list

  - your lighting-rig plan

  - a task light (such as an angle-poise lamp)

  - a template for your cue sheet.

Grouping individual lanterns

The first stage in plotting is likely to be putting lanterns into groups. Creating groups means that you can quickly bring up and mix your lighting states.

A group of lanterns is several lights working together to give a particular look, such as **general cover** or warm colours; to light a specific area of the stage (DSL for example), create a special effect (sfx) and so on.

You could also group lanterns by their position on the rig, such as those at the front lighting bar, **sidelights** and so on.

A lantern could be in more than one group, and you will often use more than one group at a time.

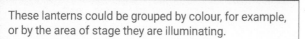

These lanterns could be grouped by colour, for example, or by the area of stage they are illuminating.

Identifying and documenting lantern groups

You will need your lighting plot and script (or detailed performance notes).

Creating your lighting cue sheet

This document is your ultimate guide to operating the lighting for your production. It plots precisely which groups are in use for each cue along with their intensity and the timings involved.

DESIGN TIP

Make separate notes on **why** you are making decisions. These will help you to analyse and evaluate your design.

DESIGN TIP

Note that blackouts are a cue in themselves. So are all transitions.

LOOK HERE

Go to www. illuminatepublishing.com for a detailed cue sheet example.

RIGGING AND FOCUSING

This process takes its name from the rig, which, in this case, is the construction of bars from which the lanterns are suspended.

FOCUS

The method by which lanterns are positioned and focused.

ASSESSMENT CHECK

You should supervise the rigging of your lighting design. This will help you towards AO2: 'Apply theatrical skills to realise artistic intentions in live performance.'

PREPARATION

Complete the checklist on page 178.

Gather all your resources.

Check your rigging diagram.

Set up your lighting desk.

Switch on the dimmer rack.

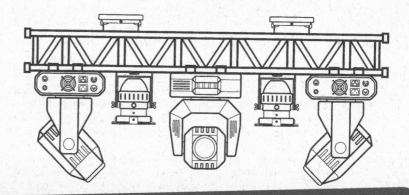

DESIGN TIP

These rigging notes are for your information as you supervise the process. (You will not be rigging the lights yourself.)

Steps for safe and successful rigging

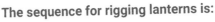

NB: Lanterns should be checked before rigging by a qualified person.

NB: Nobody should be underneath the rig when lanterns are being mounted.

Check that all climbing equipment can be secured and 'guarded'.

Check that all the lantern attachments, such as barn doors, gels, gobos and the safety bond work properly and are secure.

The sequence for rigging lanterns is:
1. Hook over bar and tighten wing nut.
2. Attach safety bond.
3. Point the lantern towards the area you want to light.
4. Adjust shutters and barn doors.
5. Plug in the lantern, wrapping any extra cable loosely around the bar.

Focusing

Focusing involves fine-tuning a lantern's beam size, shape and spread.

Each lantern needs to be adjusted so that it lights the required area precisely. You might want a tight, round spotlight to pick out an individual actor. Alternatively, you might focus a group of lanterns for a subtle wash of light. For this effect, look to make the edges of the beams very soft.

You need a minimum of two people, but three are better. Ideally, one will rig and focus; one brings up the working light on the desk and the third moves around the performance area as the subject for the lighting so that the focusing effect can be seen.

DESIGN TIP
You will nearly always want to light the performer, not the floor!

LOOK HERE
Use the information on pages 22–25 and 32–33 to guide your positioning and focusing.

A technician needs the following equipment, so provide them if you can:

an adjustable wrench
(to tighten and loosen nuts)

heat-resistant gloves

a small torch or headlamp

a tool belt or pouch

To focus a lantern, the following actions might be required:

- Moving shutters or barn doors
- Inserting or removing coloured filters and gobos (Gobos get very hot!)
- Moving lenses backwards or forwards.

House lights need to be off and one lantern needs to be focused at a time. Some lights can be brought up together to test their combined effect.

DESIGN TIP
Try to get rigging and focusing correct first time to avoid having to get the people and equipment together again and doing tasks more than once.

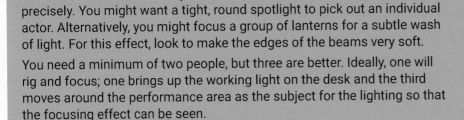

ASSESSMENT CHECK

Throughout Units/ Components 1 and 2, you should adopt safe working practices.

This is also covered in AO3: 'Demonstrate knowledge and understanding of how drama and theatre is developed and performed.'

HEALTH AND SAFETY IN LIGHTING DESIGN

Any activity that involves electricity and hanging heavy objects above people's heads needs to be treated with a great deal of care. Stop and think about the risks for a moment!

If I'm not allowed to rig lights, why do I need to know about health and safety?

The exam board does not want you to take on much responsibility for your own and other people's safety when it comes to lighting. Your school must not allow students to put themselves or others at risk either.

However, there are good reasons why you still need to know about it:

- Everyone bears some responsibility for the safety of their environment. If people look out for potential dangers, the better it is for everyone.
- Assessing risks and avoiding hazards is part of being a responsible member of the group.
- You are expected to show your knowledge and understanding of health and safety issues.
- If you progress to make your living in this field, you need to consider health and safety issues and how to tackle them.

Take notes on any risks and hazards you encounter in your practical work. As well as making sure that they are attended to by an adult, you could mention them in your portfolio if you design lighting for Unit/Component 1.

Using your common sense

Many dangerous situations can be avoided when people are sensible. Here are some basic issues to be aware of before your lights are set up.

! Hazards	Safety measures ✓
⚠ Loose electrical cables	✅ Tape them down or cordon off the area.
⚠ Damaged cables or electrical items ⚠ Lack of or out-of-date PAT (electrical safety) test label	✅ Report the problem immediately to someone in authority.
⚠ Having the wrong tool for a job, such as a knife instead of a screwdriver	✅ Find out what the right tool is and make sure it is available and used.
⚠ Working at height	✅ See 'Rigging and focusing', pages 34–35.
⚠ Unsecured lanterns or fixtures on the lighting bars	✅ Make sure no one is underneath. Ask a suitable person (not yourself!) to attach a safety bond (cable).
⚠ Hot lanterns and gobos	✅ Wear safety gloves.

OPERATING THE LIGHTING

I don't need to operate the lights, do I?

You are not required to operate the lighting desk, but there is no reason why you shouldn't. If you design the lighting for Unit/Component 1, learning how to operate the lighting and evaluating your success would be very useful for your portfolio. Similarly, operating skills will be impressive if you design lighting for Unit/Component 2. Most importantly, perhaps, it is a thrilling, satisfying experience.

Operating lighting equipment

The following items need to be in place:

- a working lighting desk that you have been able to practise using
- rigged and focused lanterns
- a task light (angle-poise)
- script (if applicable), marked up with the cues (two scripts are ideal – one for your assistant)
- your completed cue sheet.

If there is a sound operator, you will need to co-ordinate certain effects with them. You might need to fade sound and lights precisely at the same time, for example. Unless you are wearing cans (linked headphones), it is wise to operate sound and lights next to each other.

Practising lighting operation

- Take time to check that you are comfortable using your lighting desk. Your preparation could include labelling master channels with group numbers – on a manual board. (You can write on masking tape and it is easily removed.)
- It is useful to have at least one person 'walking' the acting area with a marked-up script. They can work cue to cue with you. The script will keep you in time with the action and enable you to see where cues need to happen, such as on a particular word in the performance.
- Make sure you practise transitions, as well as changes within cues, such as dimming and intensifying lighting states.
- If there are long fades and you are using a manual board, make sure that you can operate them smoothly. This is a benefit of a manual desk, as you can 'feel' the action.

FOCUS

Advice for the lighting operator.

ASSESSMENT CHECK

You can use your lighting knowledge and skills to realise artistic intentions in live performance (AO2).

LOOK HERE

See 'Plotting the lighting design', pages 32–33, for details on cues.

Some additional health and safety points

Beware of blackouts! In rehearsals, always call out that you are about to do them, so people are not unexpectedly plunged into darkness.

Be very aware that flashing lights can trigger epilepsy.

FOCUS

Your design role during final rehearsals.

DESIGN TIP

If you are struggling with a technical aspect, ask your group if you can run a cue again. This is the purpose of the techs.

ASSESSMENT CHECK

Rehearsals give you the chance to adjust and practise your design so that it will operate as smoothly as possible in performance.

This demonstrates your knowledge and understanding of how drama and theatre is developed and performed (AO3).

TASK 1.17

1 Update your notebook and script with any issues to be resolved before the dress rehearsal.

2 Arrange some time to work things through with other designers if there are any clashes.

LOOK HERE

Technical equipment doesn't always work properly. Use the troubleshooting guide on page 61 to help you cope.

TECHNICAL AND DRESS REHEARSALS FOR LIGHTING DESIGNERS

These are the final rehearsals before the performance.

The technical rehearsal

Technical rehearsals ('techs') are lengthy rehearsals because they need to let lighting and sound operators test their designs in practice.

At the same time, the director and other designers are checking that all the technical aspects of the production work smoothly and harmoniously. The performers get to experience the piece with the design elements in place.

You will need to decide as a group whether to run the production in its entirety or move from cue to cue, missing out certain sections. All the different design roles will need to work closely to make sure that everyone is confident that the process can be repeated when the piece is performed without interruptions.

During technical rehearsals, make sure performers know which areas of the stage will not be lit during particular lighting states. These areas could be marked with tape so that cast and crew can practise moving around safely.

Making technical and artistic improvements

Unlike set and costume designers, who will have completed the bulk of their job by now, you are likely to be heavily involved in the tech. Even if someone else is operating the lighting, you need to guide them through the cues and make adjustments to levels, timings of fades and so on.

You will also need to watch the acting area and check that:

- lighting states allow all sections of the audience to see the actors
- coloured lighting works harmoniously with set and costume
- practical special effects are managed successfully
- the lighting design overall is working well in practice.

The dress rehearsal

The important thing about the dress rehearsal ('dress') is that is runs through the whole production without interruption, except in an emergency. The performers can experience the whole show with all the technical elements, but without an audience to see the actors. The lighting designer can test that the lighting design can be carried out successfully.

Until the dress, none of you will be sure that the performance can run smoothly. For lighting, these are some issues you might face:

⚠ Lighting problem	Possible solution 💡
Lack of time between cues in a specific section.	Simplify your design by removing or changing a cue to make it manageable.
The show is 'running away with you' in general. It is a struggle to keep track of the cues, desk, script and stage at the same time.	Don't panic! Get through the dress rehearsal as best you can. It might be a particularly demanding design or production. Practice as much as possible before the performance. Consider simplifying the cues.

EVALUATING YOUR LIGHTING DESIGN

Examining the detail of your design

Once you are clear about what evaluation is and the best way of approaching it, you can focus on assessing the success of your lighting design.

Whenever you evaluate, you should make at least three different points. These points should be illustrated with specific examples. Each time, you should also explain the reason why you have made a particular value judgement. You should highlight anything that could have gone better.

FOCUS

Placing a value judgement on design.

ASSESSMENT CHECK

This part of the design process is the essential element of AO4: 'Analyse and evaluate your own work and the work of others.'

SIGNPOST

Use the evaluation guidance on page 80 before you start.

> ## TASK 1.18
>
> 1   Copy and complete a table like this one (some examples have been included). The notes will provide a solid basis for your evaluation writing.
>
> | Lighting design evaluation | | | |
> |---|---|---|---|
> | **Design element** | **Example/ moment in the play** | **Evaluation** | **Reason for evaluation** |
> | Pre-set lighting state – down-lit white fresnels over the stage. Enhanced by fog machine. | Before the performance began. | Engaging and created powerful atmosphere. | Audience feedback suggested that the eerie atmosphere was established from the start of the play. This was a key part of our artistic intentions. |
> | Practical special effect – camp fire plus key light. | Hansel lights a fire in the forest. | Convincing in setting scene and contributing to action. | The practical effect of the red lamp in the 'fire' was operated well by the actor. Gradually increasing the intensity of the key light on her face gave a convincing illusion of a fire. |
> | Use of cobalt blue filter from side of stage. | The moonlit forest. | Atmospheric; helped in characterisation. | The blue lighting that side-lit the acting area created an atmosphere of fear. Lighting combined well with the soundscape to emphasise the characters' feelings. |
>
> 2   Expand your notes into three paragraphs of evaluative writing. Remember that you should compare your finished lighting with your agreed artistic intentions.

LOOK HERE

More examples of analysis and evaluation can be found in Chapter 7 of this book.

LIGHTING DESIGN VOCABULARY

AML (automated moving lantern) Operated digitally, these lanterns can swivel and tilt.

Atmospheric A sound, for example, that creates a strong feeling or mood.

Backlight/backlighting Lighting that comes from the back of the acting area.

Barn door A metal attachment that slides into the front of a lantern, with hinged flaps to control the beam.

Birdie A miniature lantern ideal for hiding in small parts of a set or along the front edge of the stage.

Blackout A moment when all the lights are dimmed, often suddenly.

Channel A number given to a **lantern** that corresponds to a number on the **lighting board** or **desk**.

Colour count A record of the number of gels of each colour required.

Colour palette A complementary set of colours that belong to a group, such as pastel or dark.

Cross-fade Fading up one lantern or group while fading down another.

Cue sheet A list of cues along with timings.

Digital Using computer technology. Digital lighting desks, for example, are programmed using software.

Dimmer/Fader A way of controlling the intensity (brightness) of the light. These are often manual or digital sliders.

Dimmer rack The control centre for changing the **intensity** of each channel.

Fade A gradual increase or decrease.

Fill light Working with a **key light**, fill light is less intense (bright) and is often used to lessen shadows.

Filter/gel A piece/sheet of coloured plastic/resin that fits at the front of a lantern to change the colour of the beam.

Flood A lantern that produces a wide spread of light; a broad cover of light.

Focus Adjust the angle and beam size of a lantern so that it lights the exact area required.

Fresnel A type of lantern that is good for lighting large areas and which blends easily with other fresnels or spotlights to create a wash of light.

Gel See **Filter**.

General cover Lanterns that provide overall lighting to the acting area.

Gobo A metal cut-out plate that fits in front of a lantern and casts a shadow shape onto the stage (such as a tree outline, window frames and so on).

Intensity The brightness of lighting. Intensity is generally measured as a percentage (such as 60%).

Key light The main, strongest, most intense light, designed to copy the main light source (natural or artificial) in the real world.

Lamp The technical name for a light bulb.

Lantern The technical term for a **lighting fixture** that contains a light source, such as a lamp.

LED (Light Emitting Diode) Lighting fixtures that use less energy and create less heat than other types of lantern. LEDs are the most popular type of fixture in professional theatres.

Lighting desk/board/console The means of operating the lighting, with channels, dimmers and faders.

Lighting fixture A stage light unit.

Lighting plot The diagram that shows where the lanterns are hung on the rigging.

Lighting state The way a lantern or group of lanterns is used on stage. For example, a certain lighting state could create a moonlit effect.

Manual Operated by hand as opposed to digitally.

Naturalistic A set or lighting effect, for example, with characteristics of reality; having the appearance of a real place.

Non-naturalistic A set or lighting design, for example, that aims not to look like a real place.

Pace The speed with which lighting effects transition from one to the next.

Par can A type of lantern that produces a very strong beam of light.

Plotting The process of creating a cue sheet to show what light effect happens when and where. This could be on paper or a computerised lighting board.

Practical effect A lighting effect that is operated or worn by a performer.

Profile spotlight A versatile lantern that can be used to create tight spots of light or bigger areas as required.

Rig The bars that lanterns are hung on.

Safety bond/cable/chain The metal chain or cable that attaches the lantern to the rigging.

Sidelight Light that shines from the side of the stage, perhaps from the wings.

Silhouette The dark shape of a person or object against a lighter background.

Snap A sudden change such as a **blackout**.

Special effect A lighting effect that has a specific purpose, such as a colour wash to suggest a flashback.

Spotlight A type of lantern that can create a tight circle of light or a larger, softer-edged one.

Three-point lighting A method that shines light from three different directions to give good coverage.

Transition A change between lighting states, such as a snap or a fade.

PRACTICAL GUIDE TO SOUND DESIGN

FOCUS

The power of sound in theatrical performance.

ASSESSMENT CHECK

This section develops your ability to create and develop ideas to communicate meaning (AO1).

You will learn how sound designers create mood and atmosphere.

You will also gain insight into how and why choices are made, which will help you in Unit/Component 3.

INTRODUCTION TO SOUND DESIGN

How can I design sound as part of this course?

You can opt for sound design in either or both of the practical sections of the course. If you choose to work as sound designer in Unit/Component 1, you will work in a small group and help to develop the piece, but your specific responsibility will be to create a sound design for the performance. Unit/Component 2 is similar, but you will work with a script.

Unit/Component 3 is the written exam. Working practically with sound will give you the knowledge and understanding to write confidently about sound in your set text or a performance you have seen.

Sound in the real world

Sound is one of the five senses that connect human beings with the world. We hear things in the womb before we are born, and it is generally accepted that hearing is the last sense to fail when we die. Sound is possibly the most evocative sensation.

We are not particularly conscious of many of the sounds that most of us hear every day. Traffic noises, people chatting, bird song, the wind and so on often fade into the background. Our brains filter them out so that we can focus on more important sounds.

Other sound choices, such as our ringtones and the volume of our video games, are very conscious. Similarly, we choose our music to suit our situation and the mood we want to create.

Then there are the sounds that are signals in our life, such as a doorbell, text alert, smoke detector or siren of an ambulance. This kind of sound alerts us to actions that we might need to take.

TASK 2.1

1   Take a few moments to listen carefully and identify all of the sounds you can hear right now. Note them in a chart like this one (some examples have been included for guidance.)

Sounds in life		
Closest sound: Computer whirring	**Sound(s) that suggest mood and atmosphere:** Breeze, clock ticking, songbirds, crows…	**Intermittent sound(s):** Toddler whinging
Most distant sound: Football on playing field (whistle, shouts, ball being kicked)	**Constant sound(s):** Clock ticking	**Other sounds:** Car door slamming

2   On a scale of 1 to 5, at what level of volume would you place each sound?

3   Finally, try to imagine the blend of sounds you are hearing as a **soundscape** for the stage. What sounds might you take out or add in order to add meaning or atmosphere?

Sound and the stage

In the theatre, the sound designer re-creates many different types of sound to convey meaning and add atmosphere to a production and fit into the harmonious world of the stage. Every sound is included for a reason, including those that help to create location. The sounds feed the imagination of the audience.

Different types of stage sound

There are broadly two types of theatre sound. **Diegetic sounds** are those that seem to come from the world of the stage, such as a scene's background noise, doorbells, music that is put on by an actor, phone ringtones. **Non-diegetic sounds** are those used to add mood and ambience for the audience, such as **atmospheric** sound effects and music. Non-diegetic sounds would not be 'heard' by the characters.

TASK 2.2

Look at this image on the right from *The 39 Steps*. Imagine you are creating a soundscape for it.

1   What sounds would you create? Describe them here.

An atmospheric soundscape	
Diegetic sounds	**Non-diegetic sounds**

2   For each sound, add a volume level from 1 to 5 to create the blend of sounds that you think is suitable. Think about the atmosphere you wish to create.

3   Using CDs, online sound effects and/or (with permission from your teacher) a smartphone, create a version of your soundscape. Even if you are not able yet to mix the sounds, you will be able to blend at least three.

4   Play your soundscape to others. Note their responses regarding the meaning and atmosphere your blend of sounds create for them.

-   Was it what you hoped for?

-   What could you change to achieve your desired effect?

ASSESSMENT CHECK

This section will get you started with some of the technical knowledge needed for AO2: 'Apply theatrical skills to realise artistic intentions in live performance.'

HOW TO PRODUCE SOUND FOR THE STAGE

Resources for producing sound

Every professional designer needs to understand the mechanics of how sound is produced and most professionals will have significant skills and knowledge. Once you have gained a good understanding of the technical aspects of theatrical sound design, you will be able to unleash your creativity. At GCSE level, it is your design that is assessed, but you need to have sufficient knowledge and understanding to create and transmit sounds for the stage.

As a sound designer, your tools are:

- **sources** of sound (microphones, CDs, **digital** recordings, musical instruments)
- mixing desk (**manual** or digital) and **playback device**
- **amplifier** (produces the signals for the speakers)
- **speaker** (broadcasts the sound).

If we add an 'H' for the person who **h**ears the sound, we can make a mnemonic for the sequence of sound production:

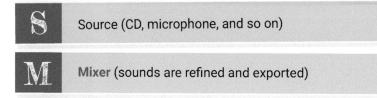

S — Source (CD, microphone, and so on)

M — **Mixer** (sounds are refined and exported)

A — Amplifier (signal is boosted)

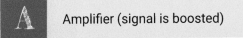

S — Speaker (sound is transmitted)

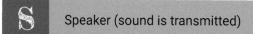

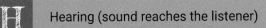

H — Hearing (sound reaches the listener)

TASK 2.3

Draw a flow chart to show your understanding of SMASH. Use symbols to help you include details.

Getting to grips with your resources

Experiment with sound technology until you feel confident. It can be quite easy to produce impressive results.

TASK 2.4

Complete this table to take stock of the sound equipment you have available.

Number of speakers, their positions and if they can be moved	Mixing desk: manual or electronic? Number of channels?	Playback device: type and details	Other resources

DESIGN TIP

If your mixing desk runs from a laptop, check what your operating system provides. Apple has a free version of *QLab*, for example, which enables you to mix and pre-programme sound **cues**.

Sound sources

The source of a sound is simply the place where you 'grab' the sound you want. You can find a piece of music, for example, on a CD, online music service or, with the help of microphones, from live instruments or voices.

Mixing desk

As its name suggests, a sound mixer is the device where a designer or technician refines and blends sounds. Digital mixers are more complex than manual ones, but work on the same principles.

If you don't have a mixing desk, sounds can be mixed and edited in software and played through a computer or amplifier during the performance.

DESIGN TIP

Store all your sourced sound effects into a computer file in a folder that you can find easily for editing and/or mixing.

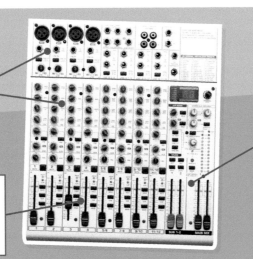

The input section is where the raw sound enters the system. You can then balance the sound. This might be to equalise it (improve tone) and add effects (such as **reverb**). Several channels mean you can mix several sounds.

Once the sounds have been adjusted, a **fader** is used to set the volume of each sound. Each input can then be routed to one or all of the outputs.

The output section also has faders. These are where the final volume for the blend of sounds is adjusted. The mixed sound(s) go from here to the amplifier(s).

Amplifier

To amplify means 'to make louder or bigger'. In sound design, the amplifier (amp) boosts the signal from the mixing desk to a level where it can be 'read' by the speakers.

Some venues have more than one amplifier. One might connect to the speakers on stage, for example, and another to speakers in the audience.

Speaker

Speakers might be the piece of equipment you are most familiar with. They broadcast sound! Find out early on what speakers you have and whether they are fixed or moveable.

Microphones

In larger spaces, performers sometimes struggle to make themselves heard. This is an issue for sound designers, particularly as you might want to use other sounds under dialogue. In a smaller space, you might not need a microphone, but might want to create specific effects, such as a voice-over.

Radio mics are used in many theatres to amplify actors' voices. Your school or college might have some or can hire them. If so, it is part of your job to make sure they are working and fitted properly.

Floating mics tend to be positioned at the front of the stage. They can be problematic unless used and positioned carefully. They tend to pick up unwanted sounds, such as footsteps on stage.

Hanging mics are suspended above the stage. Again, they will pick up all the sounds on the stage, not just voices.

LOOK HERE

For more on using sound software, see page 61. For advice on positioning speakers, see pages 56–57.

FOCUS

Developing ideas and making approximate costings of equipment and materials.

ASSESSMENT CHECK

For Unit/Component 1, you need to show that you have researched and experimented with different sound effects and their suitability for your sound design (AO1).

TASK 2.6

Repeat Task 2.5, but search specifically for clips from musical theatre. **Analyse** the sounds using the same table.

RESEARCH FOR SOUND DESIGN

Where can I find inspiration for sound design?

If you are new to sound design, an effective and fun way to learn is to study how the professionals work.

TASK 2.5

1. Search the internet for something like 'best sound design'. It should produce a wide choice of videos and articles to inspire you. They might be mainly about film sound, but the basic ideas are the same. Watch, listen and read, and use your notebook!

2. Now turn away from your screen as you play some film trailers. Listen carefully, using headphones if possible. You should be impressed by the clever use of sound to create mood and atmosphere as well as suggesting location, **genre** and style. One trailer for *La Haine*, for example, ends with the slam of a garage door. It is highly effective!

3. Fill out a version of the following table using two or three different film trailers. (This example is based on *Titanic*.)

Analysis of sound design: film trailers	
Title: *Titanic*	
Use of voice (dialogue, monologue, voiceover)	**Montage** of character voices. Short clips from key moments in film. Chilling shouts and screams gradually increase after ship hits iceberg.
Diegetic sound	Waves. Water gushing into the ship. Hull creaking slowly.
Non-diegetic sound	**Echo** on voices suggests the past. Bells (single chimes) are like ship bells and church bells at a funeral. These bells are at the start and end of the trailer.
Music	Orchestral soundtrack suggests romance, drama and tension at different moments. Use of Celine Dion song is moving.
Impact on audience	Strong sense of genre – Action and Romance comes from music and sound effects. Layering of music, dialogue and effects creates different atmospheres. Excitement, panic and sorrow suggested by varied **pace** and volume.
Useful ideas for my stage sound design	Different volumes and pace of music and sound create different moods. Could I use actors' voices off stage to suggest memories? A simple sound could be repeated at different moments to suggest theme or time passing (motif).

Finding the sounds you need

If you need an ambulance siren, you will probably need to look online. There are many websites that provide free sound effects. Others might charge a small fee. There are also sound effects CDs available. Some are general; others specific. Don't buy any until you know just what you need.

There is also the possibility of recording your own effects. For instance, you might not be able to find the exact playground sound effect that you want. You could take out a microphone with a simple recording device (or possibly a smartphone) to record the right sound.

Don't settle for the first effect you find. Select the effect that exactly fits the meaning, mood and style for your drama piece.

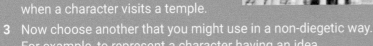
How do I find technical sound support?

If you are not quite confident yet, or need further help:

Read...
For additional technical information, refer to stage sound books.

Watch...
There are many online videos and guides that should help.

Ask...
Consider your human resources. Are there people in your school who could help? Approach the music department. They are very likely to have staff and students with the skills you need.

Visit...
Local theatres should have a sound specialist. They will probably be keen to share their expertise. Is there a local youth theatre that encourages technicians as well as performers?

Continuous research

Make sure that you visit your group's rehearsals regularly. You are likely to be inspired with new ideas, or note the need for:

- new or different sound effects
- opportunities for performers to be involved with sound effects.

If you discover that your performers do need radio mics, or you want to use floating mics, for example, find out if you can hire them.

FOCUS

Combining sounds and being adventurous as you put your sound design together.

ASSESSMENT CHECK

Choosing, finding and building sounds are important aspects of AO1. You are also beginning to apply the theatrical skills needed for AO2 and developing knowledge and understanding of drama and theatre (AO3).

DESIGN TIP

If permitted, you could download suitable software or an app so that a phone or tablet could be used as a recording device.

DESIGN TIP

Listen out for what you don't want to hear! Recording an outdoor sound on a windy day, for example, is pretty much impossible.

Do we have to pay for the music we use?

Your school or college will have its own policy regarding copyright and royalties, and might already have a licence to play your choices of music to the general public. It can be a complicated issue, so make sure you check with your teachers.

SOURCING, CREATING AND MIXING SOUNDS

Can I make my own recordings?

You might want, for example, the sound effect of a bath filling or emptying. It is possible to create it yourself – with a recording device and patience. How authentic it sounds is something you will need to discover! You might end up with something different but magical. Simply taking a recording device out and about with you and recording in different locations can provide very useful sound material. Similarly, experimenting with musical instruments can produce effects that will be unique to your design.

Styles and places

Trying different locations for your effect recordings can produce interesting variations. Recording in a small space like a bathroom will generate a different effect from that in a big, empty space. Experiment to find styles of sound that suit your group's artistic intentions.

Music

You are familiar with where to find the music you like. You might be knowledgeable about different types and styles of music. But, can you select music that will enhance the performance you are involved in?

TASK 2.8

Imagine you are working on a devised piece about the threat of climate change. The **structure** is episodic, and the style is **non-naturalistic**. You need to find a piece of music to use during each scene change. Research three different types of music that might be suitable; then complete the following chart.

Specific music requirement: Scene changes		
Music type	Suggested piece	Notes on meaning and atmosphere
Classical music (Orchestral? Chamber?)		
Modern instrumental (Atmospheric?)		
Contemporary song with lyrics (Try your own ideas here.)		

How do I create a particular mood for a scene?

Your sound design is made up of all the individual sounds you source and mix. They must have a sense of belonging together.

Let's suppose that you want non-diegetic sound or some music that will build tension or romance underneath onstage dialogue. This is **underscoring**.

You might find music tracks that are up to 15 minutes long, so you should be able to find a piece suitable for your scene. If you have the right technical equipment (*Audacity*, for example), you can edit tracks to put together particular sections.

DESIGN TIP

If you are searching online for underscoring pieces, try something like 'ambient soundtrack'. Streaming services like Spotify are a good place to start.

MIXING SOUND

Live mixing

Live mixing of sounds occurs in performance. At some point, you will probably want to combine sounds. This is done by bringing up individual channels on your mixing desk so that sounds come in, are added to and are taken out. This is fine as long as you are not setting yourself too many things to do at once. You can set volume levels during the **plotting** process (see 'Plotting the sound design', on pages 58–59).

Pre-recording soundscapes

You could combine a number of sounds onto a single track to make operating easier. If you have sound-mixing software, you will be able to do this quite easily. You could start with some music as your base sound, for example. Then, using timing controls, set sound effects, such as echoing voices and a siren, to come in and go out automatically. You can set the relative volume levels as you go along. Then, come performance time, it is simply a matter of hitting the space bar on your laptop!

TASK 2.9

Experiment with both live and pre-recorded mixing if you can.
- Which method do you prefer? Why?
- Which will be most useful or effective in your performance?

Live sound effects

Does all my sound design have to be recorded?

It is most certainly possible to create **live sound** during the performance. You could play a musical instrument, for example, create thunder with a metal sheet, or ring a real school hand bell.

Depending on the style of your production, the performers could create sound effects as part of your sound design. A **drone**, for example, can be made by the cast, or they could make percussion sounds by tapping different parts of their bodies or costumes. Generally, this kind of sound design suits a non-naturalistic performance style.

In one production of Richard Shannon's play *Sabbat*, performers made whistling noises with their voices and also used an old wind machine to create atmosphere. The audience saw them creating their own sound effects and it had a powerful impact. In this scene, an actor plays hand bells to accompany a song. (Music and sound design by John Biddle.)

ASSESSMENT CHECK

In creating your own sounds, you will be using complex theatrical skills in order to realise your artistic intentions (AO2).

DESIGN TIP

You, and your performers, will need plenty of practice for live sounds to be successful in the performance.

TASK 2.10

Think about the performance you are working on now or a one you were recently involved in. Find a particular moment in the piece at which a live sound effect could be included.

- Why is that moment suitable?
- What sound effect would you use?
- How would the effect be produced?
- What impact are you trying to achieve?

TASK 2.11

Study the sound design ideas you have so far. Where might a period of silence be effective?

Silence has impact

Silence has a definite place in sound design. In a performance that might be quite full of dialogue, music and sound effects, quietness can make a significant impact. It gives time for the audience to pause and think and, depending where the silence is placed, can be a very effective contribution to mood and atmosphere.

HEALTH AND SAFETY IN SOUND DESIGN

Using your common sense

Many dangerous situations can be avoided when people are sensible. Here are some basic issues to be aware of when using sound equipment:

! Hazards	Safety measures ✓
⚠ Loose or unsafe electrical cables.	✓ Tape them down or cordon off the area. ✓ Don't use electric cables outdoors.
⚠ Damaged cables or electrical items ⚠ Lack of or out-of-date PAT test label.	✓ Report the problem immediately to someone in authority.
⚠ Having the wrong tool for a job, such as a knife instead of a screwdriver.	✓ Find out what the right tool is and make sure it is available and used.
⚠ Damaging ear drums. This applies to people wearing headphones as well as in the rehearsal and performances spaces.	✓ Check – beforehand – that volume levels are not too loud.
⚠ Startling people with sudden, loud sounds during rehearsals ⚠ Negative effects of sudden loud noises or loud continuous sound.	✓ Fade sounds in during practice sessions. Warn people if you are about to bring up loud sounds. ✓ Monitor sound levels carefully. ✓ Post a notice in the show programme or in the performance space as a warning.

FOCUS

Some rules and reminders for keeping yourself and others safe.

ASSESSMENT CHECK

Throughout Units/ Components 2 and 3, you must adopt safe working practices.

This is also included in AO3: 'Demonstrate knowledge and understanding of how drama and theatre is developed and performed.'

DESIGN TIP

In practice, health and safety needs to be your top priority!

SPECIAL SOUND EFFECTS

What are special effects in sound?

As with lighting special effects, it can be tricky to decide what makes a special effect as opposed to a regular sound effect. For now, we will define a special sound effect as one that has additional features such as reverb, echo and **pitch-shift**.

You can add these effects to voices, instruments and other sounds.

Reverb

Reverb is short for 'reverberation'. Sound waves hit surrounding surfaces and we hear the original sound plus its sound reflections. Reverb is always there to some degree, but we don't often notice it. Reverb **is** noticeable when we increase the effect of sound bouncing back to us. This adds depth and fullness to a sound. The sound becomes somehow longer and weightier. It then gradually dies away.

You can record a sound effect in a specific space to affect the reverb acoustically.

TASK 2.12

Take a simple recording device (a phone with a suitable app is fine) to a variety of spaces, such as a cupboard or small bathroom and a large hard-surfaced space such as a sports hall.

In each space, record your voice saying the same thing. You could also take a percussion instrument to experiment with.

- Which space(s) gives you the most reverb?
- Why do you think that is?
- Can you describe what you do and do not like about the special effect created?
- Is there a moment in your devised or scripted piece where it would be useful?

Echo

Echo is another specific quality that can be added to an existing sound effect. Echoes occur when sound bounces off surfaces that are at least 17 metres away from the source of the sound. Echo is different from reverb: the sound has time to repeat rather than blend into the original one.

How do I add reverb and echo?

You can add these effects easily and effectively with the help of technology:

- Digital **sound desks** are likely to have reverb and echo settings.
- *QLab* (the Mac sound programme) and Windows-compatible software, such as *Audacity* and *CSC Show Control*, should have reverb built into them.

Your music department might have a reverb unit you can feed into your mixing desk. Most reverb units have a range of settings, which could include echo.

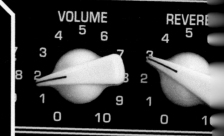

This vintage guitar amplifier has a reverb control.

TASK 2.13

Using reverb or echo to add meaning or atmosphere

1 Choose a sound effect from the design you are working on. Alternatively, think of a sound that is rather 'flat', such as a ball thudding onto a rug or long grass.

2 Fill in the following table. (An example has been included to guide you.)

Sound effect	Echo or reverb	Notes on the special effect and meaning or atmosphere
Pre-recorded voice of narrator	Auditorium-style reverb added	• Reverb gave the narrator's voice much more depth. • It sounds more important and more powerful.

Pitch-shifting

People might think about singers who can't stay in tune when they consider pitch-shifting! There are many uses for this technology, however. You could alter a sound effect, for example, by having three differently pitched versions of the same effect. One would be left at its original pitch. One could be pitch-shifted to 10 per cent below the original, and the third copy could be pitch-shifted to 10 per cent above. The final version – the three mixed together – should have a richer, thicker sound.

High-pitched sound

Sound at low pitch

TASK 2.14

1 Pick one of the additional special effects in this section (reverb, echo or pitch-shift).

2 Conduct some research and explore the effect in practice on some potential sounds for your design.

3 Create a short presentation for other students who are interested in sound design, or for other members of your performance group. (Your presentation could be live or recorded.) Explain the impressions the different effects should make on the listener.

 DESIGN TIP

By experimenting, you will discover what type of special effect lends the right meaning and atmosphere to your sound design.

TASK 2.15

1 Practise drawing up each type of document as you go along with your design, so that you are confident by the time you are working on an actual production.

2 Work through all of the documents detailed here in the order they appear.

HOW TO DOCUMENT YOUR SOUND DESIGN

What documents should I produce?

You should create a source sheet, which details whether each sound you use is live or a piece of **recorded sound**. You should also put forward a **cue sheet**, which shows the source, order, length and output level of each cue.

These plans and tables can look complicated, but the advice on these pages will help you to complete excellent documents.

Why should I have these documents?

Source and cue sheets provide the sound operator (whether this is your or a technician) with plans to follow.

The documents will help you practically as well as going in your portfolio and being seen by the examiner who watches the scripted performances.

A sound plot is not essential, but does show you (or anyone else) what speakers are used and where they should be positioned. It should include a key that explains any symbols used in it.

The completed cue sheet and source sheet contain all the information needed to complete the design and operate the sound during the production.

Source sheet

A simple list like this is fine:

Sound	Source
Introduction music	Found
Owl hoots in the distance	Found
Sound montage of wind with occasional owl hoot	Mixed from two found sources
Suspense music underscore	Original
Cockerel crowing in the distance	Found
Gentle wind with birdsong	Mixed from two found sources
Forest effect	Mixed from three found sources
Fire effect	Found
Thunder clap	Found

Cue sheet

You cannot plot the sound for the production until you know what your music and effects are going to be. So, you will already have marked your sound ideas on your script or notes. You might even have an early version of a cue sheet as well as a source sheet.

The key to the sound plot on the following page explains the different types of speaker that are detailed in a cue sheet.

Sound plot

This diagram is not essential, but will be useful (and should be included in your portfolio if you design sound in Unit/Component 1, for example). It shows the positioning and type of speakers to be used in the production.

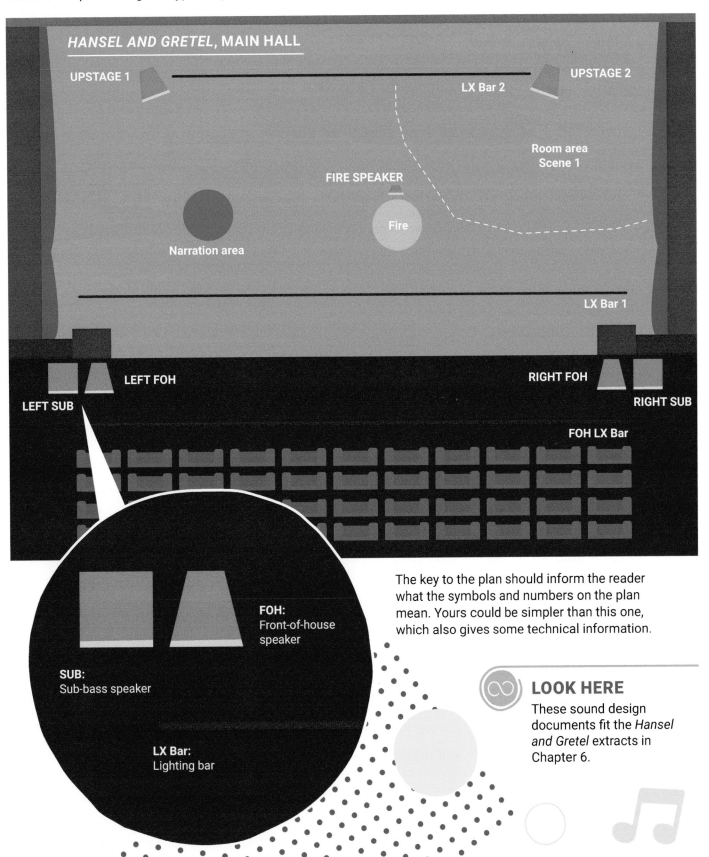

HANSEL AND GRETEL, MAIN HALL

UPSTAGE 1

UPSTAGE 2

LX Bar 2

Room area
Scene 1

FIRE SPEAKER

Fire

Narration area

LX Bar 1

LEFT FOH

RIGHT FOH

LEFT SUB

RIGHT SUB

FOH LX Bar

FOH:
Front-of-house speaker

SUB:
Sub-bass speaker

LX Bar:
Lighting bar

The key to the plan should inform the reader what the symbols and numbers on the plan mean. Yours could be simpler than this one, which also gives some technical information.

LOOK HERE

These sound design documents fit the *Hansel and Gretel* extracts in Chapter 6.

FOCUS

How to position sound equipment for the best effect.

ASSESSMENT CHECK

This section will help you to gain the specific knowledge required for AO2.

DESIGN TIP

Add your own notes to the table as you progress with your design.

POSITIONING SOUND EQUIPMENT

An important aspect of your sound design and practical skills is taking care with the placement of your speakers.

As a general rule, you would have at least one speaker for each section of the audience.

Where do I put moveable speakers?

If the sound speakers in your performance area are fixed, you need to consider that in your design. It is likely, however, that there will be some speakers that you can position yourself. Ask the music department. The table below indicates ideal placements in common configurations.

Once they are in position, you might need to secure speakers with safety bonds or cargo straps.

Minimum number of speakers and their positions		
Stage configuration	**Position of speakers**	**Notes**
Proscenium arch / end on	Front of stage – left and right	If possible, all speakers should be positioned at ear height for the audience.
Traverse	Facing the audience from the acting area (minimum of 2)	See above.
Thrust	Front and sides of stage (3 in total)	See above.
In the round	All four sides, facing the audience	Ideally, these speakers would be hung discreetly above the acting area.

Are mini-speakers useful?

The short answer is that it depends on your sound design. One good example of their use is on stage as part of a diegetic sound device, such as a radio or phone. You could use a powerful bluetooth speaker that the performers would activate themselves. This is a good example of directional sound.

DESIGN TIP

For Unit/Component 1, the diagram that you draw in Task 2.16 should be included in your portfolio.

TASK 2.16

Draw a plan diagram of your performance space. Pick a simple icon to show the position of your speakers. Be sure to mark the position(s) of the audience too.

Note that 'left' and 'right' in sound usually refers to the audience's right and left, rather than stage left and stage right. (Think about where the sound operator is likely to be.)

Sub-bass speakers produce very low-frequency sounds. They produce the 'thump' in music tracks. They can be useful for sound effects such as thunder.

FOH speakers produce mid- to high-frequency sounds and are the most common type in school halls, for example.

The fire speaker in the plan on page 55 is a small speaker concealed within the fire set on stage and used to make fire crackle sounds. As in lighting, this kind of speaker is called a 'special'.

Is there an ideal place to position the sound desk?

The best place for the sound desk is in the audience area. (Why do you think this is?)

In some venues, there is a 'box' at the back of the auditorium where technical equipment is fixed. Sometimes, these have a sliding window that allows the sound operator to hear what the audience is hearing.

The other element to consider is communication with the lighting operator. There are likely to be times when lighting and sound effects should be **synchronised**. If they can't sit near each other, how could the operators for sound and lighting communicate?

TASK 2.17

1 Walk your performance space with your teacher or other human resource. Identify the ideal location for your sound desk and establish whether it is a practical and safe site.

2 When you have settled on the best place for the sound operating equipment, use a simple icon to add to the diagram that you made in Task 2.16. Add a key to your sketch.

FOCUS

Creating the cue sheet that will guide you through a performance.

ASSESSMENT CHECK

A cue sheet will help you to successfully realise your artistic intentions (AO2). It is useful evidence for your Unit/Component 1 portfolio.

DESIGN TIP

Don't try to plot the performance until you have sourced your sounds and know where in the performance you are putting them!

DESIGN TIP

Remember that your design should indicate at least **five** sound cues in Unit/Component 1, and at least **four** in Unit/Component 2.

PLOTTING THE SOUND DESIGN

As sound designer, you are contributing to and supporting a performance as a whole. So, the sound operator needs to be able to run the 'sound show' smoothly and accurately. Plotting the sound and creating the cue sheet makes this possible.

What is plotting sound?

In this book, we use the term **plotting** to mean the act of fixing the sound for every part of the production. The **cue sheet** should record details of every sound cue decided. If you have sound design software, record each cue digitally as you go along.

You will need to make several decisions for each cue, including:

- what the sound is and from where it is sourced
- when it happens
- how loud it is
- how long it lasts (Does it **snap** off or **fade**?)
- what sounds are combined (if not plotted in software)
- the type and length of **transitions**.

Conditions for successful sound plotting

Don't underestimate the amount of time plotting will take. You might need more than one session if the performance is lengthy or complex.

- Make sure you plot sound in the performance space that you will be using!
- Choose a time when you can have the space to yourself. There is no point trying to plot during a rehearsal or when people are talking loudly. Setting volume levels, for instance, requires quiet and concentration.
- Collect everything you need, including:
  - your annotated script and notes
  - sound equipment
  - prepared sound effects
  - a task light (such as an angle-poise lamp)
  - a template for your cue sheet.
- You might also find it useful to ask an assistant to read lines of dialogue and check volume in various parts of the audience areas.

Understanding the terminology of sound levels

Unless you have worked with a sound desk before, you would probably expect that 0 on a fader would mean that the sound was off... In fact, sound is measured in **decibels**, which is a complex unit using a scale. All you really need to know is that 0 decibels is in fact quite loud.

TASK 2.18

Experiment with the faders on your sound desk, keeping your drama piece in mind. Make notes for yourself or use masking tape to label points on the scales that are quiet, average and loud.

Creating your cue sheet

When you have good sound conditions and clear understanding of both your design and the technology, you are ready to plot the production.

TASK 2.19

1 Lay your script and a cue sheet template around your sound desk. If you have a software package for storing your cues, bring it into action.

2 Starting at the beginning of the show, work through the production cue by cue and scene by scene to build and chart each sound cue. (An example is given to show you how it works.)

3 Check that cue numbers are clearly and correctly marked in your script so that the operator can track approaching cues. You could add '6a', '6b' and so on, if needed.

4 Continue to fill in your cue sheet until you have plotted the entire production.

DESIGN TIP

Take your time with plotting. Continue to check that you are supporting the artistic intentions of the piece. If you miss a cue, add it later, as '3a', for example.

Sound cue sheet						
Cue number and script page	Cue signal	Sound	Playback device (if more than one)	Level (dB)	Transition	Notes with timings
1 pre-set	House open	Play music	CD player	−10		Pre-set from time house is open. Visual.
2 p1	Visual – actors walk on	Music off		All out	Fade out	Over 10 seconds (in time with lighting transition).
3 p3	"Come over here!"	Soundscape 1	Laptop	+6	Fade up	Over 5 seconds – gradual fade up.

ASSESSMENT CHECK

Here, you are applying your theatrical skills to realise your artistic intentions (AO2).

OPERATING SOUND EQUIPMENT

Creating impact for an audience involves delivering sound cues skilfully in performance. You will need these items in place:

- a working sound desk that you have practised using
- playback device(s), such as a laptop and sound software, CD or mp3 player
- speakers
- a task light
- script (if applicable), marked up with the cues
- the completed cue sheet.

A complex set of sound equipment at Helsinki City Theatre.

ASSESSMENT CHECK

You can use your knowledge and skills to realise your artistic intentions in performance.

TASK 2.20

Practise operating sound, even if you will not be responsible for it in the final rehearsals and performance.

1 Set up your equipment and test that it is working.
2 Run through all your cues and check them for volume and effect.
3 Refer to 'Troubleshooting', on the following page, if needed.

Facing the challenges of operating sound

You might not be operating the sound for your production. It is not a requirement for the assessment, but you should know what the challenges are. Remember too that operating sound sensitively will be a significant aspect of the performance.

For now, let's assume that you **are** the sound operator. An early hurdle you might face is equipment not working properly. Your human resources are likely to have more experience than you, so do ask them for support.

DESIGN TIP

Set up a small angle-poise light next to you.

Troubleshooting

Here are some common issues and suggestions for overcoming them.

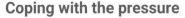

Problem	Checks and possible solutions
No power to desk.	Are other electrical items working, such as the angle-poise lamp? If so, the problem lies with the desk's connection to the electricity supply. Check sockets and cables.
One element of the system, radio mics, for example, is not working.	Is it reaching the desk? Does a light come on for it? If so, the problem is in the output. If not, it is in the input. Is it plugged in to the right socket?
Everything seems to be coming in, but there is still a fault.	There must be a problem with output. Are the **masters** up? Can you isolate the issue by eliminating things that are working?

Coping with the pressure

If there are a number of cues that are close together, the operator is under pressure to get the timings right. Badly timed sound cues can make a mess of things for the cast and for the audience.

Using software

If you are using software to operate your sound, you are hopefully simply pressing the space bar to trigger the next cue. However, you need to be very familiar with the software so that you know what to do if you fall out of sequence or trigger a cue too early. Practise as much as possible.

Operating a manual desk

You are likely to be busy with both hands and working much harder if you do not have pre-programmed effects. Prepare as much as possible to simplify the process. This could mean labelling master channels, for example. You can write on masking tape, which is easily removed. Always use your pre-set sections to prepare the next cue, and stay focused so that you are always ready for the next cue.

Practising sound operation

You should already be familiar with your sound desk and playback devices, but take time to ensure that you are comfortable using them. Go **cue to cue** through the script, practising the types of fades and effects that you are aiming for. Make sure you can operate them smoothly.

The script will keep you in time with the action and enable you to see where cues need to happen, such as on a word in the performance. You will begin to realise that you can 'feel' the action.

Live music

Many theatrical performances include a band or live performance on stage. This has implications for the sound designer and operator. If you do have instruments on stage, establish how these requirements fold into your sound design and operation. Practise this aspect as early as you can in the design and rehearsal process.

DESIGN TIP

The key to technical troubleshooting is to work through things logically and try to isolate exactly where the problem is. Only then do you stand a chance of fixing it!

DESIGN TIP

QLab (for Mac) is very useful for assembling and mixing sounds. It can also simplify the control of lights, video playback and the settings on a digital mixer.

DESIGN TIP

Be very aware of radio mics and when they need to be live. Keeping their fader down or channel muted at all other times is very important.

ASSESSMENT CHECK

Rehearsals allow you to adjust and practise your design so that it will operate as smoothly as possible in performance.

This demonstrates your knowledge and understanding of how drama and theatre is developed and performed (AO3).

LOOK HERE

The notes on pages 60–61 will help you to put everything in place before the tech.

DESIGN TIP

If you are using *QLab* or *SCS*, the software can trigger sound cues as well as lighting ones. This can be very useful if you want to precisely co-ordinate a blackout, for example.

DESIGN TIP

Sound levels vary depending on how full the space is. So, you might need to turn up the volume if you have a full house!

TECHNICAL AND DRESS REHEARSALS FOR SOUND DESIGNERS

The final rehearsals are your chance to check that you have a creative sound design that works well in practice. You might have a lot of equipment to set up, so try to complete this before the technical rehearsal ('tech').

The technical rehearsal

Techs are lengthy because they must allow lighting and sound operators to test their designs. At the same time, the director and other designers are checking that other aspects of the production are working smoothly.

Decide as a group whether to run the performance in full or move from cue to cue, missing out some sections. Make sure that everyone is confident that the process can then be repeated without interruptions.

As sound designer, you are likely to be heavily involved in the tech. If someone else is operating the sound, you need to guide them through the cues and make adjustments to levels, timings of fades and so on.

You will also need to watch the acting area to check the following points.

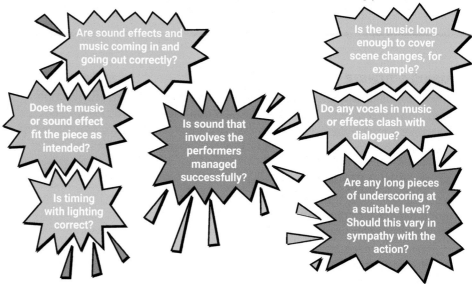

You (or an assistant) should also move around the audience area to hear volume levels. It is likely that levels and timings will need to change for some cues. Set these as you go along, even if it means holding up the tech for a couple of minutes.

If you or the sound operator are struggling with a technical aspect, ask your group if you can run a cue again. This is the purpose of the tech.

TASK 2.21

1 Update your notebook and script with any issues to be resolved before the dress rehearsal.
2 Arrange some time to work things through with other designers.

The dress rehearsal

The dress rehearsal ('dress') runs through the whole production without interruption. The performers can experience the full show with all the technical elements, but without an audience. You can test that the sound design can be operated successfully and works effectively in performance.

EVALUATING YOUR SOUND DESIGN

Once you are clear about what **evaluation** is and the best way of approaching it, you can focus on assessing the success of your sound design.

Examining the detail of your design

You need to provide a careful evaluation of your design skills demonstrated in performance. The only way that you can do this really well is to give detailed examples.

Whenever you evaluate, you should make at least three different points. These points should be illustrated with specific examples. Each time, you should also explain the reason why you have made a particular value judgement. You should highlight things that could have gone better.

It is very important to compare your finished sound design against your artistic intentions. Check your notes and make sure you include the success of this aspect in your evaluation.

Try not to repeat yourself when you evaluate. Discuss different types of sound and use a wide technical vocabulary.

TASK 2.22

1   Complete a table like this (some examples have been suggested). The notes will provide a solid basis for your evaluation writing.

Design element	Example / moment in the play	Evaluation	Reason for evaluation
Pre-set music	Before the performance began.	Engaging. Helped to create mood and place piece in time.	The music was chosen to put the audience into the right time period and to create the mood we wanted in our artistic intentions for the start of the piece.
Underscoring	The increasingly tense duologue between the two characters.	Atmospheric and contributed to action.	The underscoring track that I mixed included the use of reverb, which added depth. The pace increased as it went along, but was quiet enough for the actors' voices to be heard clearly.
The live sound from the performers	The end of the piece.	Successfully performed. Suited the ending.	As the performers linked hands and moved around the stage, they used their voices to make a humming sound. As they varied pitch and volume, there was a strong sense of their connection. I do wish that it could have been a little louder.

2   Expand your notes into three paragraphs of evaluative writing.

FOCUS

Placing a value judgement on design.

ASSESSMENT CHECK

This part of the design process is the essential element of AO4: 'Analyse and evaluate your own work and the work of others.'

SIGNPOST

Use the evaluation guidance on pages 80–81 before you start.

DESIGN TIP

No process is complete until you reflect upon it. Evaluation is a skill that will be important in all your exam subjects.

SOUND DESIGN VOCABULARY

Amplifier A piece of equipment that produces the sound for the speakers, primarily used to increase volume.

Constant sound An uninterrupted sound.

Cue sheet A list of cues with timings.

Cue to cue Going through a play from one sound or lighting cue to the next, missing out the parts in between.

Diegetic sound A sound that the characters would hear within their world, such as a phone ringing.

Digital Using computer technology. Digital lighting desks, for example, are programmed using software.

Directional sound Sound technology that produces a sound in a highly focused way, particularly so that the sound travels a long way. It also refers to the location and angle of a speaker, for example using an offstage speaker to suggest the location of a car.

Drone A constant sound that is often in the background. Drones are often used in non-naturalistic sound effects and are very good for creating atmosphere such as tension.

Echo The effect that occurs when a sound bounces off surfaces.

End on A stage configuration that places the audience on one side of an open stage.

Fade A gradual transition from quiet to loud, or vice versa.

Fader A device to control the volume of a sound.

Floating mic A microphone positioned on the front of the stage.

Hanging mic A microphone suspended above the performance area.

Intermittent sound A sound that is not constant; it comes and goes.

Live sound A sound that is played directly for the audience.

Manual Operated by hand, rather than digitally.

Mixer A device that can change and combine sounds.

Montage A sequence or joining together of sounds to make a new piece of sound.

Naturalistic A set or lighting effect, for example, with characteristics of reality; having the appearance of a real place.

Non-diegetic sound Sound that can be heard by the audience, but would not be heard by the characters (such as atmospheric music to encourage the audience to feel something).

Non-naturalistic A set or lighting design, for example, that aims not to appear like reality.

Pace The speed with which lighting or sound effects transition from one to the next.

Pitch-shifting Altering the pitch of a sound which, when mixed with other differently pitched versions of the same sound, makes it have a richer, thicker sound.

Playback device The means through which recorded sound is played, such as a CD player or smartphone.

Plotting The process of creating a cue sheet to show choices of what sound happens when.

Proscenium (arch) A stage configuration where the audience are where the 'fourth wall' of a room would be – similar to **end on**, but with the addition of a picture-frame effect around the stage.

Radio mic A microphone that is worn by a performer, often taped to the cheek.

Recorded sound Sound that is captured electronically, such as onto a computer file.

Reverb The effect that occurs when sound waves hit surrounding surfaces and we hear the original sound plus its reflections. Adding reverb to a sound makes it longer and weightier.

Snap A quick and sudden transition, such as from loud to silent or a blackout.

Sound desk The means of operating the different sounds.

Soundscape An effect made up of several sounds to give the impression of a city street, for example.

Source Where the sound comes from, such as a computer file. Also used to describe the sound itself, such as a bell ringing.

Speaker The device that transmits the sound. Its volume level can be altered.

Structure The way that something is sequenced, put together or built.

Synchronised Two or more sounds operating at the same time.

Transition Movement between sound cues, such as fade and snap.

Traverse A stage configuration where the audience is in two parts that are seated opposite each other along two sides of the stage.

Underscore Sound (often non-diegetic) that is played quietly while performers are speaking, to add atmosphere.

PRACTICAL GUIDE TO SET DESIGN

ASSESSMENT CHECK

In the beginning of your journey as a set designer, you will start to understand how drama and theatre is developed and performed (AO3).

DESIGN TIP

Pay attention to your **pre-set**. This can include light and sound too and is seen or heard before the performance begins. It establishes setting and style and lets the audience think, 'I know where we are.'

INTRODUCTION TO SET DESIGN

What is a set designer?

In a sense, you are already a set designer. You probably have opportunities to influence the layout and colour scheme in your bedroom, for example.

Your choices are influenced by practicality, style, comfort and image. An observer might also learn something about you based on the books or games on your shelf or the posters on your wall.

A set designer is very different from an interior designer, however: they think about space from the audience's point of view, not the occupant's. This means that they help to communicate meaning, artistic intentions, style and atmosphere through the **scenery** they design and the stage furniture they select.

What can you tell about the person who occupies this room? What clues give you those ideas?

How can I design sets as part of this course?

You can opt for set design in either or both of the practical sections of the course.

If you choose to work as set designer in Unit/Component 1, you will work in a small group to devise a piece of theatre. You will help to develop the piece as a whole, but your specific responsibility will be to design the set.

Unit/Component 2 is similar, but you work with a script instead of devising your own drama.

Unit/Component 3 is the written exam. When you evaluate a performance you have seen, you might have to write about set design. Practical work will give you the knowledge and understanding to write confidently.

How can set design communicate meaning?

We all 'read' peoples, places and situations, but do not always realise it.

TASK 3.1

Study this set for *Blithe Sprit*, then answer the questions, giving specific examples from the set.

1. What room is shown?
2. The play is set in the 1930s. Are there any clues to this? (Look at styles and shapes of **furnishings**, scenery and fabrics.)
3. What seems to be the economic background of the people who live in this house? (Do they seem wealthy? How does the set suggest this?)
4. What **colour palette** is used?
5. What mood or atmosphere is suggested? (Consider, for example, whether colours are light or dark and whether there is clutter or space. Does the set suggest a calm life or hectic one?)

Creating a location (place)

Location is a key starting point for most set designs. A set designer must be able to design both **interior** and **exterior** locations. The following tasks will help you to explore these in more detail.

Interior spaces

TASK 3.2

1 Look around the room you are in and notice its shape and features.
2 Now imagine it as a theatre set.
3 In a group, discuss what elements you should keep in order to maintain the room's meaning as, for example, a classroom or drama studio.
4 Then share ideas on how you could re-create the space for staging a drama **in the round**. Think about your audience, furniture, scenery, lighting fixtures and flooring.

Exterior settings

TASK 3.3

This scene from *The Woman in Black* uses back projection to place the character outside a mansion.

1 Imagine that you have been asked to create a set design for the same location, but without the use of projection. This means that you would have to place **constructions**, stage furniture and/or **props** on the stage. You could also consider a painted backdrop. You have a small budget of £100–200.

Use a chart like this to note down items that you could include.

| Location set design: Mansion exterior | | |
Scenery (flats, backdrops, etc.)	Furniture	Props
		Plant pots.

2 Next, imagine that a set designer has a budget of several £1000s and is designing the same exterior location, for an **end-on** stage configuration. The designer has provided this sketch ⟶

Work with a partner to give oral feedback to the designer.
  • What do you like about the set design? Why?
  • How could it be improved?

3 Now **you** are the set designer in a school production of the same scene from *The Woman in Black*. It is an end-on stage configuration. Draw and label your own design.

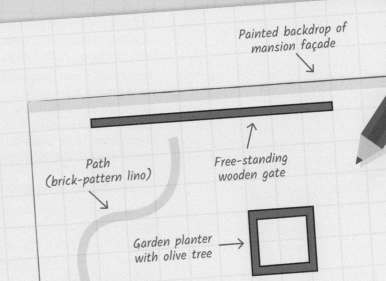

Painted backdrop of mansion façade

Path (brick-pattern lino)

Free-standing wooden gate

Garden planter with olive tree

FOCUS

Naturalistic and non-naturalistic set designs.

ASSESSMENT CHECK

Learning about different set styles will help your knowledge and understanding of drama and theatre, working towards AO3.

TASK 3.4

Study the set, right, for *Crocodile Fever*. Write down three details of the design that make it look like a real kitchen. Remember that set design usually includes large props, furniture, **set dressings**, furnishings and accessories, as well as the 'frame' and 'backdrop' of the space.

TASK 3.5

Write down three thoughts or questions that spring to mind when studying the set on the right. These could be linked to the set itself, the performance or the characters within it.

TWO STYLES OF SET DESIGN

Although there are many ways of categorising types of set design, it is helpful to start with these two basic ideas of **realistic**, **naturalistic** sets and **non-naturalistic** sets. They are clear and recognisable styles, and the choice between the two is one of the first decisions a set designer makes.

Naturalistic sets

A naturalist set could also be described as 'realistic'. It aims for immediately recognisable locations and to make the set appear as natural as possible. The audience does not need to use their imagination to understand the setting, as the **illusion** is complete.

A highly detailed set for *Crocodile Fever* at the Traverse Theatre in Edinburgh.

Non-naturalistic sets

A **representative** or non-naturalistic set might include key items that 'shout' the location within an otherwise **stylised** setting. The set on the right, for example, creates the illusion of a bedroom, but leaves scope for the audience to **interpret** the setting. Lighting and sound can be effective in enhancing meaning with this type of set design.

The use of a non-naturalistic set does not have to be restricted to non-naturalistic texts. They can be used to 'modernise' older plays or 'move' the original location.

The minimalist pre-set for a student production on a thrust stage at the University of Michigan.

The space you are designing for

Other important points in the early stages of set design are the size of the space for the set and what the stage configuration will be. Your teacher will be able to tell you if the performance will be in the drama studio or the hall, for example, and help you with the layout of the acting area and where the audience will sit.

Pay attention to safety issues in your design. It could be very difficult to remove hazards once the set has been constructed.

RESEARCH FOR SET DESIGN

Don't start online! Your first instinct might be to browse the internet, but there is no better place for inspiration and information than the real world.

FOCUS

How to start generating ideas for you set designs.

Ask...

If your set text or devised piece is set in the 20th century, try talking to your family and their friends. You can't beat first-hand experience, and they might have photos.

ASSESSMENT CHECK

This research will help you towards AO1: 'Create and develop ideas to communicate meaning for theatrical performance.'

You are also required to describe your research findings.

Visit...

Museums and galleries often have exhibitions linked to particular periods in history. You might get ideas for furnishings and props as well as the set. A visit to a heritage site can be highly inspirational. These places include back-to-back terraces, art deco houses and so on. Take notes and photos, if permitted.

Watch...

There have been some entertaining television documentaries on social history. *Turn Back Time*, for example, placed different families in various historical eras. *A House Through Time* put a modern family in a house that changed to show life from the 19th century to the present day.

Track down some films that are made or set in the period for your drama. Focus on the settings as you watch.

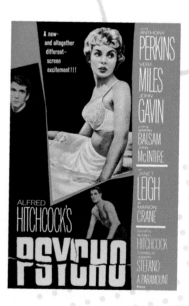

Online research

Use specific key words in your internet searches. Furniture is a good place to start, and 'Ikea 1970s', for example, should bring up some very useful images. A heritage website will also provide inspiration and information.

Just a couple of props and furnishings or pieces of stage furniture will give your set an authentic feel and help to communicate meaning. It is important to reflect the social and economic contexts of your drama.

If your design allows it, a print or painting that strongly identifies the period or social context is well worth hanging on a wall. This 1960s film poster adds atmosphere as well as a sense of the period.

TASK 3.6

1 Search for '1930s house interior' and choose an image that interests you. (If you want to, narrow down your search by specifying 'working class' or 'art deco', for example.)

2 From it, pick an item or two that you might be able to use in a set.

3 What colours and patterns from the image might also be suitable for your set?

ASSESSMENT CHECK

Consideration of the use of performance space, including levels, is included in AO1.

DESIGN TIP

Take care to ensure that seats, steps or platforms are sturdily built and safe to use.

DESIGN TIP

Think carefully about where levels could be used in the acting area. Performance should still be versatile, and sightlines considered.

USING LEVELS IN SET DESIGN

When writing about your own set design or one that you have seen, the use of levels is an important consideration. As well as adding interest, raising areas of the acting area offers potential for:

* creating more than one location
* enhancing a split focus (with the aid of lighting)
* suggesting power relationships.

How to include levels

Professional productions might use expensive methods to create levels, but they can be created without spending much at all. For example:

* Purpose-made staging blocks might be available in your school. Some versions are stackable. Alternatively, you might be able to borrow blocks from another learning setting, your local hall or a theatre nearby. If not, it is possible to hire stage blocks reasonably cheaply.
* If there is a fixed stage (in the hall, for example), you could design a set with some action taking place on the floor and some on the stage.
* A technical department might be able to build some simple levels.
* Actors could sit or stand on low benches, chairs or stools.

Professional set designers often include more than one level in their designs. This one by Tony Ferrieri for *The Morini Strad* takes place in a stringed-instrument repair shop. The platform is in the shape of a violin. The polished wood tones also match the material of a violin.

Writing about levels in set design

You should explain the significance of levels in the set design you are writing about. Ask yourself questions similar to those below.

* How are levels used by performers? Be specific here. (A character or location might be associated with a level. Characters might use a level to show that they have power at a certain moment.)

* How high are the levels? Why? (There might be a variety of heights to add interest and meaning.)

* What shape are the raised sections? Why? (Straight edges might suit the severity of the court setting.)

* How have the levels been positioned in this set for *The Crucible*? Draw a quick sketch.

HOW TO DOCUMENT YOUR SET DESIGN

Set designers need to produce their designs very early in the process as lighting, in particular, cannot be designed without knowledge of the set. The director and performers also need to lay out the rehearsal area in a way that represents the set.

What documents should I produce?

All types of theatre designer must be able to show their design ideas long before their designs are actually created. Sketches, ground plans and models are useful ways of doing this.

Clear drawings and ground plans are required for Units/Components 1 and 2. These do not need to be drawn to **scale**, but showing scale on the ground plan, in particular, is very useful. When your set is constructed, the builders will use the ground plan to check measurements.

Set designs are created for a specific space. Produce plans that reflect the size of this space as well as the appropriate stage configuration.

Drawings of the final design

This example draft sketch shows a design idea for Oscar Wilde's Victorian social comedy *The Importance of Being Earnest*. It includes enough detail to base a ground plan on.

FOCUS

- Clearly presenting your set design as a ground plan.
- Using 3D models to visualise the design.

ASSESSMENT CHECK

Your ground plans, sketches and models will show that you can create and develop your ideas (AO1) and apply your theatrical skills to realise artistic intentions (AO2).

Two portraits are hung at either side of the doors.

Three **flats** are joined to make a **run** at the back of an end-on stage configuration.

The centre section is hinged to form outward-opening **French windows**.

Two more flats are free-standing centre left and centre right.

Two chairs and a small table stand on the rug.

A large Victorian-style rug centre stage.

Find out the exact size of the area you are designing for. Then you can work out a realistic size for the scenery you are placing in it.

Let's say that your stage area for an end-on configuration is: 5 metres wide by 4 metres deep.

- You have allowed 1m behind the run of flats at the back so that the doors can open outwards. This means the acting area will be 5m wide and 3m deep.
- The two outer flats at the back are going to be 1m wide. The centre one will be 2m wide to include the opening doors.
- Your **free-standing flats** are 1m wide (2m high works well).
- The rug is 2m square, laid at an angle.
- A net/voile curtain does not appear on the sketch, but will be added to the ground plan.

Ground plans

A ground plan is a bird's eye view. If you are looking straight down you would see width and depth, but not height. It should represent the performance space, 'including entrances and exits, audience positioning and stage furniture (as appropriate)'.

The information and sketch on the previous page can be transformed into a ground plan at 1:20 scale, below.

Use an ordinary metal rule to create a 1:20 scale: 5cm on the plan represents 100cm (1 metre) on the stage. Simple annotations and a key help to make details clear.

TASK 3.7

Drawing a ground plan

1 Sketch a **simple** set design for the play you are working on.

2 Measure the performance area in whole or half metres. (Anything else will be complicated to use on a ground plan.)

3 List the dimensions (measurements) of the stage area and the width and depth of all items of scenery to be included.

4 Go on to draw a 1:20-scale ground plan of your design.

5 Add annotations, such as 'rug', main measurements and a key that explains any symbols you use. Note the scale here too.

6 Share your sketch and ground plan with a group member. If they can't understand them, note where the difficulties are, and try again!

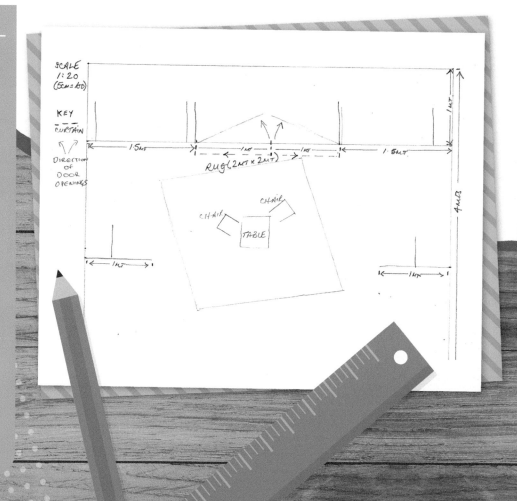

3D models

You are not required to make models, but they are an excellent form in which to show your set designs. Models are widely used because:

- they allow the director and performers to visualise the set clearly
- free-standing parts of the model can be moved around during design meetings, aiding discussion and decision making
- they give valuable information to the set builders.

If you choose to make a 3D model of your set, you might need:

- ○ Paper, pencils, paints and small brushes
- ○ Collage items (magazines and so on)
- ○ Foam board
- ○ Plasticine
- ○ Lolly sticks
- ○ Cardboard
- ○ Plywood offcuts
- ○ Scraps of light weight fabrics
- ○ Glue sticks
- ○ Electrical tape
- ○ Sculpting tools
- ○ Dressmakers' pins
- ○ Cotton reels (about the right scale for tables)

LOOK HERE

Follow the checklist in 'Health and safety in set design', page 77.

DESIGN TIP

Start gathering useful modelling materials as soon as you begin the design process.

White card models

These 3D models are relatively quick and easy to make because they are not detailed. You simply use cardboard. They allow you to experiment with, for example, positioning flats. Moving elements of the model around enables you to see what effects are created in terms of entrances and exits, for instance.

The pictures below show **white-card** elements of a set design for *Hansel and Gretel*. The maker has experimented with **book flats** in different positions.

DESIGN TIP

Include an 'actor' that can be moved around the 'set'. This is very helpful in understanding the space for various scenes. (At 1:20 scale, you could make your figure 7cm tall.)

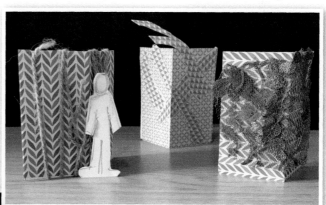

These book flats have been made from 10cm-square sheets of card, scored and folded to be free-standing. They are at 1:20 scale. The textures are experiments with origami paper, fabric and string for a non-naturalistic forest effect.

Model boxes

Model boxes are generally made when a designer is fairly certain of their set design. They can be seen as more complete versions of white card models. They can be as simple or as highly detailed as you wish. Some model boxes even include lights!

A model of the set for *Kindertransport* at Coventry Belgrade Theatre by Juliet Shillingford.

A fairly quickly made model box, developed from the ground plan on page 72.

TASK 3.8

Making a 3D model

1 Choose a design from which to create a model box or white card model. You could use the ground plan from Task 3.7.

2 Gather the materials to work with.

3 Make your model at a scale of 1:20.

4 Take feedback on your model and make the necessary changes if you can.

UNDERSTANDING YOUR RESOURCES

Materials, tools and equipment

At an early stage of the design process, you should make yourself aware of the materials available for creating the set.

TASK 3.9

Select from the following list the items you would like to use for your set. Then highlight which are available in your school or college.

This will give you a good starting point, but if you think you need further items, add them to the list and begin to think where you could source them.

Building MATERIALS and TOOLS

- ○ Cardboard sheets and boxes
- ○ Large pieces of sturdy cloth such as canvas
- ○ Plywood sheets
- ○ Timber strips
- ○ Staple gun
- ○ Glue gun
- ○ Heavy-duty gaffer tape
- ○ Metal brackets and hinges
- ○ Cable ties
- ○ Drill
- ○ Screwdriver
- ○ Flooring offcuts
- ○ Water-based paint, brushes
- ○ Marker pens
- ○ PVA glue

Human resources

The exam board states that 'set designers are not assessed on the set's construction.' This means that you can get help with building your set.

The most likely source of support is your technology department, especially if topics such as construction and working with resistant materials are on the curriculum. Remember that you need to be closely involved in what is made and how it is constructed. Perhaps a technology teacher or student could construct the set or scenery item while you assist, for you to paint afterwards. Discuss this with your Drama teacher.

You might not even need to build a set. You can hire or borrow items, but you need to be involved with the process, and the **design** of the set must be yours.

A Drama student mixes and chooses paint for her set.

TASK 3.10

Arrange to visit the construction rooms of the technology department. Discuss with a teacher:

- How might they set about constructing a scenery item such as a flat?
- What materials would they suggest using for your design?
- What tools and equipment would you need?

FOCUS

Practical aspects you need to know about before you create your design.

ASSESSMENT CHECK

Being aware of the possibilities and limits to your design means that you understand how drama and theatre is developed and performed (AO3).

DESIGN TIP

Ask around! There might be a family friend who has a workshop, for example, and a trailer to transport the set to school.

How to find, recycle or buy the materials for your set and meet your artistic intentions.

ASSESSMENT CHECK

By making considered choices, you are demonstrating skills required for AO1, and beginning to analyse your work for AO4.

DESIGN TIP

Be resilient. Tackle problems step by step.
If an item is difficult to get, think:

- Can you make a saving elsewhere?
- Could you use a similar but cheaper version?
- Do you really need it?

SOURCING MATERIALS FOR THE SET

Once your set design has been agreed with your group, it is time to think about the actual set.

What do I need and what will it cost?

Keep in mind while designing that you will only have a small amount to spend on your set. Don't buy anything until you know:

- what your budget is
- everything you will need to design and make your set
- where you might get it
- how much it will all cost.

TASK 3.11

Copy and complete a chart like this to keep track of what you need.

Item	Source	Approximate cost
Large pot plant	Borrow from family or friends	None
Backcloth	Pre-painted: hire for 5 days	£100? Too much?
	Make own: canvas and paint	£60? Too much?
	Make own: 2 **tarpaulins** and paint	£40?
	Make own: sewn-together sheets, rough wooden frame, paint	£30?
	Make own: cardboard boxes taped together	£10? Will they look poor?
	Watered-down PVA as fire retardant	£2
Stage flat	Ply-board sheet from DIY shop	£20
	Rough-cut lengths from wood yard	£5
	Water-based paints and cheap acrylic	£10?
	Watered-down PVA as fire retardant	£2
3ft round table	Borrow	None
Round white tablecloth	Charity shop or make?	£3?

Recycling and borrowing

It is unlikely that you will be able to buy everything needed for your set. Is everything in your design essential? Can anything be changed to something you can borrow or recycle?

Recycling here simply means making an item into something else. For example, you could fix small wheels to a table to make it a trolley. A large scarf can become a tablecloth. A green tarpaulin over a stepladder could be a mountain.

- Find out what is already available in school. Could you borrow a table? Is there an existing stage flat that you can paint over?
- Try pound shops for craft materials and acrylic paint.
- Go to builders' merchants for offcuts.
- Pallets (often free) are useful for timber or even basic furniture.

HEALTH AND SAFETY IN SET DESIGN

Taking care of yourselves

You are responsible for the set, so you need to be aware of safety issues around construction, such as the examples below. This applies even if you are supervising others building a set on your behalf.

- ! Follow all instructions and guidance given.
- ! Make sure electrical equipment has an up-to-date PAT (Portable Appliance Testing) certificate.
- ! Check cables and machinery for damage. Make them secure.
- ! Wear safety goggles and gloves whenever necessary.
- ! Some paints and varnishes need to be applied in an airy space. Open windows and wear masks.
- ! Glue and staple guns are popular with set designers: they are quick and effective. Handle all such tools and materials with care and respect.
- ! Use the correct tool for the job.
- ! Store tools and materials neatly and out of the way.
- ! Be aware of what other people are doing around you.

Taking care of performers

On stage, actors need to concentrate on staying in role and immersing themselves in the world of the drama. Your set needs to enhance this world. It must also ensure the performers' safety.

Risks to **avoid** include:
- ! Trip hazards (rugs, for instance, should be secured with double-sided tape)
- ! Unstable pieces of scenery (brace items with stage weights)
- ! Glass in windows or doors (use Perspex or leave them empty)
- ! Slippery floor finishes (avoid gloss)
- ! Unsuitable access or space for performers with impaired mobility
- ! Large or uneven steps and levels
- ! Unmarked edges of steps (try a textured surface if tape will be seen by the audience).

Making your set fire-safe

Fire regulations for public performances are very strict. (If your show is just for staff and students in school, it is not considered a public performance.) If a prop is always held in a performer's hand, it does not need to be flame proofed. However, any scenery or large prop that is free-standing **must** be made of fire-retardant material or treated to be flame proof. You could:

- ! Buy fire-retardant timber and cloth (effective, but expensive)
- ! Use fire-retardant spray for the fabric parts of your set
- ! Cover painted wood surfaces with water-based matt varnish or watered-down PVA glue (about 5 parts water to 1 part PVA).

FOCUS

Keeping yourself and others safe.

ASSESSMENT CHECK

Throughout Units/ Components 1 and 2, you must follow safe working practices. This also shows understanding of how drama and theatre is developed and performed (AO3).

DESIGN TIP

It is important to consider safety issues before you start construction. It could be difficult to remove hazards afterwards.

FIRE RETARDANT

FOCUS

Pointers for constructing the set once the design has been agreed.

ASSESSMENT CHECK

In creating a set from your design, you are demonstrating your knowledge and understanding of how drama and theatre is developed and performed (AO3).

LOOK HERE

See page 77 for health and safety tips for set construction, and page 70 for advice on including different levels.

DESIGN TIP

Make sure that your set is completed in good time. The performers need time to rehearse on it!

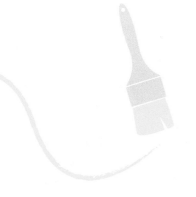

CREATING YOUR SET DESIGN FOR THE STAGE

Your responsibility

The exam specification states that you do not have to build the set yourself, as you will not be assessed on its construction. Whoever is building the set, there are some points to consider before you begin.

Which parts of the set need to function?

The most important thing to remember is that you are creating an illusion when you make a theatre set. Many aspects of your set will not need to 'do' anything. A painted shop front, for example, might not need to have a door that opens, it simply gives the illusion of a shop.

Some parts of your set, however, might need to be bear the weight of an actor, or a window might need to open and close. If this is the case, ask yourself:

- What am I making?
- How will it be used?
- Who is using it?

The answers will guide you towards the materials to use and how sturdy your construction needs to be.

Scenery on flats

You might need to make flats: upright pieces of scenery. Usually made from sheets of plywood about 1.2 metres by 2.4 metres, flats are braced and weighted so that they stand securely. Another way of making a flat is to stretch canvas over a wooden frame. Both types can then be painted.

Painted backcloths and panels

Traditionally, many stage sets had a painted cloth at the back of the acting area. It depicted the location for the play. If you have the time and resources, you could use a canvas or canvas-stretched frames. You would need to have a way of hanging them from the lighting bars or make them free-standing. Or, a run of painted flats could work just as well. Your human resources will help you to establish what is possible.

This painted cloth of a riverbank scene was created for, and can be hired from, the Yvonne Arnaud Theatre.

Be creative!

Some of the best set designs are made with non-standard materials. Try the following crafty shortcuts.

- Reinforce large cardboard boxes with gaffer tape. Use them to build pieces of scenery. Paint different sides to give varied scenes and you have an original way of changing the set.
- Ask to borrow a metal trolley from the school canteen. You could attach two different pieces of flat scenery (made from cardboard perhaps) with cable ties. Just swivel them as needed.

TECHNICAL AND DRESS REHEARSALS FOR SET DESIGNERS

The rehearsal schedule works towards a technical and then a dress rehearsal. These are the rehearsals that draw everything together.

As set designer, you should sit in the audience area for the technical and dress rehearsals. You need your notebook to hand and should change your seat every now and again to check sightlines.

Technical rehearsal

This rehearsal is for technicians and designers. It will probably be the first chance to put all the elements of the production (performers, lights, sound, costumes and set) together. Everything might look and work as planned, but take the opportunity to change things if not. If you encounter some typical problems, try the suggestions in the table below.

Potential problems	Possible solutions and timings
Parts of the set are not finished. Perhaps the edge of a flat has not been painted or a vase does not have flowers.	List outstanding tasks. Ensure they are done before the dress rehearsal (and allow time for paint and glue to dry).
A set element is not functioning properly. For example, a door isn't opening and closing smoothly.	Make adjustments so that the issue is fixed before the dress rehearsal.
A piece of set does not look or feel right. For example, a bookcase looks too empty, too full or too tidy.	Decide if you can make changes before the dress rehearsal. If not, get it done before the performance.
The actors are struggling with some aspect of the set. Perhaps they have to squeeze between items of furniture or cannot move scenery smoothly.	Make a list or annotate your design. Work with the actors after the 'tech' to rearrange the furniture or practise moving the scenery.
The set does not appear as you had hoped under some of the lighting states.	Note which scenes are causing the problem. Talk to the lighting designer before the dress rehearsal and see if you can come to a compromise in the intensity or colour of the lighting.
Part of the set is obscuring sightlines from some areas of the audience.	Sketch where problems occur. Adjust the positioning of the set if possible. Otherwise, remove the awkward seats from the audience.

Dress rehearsal

The 'dress' is the final, timed, **run** before the performance. Now that technical issues have been addressed, the actors can perform uninterrupted.

Again, watch from the audience area with a notebook. Remember to move around and look out for the following:

- Have changes from the tech been made successfully?
- Are sightlines clear from every position in the audience?
- Are set changes working smoothly and in reasonable time?
- Are the actors happy moving around the set?

If there are still issues, revisit your notes and the table above. Work with your colleagues to tackle problems. Make final tweaks as necessary.

FOCUS

- The role of the set designer during final rehearsals.
- How potential problems might be overcome.

ASSESSMENT CHECK

Rehearsals will help you to reflect upon your design, leading you to analyse and evaluate (AO4).

DESIGN TIP

Try not to interrupt the rehearsal unless there is a health and safety issue, so that you can see how elements work in real time and support the performers.

FOCUS

Placing a value judgement on drama is key to Units/Components 1 and 3. These pages will help you to develop the habit of reflecting on your work.

ASSESSMENT CHECK

Essential for AO4 is the ability to analyse and evaluate your own work and the work of others in the written exam as well as in your practical work.

LOOK HERE

'Set Design for the Devised Piece' from page 148, has more guidance on the devising process and evaluating as you go through it. See Chapter 7 for more examples of evaluation.

EVALUATING YOUR SET DESIGN

What is evaluation?

Evaluation is a skill that you will use in many of your GCSE subjects. It is the process of judging something's quality, importance or value. In other words, you give your considered opinion on how 'good' or successful something is when you evaluate it. Evaluation is a valued skill because it requires reflection and reasoning.

When do I evaluate?

You will be reflecting on and assessing the success of your set throughout any designing process.

In Unit/Component 1, the most crucial analysis comes after the production, when you evaluate the effectiveness of your contribution to the final performance. A strong ability to evaluate will contribute significant marks to the portfolio, which is a key part of the devising unit/component.

Evaluation is also an essential skill in Unit/Component 3, when you analyse and form **critical judgements** on the work of other theatre makers.

How do I evaluate successfully?

Evaluation becomes convincing when you build an argument to support your opinions. The way to do this involves giving clear examples. You should aim to use a range of vocabulary for the different evaluations you make because if you always say something is 'effective' it starts to lose its impact.

TASK 3.12

Copy the following diagram, adding some adjectives of your own. Use it when writing about your set.

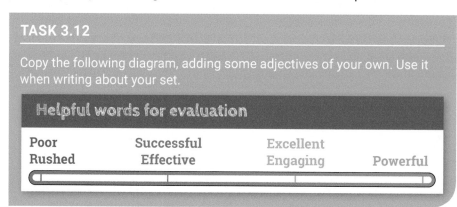

Helpful words for evaluation

| Poor | Successful | Excellent | |
| Rushed | Effective | Engaging | Powerful |

You will be expected to choose a few details from your set and give reasons why you think they were effective in performance. This student has begun to do this as well as using some evaluative words like the ones above:

Lord of the Flies by A Theatre Near U.

I believe that one **powerful element** of my set design was how it **allowed the performers** to use different **levels**. The **moment** when Jack looks down from a height onto Piggy lying on the floor is **a good example of this**. The set **helped to emphasise** the amount of control and power Jack has over Piggy. Also, the set **combined with lighting** in an **engaging** way for the audience...

Examining the details of your set design

In your evaluation, you will need to make at least three different points with examples that help to illustrate why you have made a particular value judgement.

The geometric shapes used consistently throughout this set design are simple to achieve but give flexibility and create a striking effect. (*Brokers* by Tylar Pendgraft performed by the USC School of Dramatic Arts.)

1 Copy and complete your own version of this table (examples are given based on the set design above). These notes will form a solid basis for your evaluative writing.

Set design evaluation			
Design element	Example / moment in the play	Evaluation	Reason for evaluation
Suspended frames	Pre-set and throughout the play.	Engaging. Encouraged audience to ask questions and become involved.	Encouraged the audience to think about uncertainty and things falling. Linked to the theme of the play.
Movable cubes	Scene changes.	Effective in setting scenes quickly and simply.	The fact that the boxes could be easily moved by the actors made it easy and quick to create different locations.
Use of the colour white	The moment when the character became depressed.	Powerful in creating atmosphere and helping characterisation.	The use of white in the set combined with the blue lighting created an atmosphere of emptiness and despair.

2 Once you have made your evaluation into a table like this, turn it into three paragraphs. Remember that you are evaluating. This means that you add a value judgement to an opinion and support it with examples.

SET DESIGN VOCABULARY

Backcloth A large piece of canvas or cloth which is often painted with a setting.

Colour palette A complementary set of colours that belong to a group, such as pastel or dark.

Construction Something that has been built (a set for example); the act of building.

Critical judgement Analysing the merits and faults of something to decide its worth or success.

End on A stage configuration that places the audience on one side of an open stage.

Exterior (setting/location) An outdoor space, such as a garden, street or outside a building.

Flat A tall, main piece of scenery that, as its name suggests, generally carries a 2D image.

Book flat Two flats that are hinged along their 'spine'.

Free-standing flat A braced, single flat that can stand anywhere on the set.

Run of flats Two or more flats joined as a length to achieve a wall, for example.

French doors/windows A pair of outward-opening doors often fully glazed, functioning as both windows and doors.

Furnishings Set furniture (sometimes including curtains, rugs and so on).

Illusion Something that is not as it seems; something that is not real, but often gives an impression of reality.

In the round A stage configuration in which the audience encircles the acting area.

Interior (setting/location) An indoor space, such as a kitchen or a school hall.

Interpret Express your own ideas about intended meaning; your choice where there are a number of correct possibilities.

Location The place or setting where action takes place, such as a forest, a bedroom or a park.

Model box A 3D set design, often presented within a box of some sort.

Naturalistic A set, for example, with characteristics of reality; having the appearance of a real place.

Non-naturalistic A set design, for example, that aims not to look like a real place.

Pre-set Features of the drama on stage that are already in place before the audience enters.

Props Short for 'properties' (suggesting ownership): objects that would be owned by a character such as a torch, phone, set of keys.

Realistic A set, for example, that sets out to be like real life (naturalistic).

Representative Something that represents (stands for) something else: for example, a non-naturalistic set that 'represents' and suggests rather than copies real life.

Run Either a rehearsal of the whole play, or the number of times a play will be performed (*The Crucible* has a three-week run at this theatre).

Scale The size of something relative to something else.

Scenery Parts of the set that represent locations or surroundings – on cloth or flats.

Set dressings Accessories such as tablecloths, cushions and other decorative items.

Stylised Non-realistic, non-naturalistic, where style features are dominant.

Tarpaulin Large, heavy-duty, waterproof cloth/sheet, usually of woven plastic.

White-card model A simple 3D representation of a set design.

PRACTICAL GUIDE TO COSTUME DESIGN

ASSESSMENT CHECK

As you gain awareness and understanding of costume choices, you:

- develop your ability to create ideas to communicate meaning (AO1)
- learn how costume can enhance character, period, style and mood (AO2).

INTRODUCTION TO COSTUME DESIGN

Everyday costumes

At least once every day we all use costume design skills. When you open your drawer or look in your **wardrobe**, you are choosing clothing to suit your day. Consciously or otherwise, you might be thinking:

- Am I going to be outside much and what will I be doing?
- How do I feel and what image do I want to project?
- Do I just want to be comfortable or do I want to make an impression?

Everyday make-up

Some people wouldn't leave the house without make-up. For others, they wear it for an evening out or not at all. Make-up also has strong cultural and religious meanings for some communities.

There are numerous reasons why make-up can be important, including:

- sharing your culture and identity
- boosting confidence
- helping you to feel older or younger.

How should a character be made-up and costumed?

When you design costumes for the stage, you are making decisions for a character rather than for yourself, but you can start with the same three questions above. Then go on to ask yourself these more specific questions:

TASK 4.1

1. Take a few moments to look at the people around you and what they are wearing. Apply the three bullet-point questions above to each person and put yourself in their shoes.
2. If you can, try this task in a range of locations, such as a park and a café. Build up a picture of each person. What other clothing do you imagine they have in their wardrobe?

How does their occupation (or lack of it) influence their clothing and make-up choices?

What fashions and fabrics would be available given the period of history in which the play is to be staged?

Does the character have any particular personality traits that might influence their choices? (Are they vain? Do they tend to feel anxious?)

How interested is the character in clothes and make-up?

To what extent do they care about how they look? To what extent can they afford to care?

Does the character undergo a journey through the play, or a transformation? How could that be communicated through costume and make-up?

Using costume to enhance meaning

As a costume designer, you have the power to influence how an audience perceives a character before they speak or move. Your design input might immediately inform the audience that a character is a pilot in the Second World War, for example, or an impoverished child in the 1960s.

Stylistic and artistic collaboration

Reflecting the context – such as historical and economic signs – is crucial in design. At the same time, a costume designer needs to work in harmony with other designers and the director to achieve the stylistic and artistic intentions of the drama. This might mean, for example, working within a particular **colour palette**, designing a costume that allows an actor to safely climb part of the set, or working with the lighting designer to ensure that your fabric choices will be appropriate under particular stage lights.

Costume and the actor

Costuming and make-up are very important for the actor as they help them to portray the character. Costumes also need to be comfortable enough for the actor to move freely. Costume designers will often provide **rehearsal costumes** that help the actor to behave like the character.

Removing or putting on potentially 'fiddly' garments, such as jackets, scarves and headwear, need to be practised and timed in the rehearsal room.

How can I design costumes as part of this course?

You can opt for costume design in either or both of the practical sections of the course. If you choose to work as costume designer in Unit/Component 1, you will work in a small group to devise a piece of theatre. Your specific responsibility will be to create two costume designs for the performance.

Unit/Component 2 is similar, but you will work with a script.

Unit/Component 3 is the written exam. When you evaluate a performance you have seen, you might write about costume design. Practical work will help you to write confidently about costume and make-up.

Research

Even if you are creating a contemporary (modern) world for the stage, you will still need to complete research so that your design:

- suits the personality of the character
- reflects the right economic and social contexts.

For period costumes, remember that many museums have a fashion and clothing section. Study clothing from different centuries and decades.

Also browse the internet, fashion magazines, history books and crafting and sewing magazines. Look for clothing worn by a particular type of person during the historical period of your drama piece.

TASK 4.2

Watch a few minutes of an unfamiliar television drama or film that happens to be on. Focus on one character's costume:

- What historical period is represented?
- What social and economic conditions are being suggested?
- What can you tell about the character's personality?

DESIGN TIP

Find out early on whether actors have health issues with particular fibres or make-up ingredients, so that you have time to explore options.

TASK 4.3

Ask your teacher if you can bring in some rehearsal costumes for a practical performance lesson. Afterwards, discuss how the use of rehearsal costumes affected the performance.

DESIGN TIP

Keep downloaded and bookmarked resources in a research folder on your computer. Keep magazine pages and so on in your paper folder. If you design for Unit/Component 1, these will go in your portfolio.

FOCUS

A short history of clothing to give you a starting point for including authenticity in your design work.

ASSESSMENT CHECK

This section provides useful background for your set play study and your understanding of its social, historical and cultural contexts.

A re-creation of Elizabethan hair (wig) and make-up by Alanna Sadler.

PLACING COSTUME IN HISTORY

Professional costume designers understand the relationship between historical period, including today, and clothing. What people wear is largely dictated by the society and time that they live in.

Before the 19th century

Pre-industrialisation, poorer people would typically wear **natural**, cotton, linen and wool, and **styles** were broadly modest, simple and functional. If you were wealthy, you might have silk, taffeta and satin. These fabrics could be dyed with beetroot, berries and onion skins, for example. Fashion played a significant role for those that could afford it. At the highest level of society, there were certain items that only royalty wore, such as purple velvet, gold fabric and some types of fur.

The use of make-up also has an interesting history and is used differently across the world. Very pale skin, for example, was desirable in Europe for several hundred years up until the 20th century.

The mid 19th century onwards

Industrialisation paved the way for a broader range of materials. Textile factories meant that the speed and ease of fabric production increased, allowing a wider section of the population to add variety to their clothing.

The first sewing machines were developed around the 1830s, gradually leading to **mass-produced** clothing. As home sewing machines became popular too, ordinary people could copy fashions that they saw the wealthy enjoying.

In the early 20th century, the chemical industry began to produce man-made dyes, along with fabrics such as polyester and nylon that added stretch to clothing. **Textured** fabrics such as corduroy and polyester also developed.

Some periods, such as the 1920s and 1960s, saw iconic fashion and make-up.

TASK 4.4

Look at the labels in some of your own clothing. What is the fabric made up of? Can you find out where some of the more unusual materials might have been produced?

TASK 4.5

These photographs of 1940s film star Ava Gardner show her without and with costume make-up.

1 Write a short paragraph describing her 'look' in each picture.

2 Think of at least three adjectives to describe what her made-up look says about her character (for example, *powerful*).

STYLE: WHAT WE WEAR, AND WHY

Some of the most distinctive aspects of costume design are shape and particular features of style.

Historical period

Certain times can be identified by typical clothing styles. Fashion and the availability of fabric are the major influences when it comes to shape, which might include skirt and trouser length, neckline, and so on. Oversized flared cords or jeans, for example, place a costume in the late 1960s to early 1970s. A cloche hat would be from the 1920s.

> ### TASK 4.6
>
> Look through magazines, shops and your own clothes for distinctive shapes or styles of cut. What features stand out (in terms of outline, sleeves, leg shape and length, fullness, **silhouette**)?

Social economics

A person's ability to update and maintain their wardrobe depends largely on the amount of income they are prepared to spend on clothes. Historically, only wealthier members of society could buy more than just essential garments. Today, many people shop widely and frequently for clothes.

For many decades, brand names have been an important influence on purchasing, and favoured brands command a high price tag. Displaying brand names prominently on clothes can be seen as a **status symbol**.

Identity and image

Clothing and make-up are often expressions of our character and personality. Many periods of history have **subculture** fashions, such as punk or mod, that identify the wearers as belonging to that subculture. These are often linked to other areas of popular culture or art, such as music and film.

Suitability

There are two main factors that affect the suitability of clothing.

- Someone's occupation and way of life will affect what they wear in particular situations. It needs to be practical and functional.
- Body shape and confidence levels can play their part when people think about what suits them.

> ### TASK 4.7
>
> Design a new uniform for **one** of the following (male or female):
> - manual council worker, such as a refuse collector
> - primary school pupil
> - supermarket checkout assistant.
>
> Consider suitability, socio-economic factors and identity.

FOCUS

Some of the factors that affect clothing choices.

ASSESSMENT CHECK

Here, you develop understanding of how costume design choices can create impact and communicate meaning.

Goth fans pose at a music festival.

ASSESSMENT CHECK

By exploring details of costume, you are showing understanding of how drama and theatre is developed and performed (AO3).

COLOUR AND FABRIC FOR THE STAGE

Selecting colours, patterns and materials

There are eight main considerations for costume designers when selecting which colour and type of fabric to use.

What does the period of history suggest for a particular character?

Close attention to this aspect of costume, in terms of pattern, **texture** and material, will help your designs look accurate and authentic.

Paisley patterns were introduced into Britain from India in the 18th century.

What colour palette is the set designer working with?

In the harmonious world of the stage, a unified colour theme is likely to be desired. This does not mean you have to use the same colours as the set, but you might want them to blend or have a complementary use of bold, muted or primary colours.

3 Do the artistic intentions of the theatre piece call for any symbolic use of colour?

A **stylised** drama might call for all black or all white costumes with the addition of a meaningful colour, such as red to suggest the theme of danger or violence. **Monochrome** (shades of black and white only) can be used for entire sets or costume designs and can be full of impact. Such designs have a clarity and lack of complication that could also be used alongside one or more characters being dressed in colour to emphasise them. White is very effective under coloured lights.

White often has connotations of purity and innocence, while we might associate black fabric with death or evil. Purple has links to royalty and wealth.

A play with opposing groups, such as the Capulets and the Montagues in *Romeo and Juliet*, might use an element of colour coding.

4 Warm colours and cold colours are often associated with personality types and make an impact on the audience, although they might not be particularly conscious of it.

Warm colours, such as shades of red, orange and yellow, suggest a bold, strong and confident person. Cold colours, such as shades of blue and grey, can suggest a more distant or withdrawn type of person.

This modern production of *Hamlet* in Berlin uses all-white costumes and an all-white set.

5 Even in everyday life, the appearance of coloured fabric varies in different lighting conditions, but the intensity of stage lighting takes this to another level.

A new white shirt can be glaring under white stage lights, so costume designers might knock back the brightness by running the garment through a washing machine with other items a couple of times or dye it off-white.

Coloured lights can neutralise or drain the colour from fabric. This is particularly true with subtle tones and you should always work alongside the lighting designer to test the appearance of your fabrics before you finalise your designs.

Aguecheek's bright yellow jumpsuit in *Twelfth Night* looks its best under 'neutral' lighting.

6 We all have different skin-tones, and costume designers might take account of this when they select colours for their actors. Pale skins, for example, often do not blend particularly well with yellow.

7 Mood, atmosphere and the feel of the play or character affect colour choice for costume designers. A tragic play might call for darker, more muted shades, while bright colours might suit a comedy. Professional directors are notorious for telling designers that something doesn't match the feel of their production. A design might be described as 'too fluffy' or 'not sharp enough', which the costumier has to interpret in terms of changing the shape or colour scheme of costumes.

Sequins will catch the light, but need to be used with caution!

The brightly coloured costumes in *Dream Girls* reflect the upbeat mood of the production.

8 Combinations of colours are an important consideration. Putting two shades of red next to each other, for example, tends to cancel out the tones and gives just one effect. Natural and synthetic fabrics of the same colour will appear differently under stage lights.

ASSESSMENT CHECK

You are using the key skill of interpretation here as you develop ideas to communicate meaning to your audience. This is directly assessed in Unit/Component 1 and is an important aspect throughout the course.

TASK 4.8

1 Choose a character from a play that you have been studying.
   • Would you costume this character in warm or cool colours? Why?
   • Does the historical context of the play suggest particular types of fabric, styles and patterns and make-up?
2 Sketch a quick costume design. Bear in mind the points above, as well as suitability in terms of characterisation. Add notes on hairstyle and make-up, if appropriate.

Selecting fabrics for stage costumes

In the modern world, there are very many types of material available, and costume designers need to consider a number of factors.

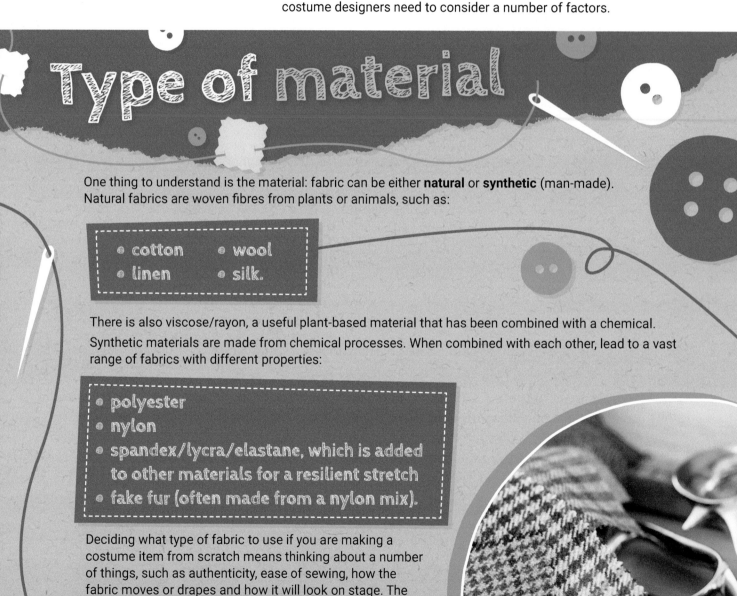

Type of material

One thing to understand is the material: fabric can be either **natural** or **synthetic** (man-made). Natural fabrics are woven fibres from plants or animals, such as:

> • cotton   • wool
> • linen   • silk.

There is also viscose/rayon, a useful plant-based material that has been combined with a chemical.

Synthetic materials are made from chemical processes. When combined with each other, lead to a vast range of fabrics with different properties:

> • polyester
> • nylon
> • spandex/lycra/elastane, which is added to other materials for a resilient stretch
> • fake fur (often made from a nylon mix).

Deciding what type of fabric to use if you are making a costume item from scratch means thinking about a number of things, such as authenticity, ease of sewing, how the fabric moves or drapes and how it will look on stage. The best way to find out if it will suit your character is to get a **swatch** so you can handle the fabric and test it under stage lights of various colours.

Weight and texture

The **weight** of fabric can be read clearly by the audience. Lightweight, flowing fabrics have more movement. If they are used with lots of fullness, they might give impressions of freedom and wealth.

Flimsy fabrics like this are not hard-wearing and therefore could suggest that the people wearing them do not do much work and can afford for their clothes not to last as long as heavier weight fabrics.

In modern clothing, the time of year and weather is a big hint as to what weight of clothing would be worn, unless it's evening-wear, when anything goes!

Corduroy.

Fabric comes in a wide range of textures such as:

- velvet
- cord
- denim
- coarse-woven
- brushed (including tweed)
- brocade/embroidered
- sequinned
- smooth.

Tweed.

Whether the **finish** of the fabric is dull or shiny affects its appearance significantly. Fabrics with a sheen include:

- satin
- silk
- taffeta (usually made from silk).

A fine taffeta dress embroidered with silk flowers.

These fabrics give the wearer an air of wealth and status, and can be expensive to use in a costume. A cheaper option is to use a synthetic version, or add **embellishments** to less expensive fabric, including:

- braid (narrow, plaited trim)
- sequins (which can be bought in strips)
- bright buttons
- jewellery
- trim, such as a fur collar or lace cuffs.

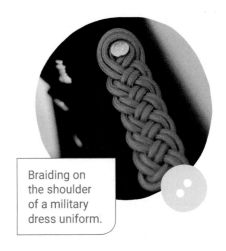

Braiding on the shoulder of a military dress uniform.

TASK 4.9

Find a simple garment from a charity shop (or use one of your own) and **upcycle** it into a more interesting and attractive version with the use of embellishments. Check the effect of the garment before and after under stage lights.

LOOK HERE

For more on altering and adapting clothing and fabric, see 'Adapting costume items' on page 96.

FOCUS

- Deciding what costume items you need – and where to find them.
- Making use of what you already have.

ASSESSMENT CHECK

A thorough understanding of your resources and materials means you can make good judgements for AO2.

DESIGN TIP

The skill of collaboration is included in your assessment, so keep notes on your work with performers and other designers.

DESIGN TIP

Selecting and sewing on decorations and trims contribute to the assessed design and creating process.

DEVELOPING AND USING YOUR COSTUME RESOURCES

There is no point designing a costume that you cannot then create, so it is essential to know what resources are available to you, including people.

Human resources

As a costume designer, you must be involved in the making and putting together of costumes, but you can supervise construction and sourcing. You will not be assessed on the costume's construction.

So, it is acceptable for someone to help you with sewing and sourcing, as long as you stay in charge of the process. It is essential that there is a process. You must not buy an entire costume, put it on an actor and say you designed it: that would just be finding a costume!

Working collaboratively

Work closely with your designing and performing colleagues to stay in touch and share ideas. Your costume will benefit from effective collaboration.

Physical resources

Sewing materials and equipment

Your school or college will give you access to at least the basic tools you need to produce your costumes. Sewing machines are ideal, but you might manage with tape measure, tailor's chalk, scissors, iron, pins, needles and thread to hand sew with. These can be bought cheaply if not available in school. Your local market is a good starting point. You might also be given a small budget for fabric and/or clothing.

Items of clothing

Have a good hunt around first in your school's costume room and family's and friends' wardrobes. Even if items are not quite what you have in mind, you might be able to alter and add items to achieve the costume you want. Make sure you get permission first, of course!

Making a costume from scratch

If you plan to make, or supervise, the main part of the costume, list all the materials you need before you begin shopping.

Finding fabric

This flow-chart should help you to decide where to source your fabric.

I need fabric.

Do I already have, or know I can get, some for free?

No

Yes

Do that!

I need less than 1 metre.

I need more than 1 metre.

Fabric needs to be a specific type or have a certain print, colour or texture.

Fabric needs to be a specific type or have a certain print, colour or texture.

Yes

Yes

No

No

Search charity shops, car boot sales for clothing or household items that can be cut up.

Search fabric shops locally or online.

Find a sheet, duvet cover or tablecloth from a charity shop or discount store.

Using historical costume patterns

Some excellent **patterns** are available for most historical periods. If you, or one of your human resources, is able and willing to sew a costume from scratch, this could be an excellent way to go. Even if you can't face making the entire costume, patterns are very useful for caps, collars and so on.

Getting the most from your budget

Priorities

It is essential to balance the cost of fabric or a garment and the way it will feel on the actor and appear to the audience. You must not overspend, but you do not want an outfit that feels and looks poor.

Making a costume does not have to be expensive, however. Remember that you can modify found garments to good effect by altering the length, shape or fit and adding **accessories**, for example. Shop around.

You need to decide on the most important aspects of your design. This will help you to spend your money wisely. There is no point buying an amazing hat, for example, if it leaves you short of money to buy the dress.

Essential extras

Accessories can make a big difference to a costume, often without costing much. Think about your character and their world. They might need a few pairs of shoes and perhaps a bag. A suit might not be finished without a tie. Allow a little of your budget for items such as socks and tights too.

DESIGN TIP

Create and update an expenses spreadsheet in which you itemise every item you buy or hire.

DESIGN TIP

You might be able to hire part of your costume. Make sure that you don't just use a whole costume off the rail, however, as this will not be **your** design.

ASSESSMENT CHECK

These practical techniques will help you to apply theatrical skills in order to realise your artistic intentions in the performance (AO2).

KEY PROCESS – SEWING

At some point in your work as a costume designer you should sew something! This book won't teach you to become a dressmaker, but these pages show you the key process that securely holds one piece of fabric to another. It really is quite easy.

You can make a bag, for example, or simple garment even if you just have some fabric and basic sewing equipment. Sewing machines are quick, but hand sewing works well too. The following are two simple hand-sewn stitches.

TACKING temporarily holds two pieces of fabric together loosely so that they can be tried on (carefully) or held in place while you sew them together permanently. It is a long up-and-down stitch that you make with the right (outer) sides of the fabric together.

BACK STITCH uses small stitches with no gaps between them. It is strong, permanent stitching which will hold fabric together securely.

BACK STITCH

MAKING YOUR FIRST PIECE OF COSTUME: A DRAWSTRING BAG

Drawstring bags were popular in Britain from Victorian times until the 1920s, and versions of it are still used today. You could make one for yourself, a friend or as part of a finished costume design.

You can buy the fabric new, but even better for developing your skills as a costume designer, would be to source, from a charity shop or second-hand sale, a garment or home furnishing item with an interesting pattern. Existing buttons or embroidery could be left on for instant embellishment. Of course, choosing and adding your own embellishments would enhance the impact of your bag as well.

Cotton fabric is the easiest to work with as it does not stretch, fray or slip around. Or you could try heavier, textured fabrics, such as velvet, cord or brocade. These bring glamour and interest, but can be more awkward to work with. You could experiment with several fabrics to make a range of bags.

METHOD

*BACK-STITCH STEPS CAN ALSO BE DONE ON A SEWING MACHINE.

YOU WILL NEED

APPROXIMATELY HALF A METRE OF FABRIC

THREE-QUARTERS OF A METRE OF NARROW RIBBON, PIPING OR CORD

PINS

NEEDLES AND THREAD

FLEXIBLE TAPE MEASURE

STEEL AND/OR WOODEN RULER

SCISSORS

IRON

A SAFETY PIN

BUTTONS, SEQUINS, BEADS AND SO ON (OPTIONAL)

1 Cut two identical oblong pieces of fabric. Your bag will end up about 4cm smaller, so 18cm by 26cm would give you a make-up bag.

2 Using a hard edge to guide you, such as a steel ruler, iron a 1cm fold onto the wrong side (inside) of the fabric over one short side of each piece of fabric. This will be the top of your bag.

3 Pin the two pieces of fabric, wrong sides together. Leave 5cm unpinned at the top on each side.

10 Back-stitch next to the tacking and remove the tacking. You now have a channel to put your ribbon through.

11 Cut your ribbon in half and attach a safety pin to the end of one piece.

4 Tack where you have pinned, about 2cm from the edge, on the long sides. Remove the pins.

9 Pin, tack and then remove the pins.

12 Turn your bag the right way out and use the safety pin to thread the ribbon through the channel of one side of the bag.

5 Back-stitch next to where you have tacked.

8 Fold the unstitched sections in half onto the wrong sides.

13 Thread the other half of the ribbon through the other channel and press the whole thing.

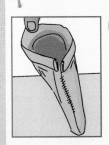

6 Unpick the tacking.

7 Press the **seam** open with the iron. Press up to the top of the bag (the unstitched section).

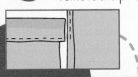

14 Sew on any embellishments, making sure that you fix them to one side of the bag only.

FOCUS

Thinking of existing items of clothing and furnishings that you can alter.

ASSESSMENT CHECK

Your imagination and creativity here will help you towards AO1: 'Create and develop ideas to communicate meaning for theatrical performance.'

Charity shops can be a source of inspiration as well as materials and resources.

LOOK HERE

See pages 92–93 for ideas on sourcing items, and pages 94–95 for the sewing techniques.

TASK 4.10

1 Look at the costume design you are currently working on.

2 Could parts of it be made, or all of it adapted, from an existing garment?

3 Could items you need be cut from a large domestic item such as a sheet? Should this be plain or patterned? Light or dark? Does it need certain qualities, such as being strong, lightweight or shiny?

ADAPTING COSTUME ITEMS

Why should I think about upcycling?

Your budget will be small and you need to stay within it. This does not mean, however, that your design cannot be creative, imaginative and effective.

You can be very successful in starting a costume with an item of clothing to upcycle. It minimises waste and is cheap. It can also help with your choices of colours, textures and patterns.

Recycling fabric

Buying a curtain, tablecloth or duvet cover that you can cut up to make an apron or skirt, for example, is a cheap and easy way of finding suitable fabric.

You can then use the offcuts to make accessories such as a headscarf, belt, collars and cuffs. This complementary use of fabric can pull a costume together and create an impression of the character.

Modifying and adapting clothing

Many items of found or cheaply bought clothing can be remodelled by:

- lengthening or shortening
- adding or removing collars
- changing or replacing sleeves
- adding accessories and embellishments
- altering the shape and fit, including padding or panelling.

Here are a few ideas:

- Buy a jacket and remove or shorten the sleeves. You could also change or remove the buttons. Perhaps eyelets and lacing could be added for a different period, such as this 16th-century-style jerkin.

- Find a skirt of suitable fabric and alter the length or silhouette.

- Remove the cuff from the gathered sleeve of a blouse to create a flare. Alternatively, add a longer cuff to suggest a different era.

- Use a cheap prom or bridesmaid's dress as the basis of a period ball gown or evening dress.

- Add sleeves in a contrasting fabric to a top to change its look.

- Customise an item with embellishments such as buttons, feathers, bows, **appliqués**, sequins, lace and beads.

HEALTH AND SAFETY IN COSTUME DESIGN

You hold some responsibility for the safety of the actors you costume and also for your own health and safety. Your examiners need to know that you have considered the risks and have acted accordingly.

Thinking about yourself as designer and maker, take care that you:

- ⚠ Use scissors, sewing equipment and irons appropriately and extremely carefully.
- ⚠ Work in adequate light.
- ⚠ Tidy away equipment carefully after use to protect everyone using the space.
- ⚠ Take frequent breaks – at least a ten-minute break every hour.

It is very important that you gather information about your actors, as they might have sensitive skin or allergies to things such as:

- ⚠ Certain metals, that might be used in jewellery
- ⚠ Specific fabrics or fibres
- ⚠ Detergents (washing powders and fabric softeners)
- ⚠ Ingredients in make-up products
- ⚠ Adhesives that might be used for masks, wigs or make-up features.

The use of make-up and hair products has potential risks. Some important considerations are:

- ⚠ Use clean hands.
- ⚠ Avoid putting your fingers in make-up in order to prevent contamination.
- ⚠ Wash brushes, sponges and applicators thoroughly at the end of every session.
- ⚠ Have a ready supply of basic cleansers, toners and moisturisers, and cotton wool pads.
- ⚠ Check beforehand with your actors that they are not allergic to any of the chemicals or ingredients in the products.

Heavy or restrictive costumes could prevent actors moving freely and potentially be dangerous. The same could be said for high-heeled footwear, for example, and very long skirts. Collaboration with the actors and the set designer should help to avoid hazards.

FOCUS

Considerations for keeping yourself, your group members and your audience safe.

ASSESSMENT CHECK

Throughout Units/ Components 1 and 2 you are expected to follow safe working practices. This also shows understanding of how drama and theatre is developed and performed (AO3).

FOCUS

The role of hair and make-up in costume design and how you can make your own interpretations.

ASSESSMENT CHECK

This knowledge and understanding should help you to:

- make an effective individual contribution to the performance in Component 2
- analyse and evaluate how meaning is communicated through costume and make-up in Component 3.

Christopher Ainslie has a completely green costume – including his hair and eyebrows – in his role as Oberon, king of the fairies, from *A Midsummer Night's Dream* (English National Opera).

HAIR AND MAKE-UP

No costume design is complete without a consideration of hair and make-up.

HAIRSTYLES

Hairstyles need to suit the characters and match the style of the costumes and period of the play. Assess whether you can work with the actor's own hairstyle in relation to the style of the play and the social, economic and cultural context of the character.

It is also important to think about the character's personality and any changes they undergo during the play. Hair that is up in a bun or ponytail, for example, could be let down at a moment in the play as an effective way of showing that a character is relaxing or is distraught, for instance. Putting hair up neatly could indicate an upward change of status.

SPECIAL EFFECTS

Ageing or unconventional looks can be aided with the use of wash-out colour sprays, but it is important not to exaggerate the use of grey unless you are aiming for comedy. Colours might be useful for a fantasy or science-fiction play or as part of an animal costume. Fake facial hair is available, but use it sparingly to avoid causing unwanted humour. Always use specialist adhesive!

Careful use of backcombing adds volume to hair, and products such as gel can smooth and flatten, both of which can significantly change a hairstyle.

If your school or college has a hairdressing department, you might find that teachers and students are keen to be involved. This is extremely helpful for you and can often contribute to those students' coursework.

WIGS

Wigs are very useful for completely changing an actor's hairstyle. A wig can create instant impact when it comes to period plays or creating styles, such as a punk Mohican, that are not easily achievable with the actor's own hair. They can also be cut and coloured as needed. They are fairly cheaply available from specialist stores.

You need to research the look you need and add this to your knowledge of the text and character to arrive at a workable design.

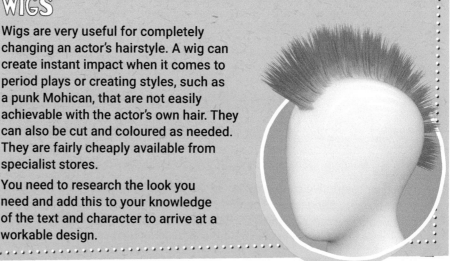

Make-up

Stage make-up is important for a number of reasons:

- It helps make facial features more visible, which helps the audience to see expressions clearly. Even when a character would not be wearing make-up, a little carefully applied lipstick in one shade darker than the lips accentuates the mouth, and eyes could be lightly lined. A base layer (foundation or powder) can be helpful in reducing shine under stage lights.
- It can help to establish period, setting and character.
- It can suggest significant aspects of a character, such as age or job.

What products should I use?

Everyday cosmetics are fine for use on stage, but always check with actors for any allergies. For more unusual looks, theatrical make-up can be well worth the expense.

As with shapes and styles of clothing and hair, different cultures and periods of history are associated with certain make-up styles. These are easily researched and should form the basis of your designs.

Useful 'extras' include:

- false eyelashes
- temporary tattoos
- stick-on jewels
- nail polish.

Have a good supply of different brushes to obtain good quality, varied effects. Keep them (and everything else you use) very clean!

Special effects

Ageing make-up should be applied carefully and sparingly or it will look comical. A useful tip is to add shading or highlighting to existing laughter and frown lines.

Bruise wheels are highly effective and easy to use when you follow the instructions. They are useful for creating a range of injuries. Similar effects can be created with inexpensive specialist products, such as scar/modelling wax or liquid latex, and your imagination. You might find that even if a bruise, for instance, is not specified in the script, your interpretation of the character could mean that it reveals something about their broader life.

Be very careful with fake blood. It often contains dye that is difficult to remove from skin and fabric. Avoid very cheap products.

LOOK HERE

Try Task 4.5 on page 86 to see how make-up can contribute to characterisation and meaning.

Make sure you follow the health and safety guidance on page 97 when trying out make-up.

TASK 4.11

Draw a detailed hair and make-up design for a character you are currently studying. If you have tools and products available, ask your teacher if you can create the look on yourself or another member of your group.

Increasing your confidence in drawing clearly presented designs.

ASSESSMENT CHECK

Improving the quality of your presentation will help you to communicate your artistic intentions in your final designs.

LOOK HERE

There are basic figure and face outlines for costume and make-up on the *Designing Drama* page at illuminatepublishing.com.

TASK 4.12

1 Browse magazines to find a standing, full-length figure of a man or woman. It is ideal if they are in underwear or swimwear.

2 Trace the outline of the figure onto plain paper. You do not need facial features or fingers.

3 On another piece of paper, have a go at sketching the figure freehand. Use short pencil strokes to create lines and curves. Be as basic or detailed as you like.

4 Look at your two versions. Decide which feels most promising and continue with that method. (You can always change your mind later.)

5 If both versions fill you with fear, try a fashion template. There are many online.

HOW TO DOCUMENT YOUR COSTUME DESIGN

All types of theatre designer must be able to show their design ideas long before the costumes, set, lighting and sound are actually created.

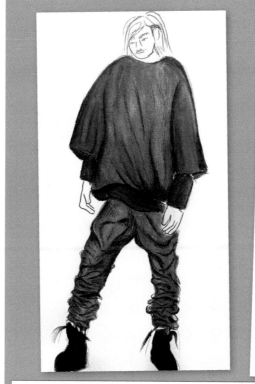

Costume design sketches by Alice Smith for Jude and Lynette in *Noughts & Crosses* at Nottingham Playhouse.

You do not need to be good at art to sketch your designs, but you certainly need to include drawn designs when working on your portfolio.

What documents do I need to produce?

In addition to making or supervising the construction of your costumes, you must produce on paper the final costume designs for two characters in Unit/Component 1.

You must also produce a costume plot or list of costumes, make-up and accessories worn by each performer, indicating any changes as appropriate.

How do I create costume designs on paper?

It is entirely up to you whether you work **freehand** or use guides such as templates. Your drawings do not have to be 'pretty': the costume details are the important things.

The first thing to discover is what method of sketching suits you best.

If you choose to draw your designs from scratch, you might find the guidance on the following page helpful.

BODY PROPORTIONS

This guide should help you get the proportion of your figures correct if you are not a confident artist, but prefer to work without a ready-made template. Fashion drawings tend to elongate the body, so you should find that the following ratio is more suitable for costume design.

The head of the figure can be drawn as an oval of any size. Two further ovals underneath will take you down to the waistline, and a further three will take you to the ankles.

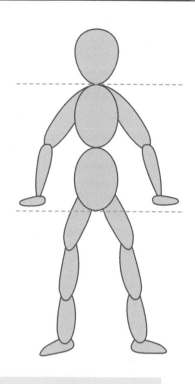

Developing your design

Below is a suggested sequence for moving from initial sketches to a finished costume design.

You will need to annotate or redraw your first designs after discussion with other designers and performers, and during and after rehearsals.

Smaller ovals can be used for hands and feet at the ends of approximated arms and legs.

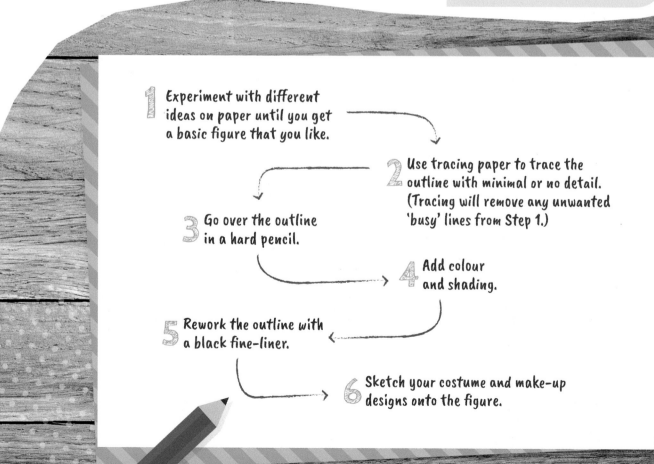

1 Experiment with different ideas on paper until you get a basic figure that you like.

2 Use tracing paper to trace the outline with minimal or no detail. (Tracing will remove any unwanted 'busy' lines from Step 1.)

3 Go over the outline in a hard pencil.

4 Add colour and shading.

5 Rework the outline with a black fine-liner.

6 Sketch your costume and make-up designs onto the figure.

Ensuring your costume fits and looks its best.

ASSESSMENT CHECK

Adjusting and fitting costumes shows that you are using refined theatrical skills and ideas and applying theatrical skills to realise your artistic intentions in the performance (AO2).

FITTING THE COSTUME

Your design needs to be 'refined and dynamic'. An ill-fitting costume will be neither of these.

To put together a costume that fits the performer early on, they need to try it on as you source, make and alter it.

Professionals continuously adjust a costume through a series of fitting sessions with the actor. This might even be right up to the performance.

Darts from the waistband of a skirt give a slim, fitted shape.

THE IMPORTANCE OF A WELL-FITTING COSTUME

Appearance

A badly fitting costume will not show your design as it should be. The silhouette will be altered if the costume doesn't hang properly, for example. Make sure that it is neither too big nor too tight.

Comfort

A badly fitting costume will hinder the actor's movements. The actor needs to be able to breathe, walk, stretch and sit in the costume. There are safety implications here too. An actor also needs a costume that will enhance the posture of their character. A casual item such as a sloppy jumper needs to be fitted to the actor, even if a 'bad' fit is a design choice.

How can I make my costume fit?

Everyone has an individual body shape proportioned in a unique way. This is why one pair of size 16 or 32" jeans will fit you very well, but a pair from another shop will not. You are unlikely to start altering the size of jeans, but it can be quite easy to adjust the fit of most garments for the stage.

The **type of fabric** a garment is made of will influence how you fit it.

Stiff fabric

This won't have much stretch, so you might need to use darts, tucks or gathers to alter the shape and make the garment smaller. Alternatively, a belt could be used to pull an item in.

Could you put a panel in the front or the back to make it bigger? For example, a panel of jersey fabric would give more ease as well as more volume. It could also add interest in terms of texture and colour

Stretchy fabric

Fabric with stretch has more ease of wear and movement. It can hug the figure but allow the actor freedom of movement.

You can try similar fitting techniques as for non-elastic fabric, above. In addition, you can alter the side seams on skirts or trousers and add elastic to necklines and waistbands.

COMMON FITTING ISSUES AND HOW YOU MIGHT SOLVE THEM

Avoid attempting to make a radical change to a sourced garment. If it is much too big or too small, get something else! Minor adjustments, however, can be very successful.

All of the following ideas can be achieved without taking a garment apart.

Too long

It is not difficult to reduce the length of everything from hems to sleeves. You could carefully cut away excess fabric and re-hem the garment, as long as the style is not complicated. If the bottom of a dress or skirt is very fancy, you might be able to take it up at the waist. You could add elastic to the bottom of long sleeves or simply fold them upwards.

If the top half of a garment looks saggy, try lifting it at the shoulders by shortening its straps or creating a dart. You need to remember, however, that the armholes will also be lifted and that it won't lie properly if the garment has sleeves. Shoulder pads are a possibility, but they are generally best in science-fiction, fantasy or costumes for the 1950s or 1980s.

Too short

Solving this can be a bit trickier than lengthening garments, but there are a couple of tricks you can try. Add borders or frills to sleeves and/or hems, for example. Simply seam them together on the wrong side. You will probably need to use a different material, so, unless you can find something very similar, choose fabric with a strong contrast (difference) in colour and perhaps texture. If you can add a piece of the same material in another place on the costume, this will give a well-finished look.

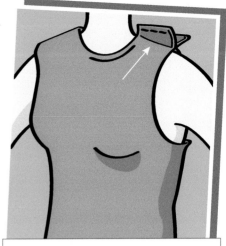

Darting the shoulders will lift the arm section of a garment. The darted section of fabric should be wider at the shoulder edge than the neck edge.

before

after

TASK 4.13

On the dress above, can you see two other places where the same white material could be added to give a considered, balanced look?

LOOK HERE

'Key process – sewing' on pages 94–95 will show you how to make a seam.

Too big

First, ask the actor to put on the costume to find out where there is too much fabric. Depending on the style of the garment, you might be able to simply sew in some elastic or add a belt. If so, carefully consider shape and size to ensure the whole costume suits the required period and style.

Another possibility would be to remove fabric by taking in the side seams. However, you can only take in side seams all the way from top to bottom if the garment doesn't have sleeves. If most of the extra fabric is around the waistline, you could try adding diamond-shaped darts on each side of the centre-front and centre-back lines.

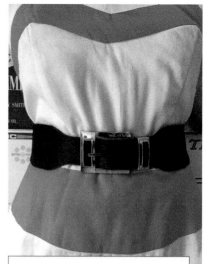

The costume designer has added a wide elasticated belt to improve the fit and style of this dress.

A good alternative might also be to add wide pieces of elastic to pull a garment in. This could be done at the back or the sides for a natural look or vertically to add a more stylised effect. You could make a feature of the gathering by adding a button or bow, for example. This would make the gather appear to be a deliberate aspect of the design.

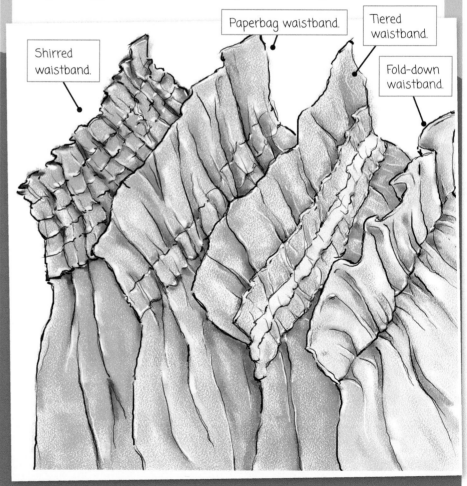

Shirred waistband.

Paperbag waistband.

Tiered waistband.

Fold-down waistband.

Necklines

Necklines can be adjusted and embellished to great effect. This is easier if the garment does not have a collar. You could add elastic, a drawstring or laces to a loose neck or one where you have removed the collar. This kind of technique can be useful for creating a period costume for characters in *The Crucible*, for example.

An infill can solve the problem of a neckline that is too low, as well as improving the appearance. Use lace or a contrasting stiff fabric.

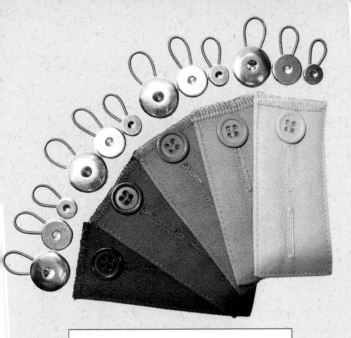

Button extenders can add a little more room and stretch to a waistband.

Frog fastenings change the style of a garment and could give you an extra inch of room.

Too small

It is often more difficult to add fabric than to take it away, but there are tricks that can solve the problem. If a garment pulls at the front because it is too tight, for example, you could move the buttons or change the type of fastening. Button extenders are useful too.

If skirts or trousers are too tight at the waist, you could move a button (or use extenders). If there is not a waistband, you could let out a seam. Another option would be to insert a panel of appropriate shape in a similar or contrasting fabric. You would probably need to cut the garment and use seams to insert extra fabric. Stretch fabrics would give extra ease. It is a good idea to balance the contrast fabric elsewhere on the costume if the panel is visible.

DESIGN TIP

Be adventurous! Costume design is a great opportunity to unleash your creativity.

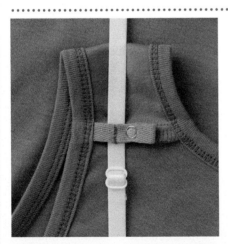

Underwear matters

If the costume has a fitted silhouette, it is very important to consider what will be underneath it. For a good fit, you need to think about the style of underwear your actors should wear. Adding bra-strap loops to a neckline will keep straps hidden.

You might also need to advise your male actors on the question of briefs or boxers if it could affect the costume!

TASK 4.14

Select a garment that you are thinking of using for your costume. Try it on the actor and experiment with adjusting the fit using some of the techniques above.

FOCUS

Final rehearsals: your last opportunity to check that your design is working well.

ASSESSMENT CHECK

Rehearsals will help you to reflect upon your design and lead you to analyse and evaluate (AO4).

TECHNICAL AND DRESS REHEARSALS FOR COSTUME DESIGNERS

The rehearsal schedule works towards a technical and then a dress rehearsal. These are the rehearsals that draw everything together.

As costume designer, sit in the audience area for the rehearsals. Have your notebook to hand and check that your costumes are meeting your artistic intentions.

Technical rehearsal

This rehearsal is for technicians and designers. It will probably be the first opportunity to put all the production elements (performers, lights, sound, costumes and set) together. If you encounter some typical problems, try the suggestions below.

Potential problems	Possible solutions and timings
An element of the costume does not look right. Perhaps the skirt looks too long or the actor is pulling the top down all the time.	Decide if you can make changes before the dress rehearsal. If not, get it done before the performance.
An actor is having difficulties with some aspect of a costume. For example, they struggle to make a costume change on stage or in the wings.	Work with the actor after the tech to see if the costume can be altered with a change of fastenings, for example. Or, another cast member could help with changing.
A costume does not look as good as you had hoped under some of the lighting states.	Note down which scenes are causing the problem. Talk to the lighting designer before the dress rehearsal and see if you can come to a compromise in the intensity or colour of lighting.

Dress rehearsal

The 'dress' is the final, timed, **run** before the performance. Now that technical issues have been addressed, the performers can run through the production uninterrupted.

Again, watch from the audience area with a notebook. Move around and look out for the following:

- Have changes from the tech been made successfully?
- Are the actors happy with their costumes and any changes they need to make during the performance?

If there are still issues, revisit your notes and the table above. Work with your colleagues to tackle problems. Make final tweaks as necessary.

DESIGN TIP

Try not to interrupt the rehearsal unless there is a health and safety issue.

EVALUATING YOUR COSTUME DESIGN

Once you are clear about what evaluation is and the best way of approaching it, you can focus on assessing the success of your costume design.

Using tops that contain lots of stretch was a very effective choice because it meant that the performers could move freely. There was good definition of their arms and legs too, which was important for the physical theatre aspects of the devised piece. One part of my design that was particularly successful in supporting our artistic intentions was the use of colour. Green and earthy colours are associated with nature...

Lord of the Flies at Theatr Clwyd. (S R Taylor Photography.)

Examining the detail of your design

Whenever you evaluate, you should make at least three different points. These points should be illustrated with specific examples. Each time, you should also explain the reason why you have made a particular value judgement. You should highlight anything that could have gone better.

TASK 4.15

1 Use a table like this (some examples have been included) to make notes for your evaluation.

Costume design evaluation			
Design element	**Moment in the play**	**Evaluation**	**Reason for evaluation**
Stretch in T-shirts	Physical theatre sections.	Effective in performance.	Performers were able to move freely and extend clearly defined arms fully.
Colour – greens and browns	Throughout, but particularly full of impact in the poem section.	Successful in supporting artistic intentions.	• I avoided making the costumes look like uniforms, but similarity suited context and added mood and atmosphere. • Combined well with set and lighting. • Addition of costume items for poem added meaning.

2 Expand your notes into three paragraphs of evaluative writing. Make sure you relate your finished design to your artistic intentions.

FOCUS

Placing a value judgement on design.

ASSESSMENT CHECK

Essential for AO4 is the ability to analyse and evaluate your own work and the work of others, in the written exam as well as in your practical work.

SIGNPOST

Read the evaluation guidance on page 80.

LOOK HERE

More examples of evaluation can be found in Chapter 7.

COSTUME VOCABULARY

Accessories Items such as bags, jewellery and small items that accompany garments.

Allergies Adverse reactions in the body (for example to breathing or the skin) to certain products or ingredients.

Appliqué A small colourful piece of embroidery – often a picture or pattern – sewn onto an item of clothing.

Back stitch A closely worked stitch done by hand.

Bruise wheel Available from theatre make-up sellers, a palette of yellows, reds, browns and cream make-up, excellent for a range of special effects.

Colour palette A complementary set of colours that belong to a group, such as pastel or dark.

Darting Sewing small, tapered folds into a garment to provide shape or otherwise alter the fit.

Embellishments Added extras such as lace, buttons, braids and so on; decorative details.

Finish The surface of fabric – usually shiny or dull.

Freehand Drawing something without a tracing or template to guide you.

Mass-produced Made in great numbers, usually in a factory.

Monochrome Black, white and grey only.

Natural In terms of fabric – not man-made. Examples of natural fabric are cotton and wool.

Pattern Design printed onto or woven into fabric, including tartan, paisley, stripes. A paper pattern is the template pieces that guide sewers as they cut cloth out to make into garments.

Rehearsal costumes Practice clothes or shoes that bear some similarity to the final costume.

Run Either a rehearsal or read-through of the whole play, or the number of times a play will be performed (for example, *The Crucible* has a three-week run at this theatre).

Seam The joining of two pieces of fabric on the wrong side.

Silhouette The outline shape of a costume.

Status symbol A possession that is seen to show someone's wealth, social position or sense of style.

Style Distinctive appearance, often typical of a particular person, period or place.

Subculture A cultural trend in society that is not the dominant one, such as goth, punk.

Symbolic use of colour The use of colour to communicate a certain meaning or represent a particular theme or mood.

Stylised Non-realistic, non-naturalistic, where style features are dominant.

Swatch A small sample of fabric that gives an idea of how an item made from it would look and feel.

Synthetic Man-made (fabric).

Tacking A fast, long, hand-made, temporary stitch to hold seams together ready for trying on or for permanent stitching.

Texture The surface feel of fabric, for example. Raised fabrics, such as velvet and cord, have a different texture from smooth ones, such as silk, which are flat.

Upcycle Taking an existing garment and changing it in some way to make something different.

Wardrobe The wardrobe department is where the costumes are produced in a theatre. Alternatively, our wardrobe is the collection of clothes we own.

Weight How heavy or light is the fabric? Does it drape or hang heavily?

UNIT/COMPONENT 1: DEVISING THEATRE – A PRACTICAL GUIDE

Chapter 5

HOW YOUR DESIGN FOR THE DEVISED PIECE WILL BE ASSESSED

The performance, the portfolio and the evaluation

This unit/component, which covers your devised piece of drama, is worth 60 marks and makes up 40 per cent of your GCSE.

Your design is assessed through the performance and your portfolio.

Go to your exam board's website for full details of the mark scheme.

Your design in the performance of a devised piece

Design role	What you need to produce
Lighting	At least **five** different lighting states for the performance.
Sound	At least **five** sound cues for the performance.
Set	An actual set for the performance, including appropriate props and set dressings.
Costume	**Two** full costumes, hair and make-up – for two different characters.

You will be assessed on your ability to:

- apply design skills which enhance the final performance to realise artistic intentions
- create a design that realises the artistic intention, including interpreting the practitoner/genre and stimulus
- make an individual contribution, sustaining audience interest.

Your portfolio: supporting evidence to accompany your design in performance

The portfolio should record three significant stages that illustrate how you researched, created and developed your ideas.	
Your portfolio can be presented in any of these forms: • a **written commentary** of between 750 and 900 words (approximately 250 for each stage) **or** • a suitably edited **blog** of between 750 and 900 words **or** • an **audio-visual recording** including the illustrative material (4 to 7 minutes for WJEC; 6 to 9 minutes for Eduqas) **or** • an **audio commentary** on the illustrative material (4 to 7 minutes for WJEC; 6 to 9 minutes for Eduqas). Whichever form you choose, you must include illustrative material for **each of the three stages**. This could include: • sketches/diagrams/plots/plans • mind maps • photographs • a model box (to be commented on for AV or photographed for written submissions) • ground plans • cue sheets • mood boards • annotated sections of script • digital media (such as sound clips, short videos of designs in progress).	**Stage 1: Research, creation and development of ideas in response to the chosen stimulus** Explain your initial ideas, research and intentions in relation to your chosen stimulus. You should explore: • how your design ideas developed from the stimulus • the theme or message that emerged for the piece as a whole • your research findings in response to the stimulus and how they influenced your design • how mood boards, for example, influenced you design • your individual contribution to the development of the piece in response to the stimulus. **Stage 2: How ideas from the chosen practitioner or genre have been incorporated to create meaning** Explain features linked to the practitioner or genre and how they have influenced or appeared in your design. You should explore: • which practitioner/genre was chosen and why • how you involved their features or characteristics in your design • how the influence of your practitioner/genre helped to communicate meaning through your design. **Stage 3: The development, amendment and refinement of ideas** Analyse how you worked through your creative ideas to arrive at a meaningful design. You should explore: • how you used feedback to improve your ideas • one or two key moments that led to the refinement of your design and enhanced meaning • changes you made towards the end of the process • how rehearsals helped you refine your design.

You will be assessed on your ability to:

• create and develop imaginative and meaningful design ideas in response to the stimulus
• creatively incorporate a range of relevant design techniques/characteristics associated with your chosen practitioner or genre
• develop design techniques to communicate meaning effectively
• make a relevant, individual contribution to the creation, development and refinement of design ideas for performance.

Evaluation of your design in the performance of a devised piece

Soon after the performance of the devised piece, you will have an exam-style session of 90 minutes in which to evaluate your finished design in performance.

In it, you must analyse and evaluate:

• your design as it appeared in the final performance
• how your design skills contributed to the effectiveness of the final performance
• your own contribution to the final performance including how effectively you fulfilled your initial aims.

DESIGN TIP

You can take two sides of A4 notes into the supervised evaluation with you. Prepare these very carefully. You can include sketches.

ASSESSMENT CHECK
You need to take an equal part in developing and communicating your group's artistic intentions with a clear and practical design that adapts in response to rehearsals. This will help you towards AO1.

YOUR DESIGN CHALLENGE

The essence of devising

DEVISE Plan or invent (a complex procedure, system, or mechanism) by careful thought.

 Devised theatre is 'a process in which the whole creative team develops a show collaboratively. From actors to technicians, everyone is involved in the creative process.'

(John Walton, theatre director)

As a designer, you will work with your group to develop form, content, style and genre and a harmonious world that has impact for an audience. Within this group dynamic, you will focus on your design element.

The process of devising

Devising drama has **collaboration** and **inventiveness** at its heart. You will work closely as a group to generate ideas that can be developed into a finished piece of theatre.

You will start from an inspiring **stimulus**. From there, you will experiment and gradually decide on:

- content, including a theme or message that you want to explore
- genres and performance styles, such as comedy, naturalism, dystopian theatre, physical theatre
- the structure, for example a linear series of improvisations, or movement backwards and forwards through time.

LOOK HERE
See page 115 for details of different stimuli and how you might use them.

When can I start designing?

Your design work will emerge from the **theme** and **artistic intentions** of your group, inspired by the stimulus. You will soon find opportunities to make design an important and interesting part of the finished piece.

Key to success is how you incorporate features of your chosen genre or practitioner. Your design should contribute to the creation of mood and atmosphere and communicate your own artistic intentions as well as those of the piece as a whole.

As the group moves through the devising process, you should be involved in each other's work. This is a **group** endeavour, and collaboration is essential for harmony in the final performance.

DESIGN TIP

Never overlook the importance of the portfolio. Record your thoughts, designs, analysis and evaluations at every stage of the devising process.

TASK 5.1

Once your group has made some decisions about content (what the piece will be about), you can develop your design ideas. Begin a table like this to get you started:

Stimulus:		
Artistic intention	**Design ideas**	
To highlight climate change as a major threat.	Lighting	• Contrasting colour palettes (to show very hot and cold environments). • Special spotlight to pick out monologues. • Special 'flashback' lighting state.
	Sound	Special soundscape for flashback scenes – could be voices arguing about climate change with an abstract tense sound effect.
	Set	• Levels to suggest power in flashback scenes and different areas for hot and cold climates • Plastic items such as bags and bottles (pollution and climate change) • Monochrome colours to tie in with costume and lighting.
	Costume	• 'Disposable' white overalls for scientist character (suggests world is becoming uninhabitable). • Contrasting warm and thin clothing worn for alternate scenes (unstable climate). • Muted monochromes (hints at severity of situation).

The portfolio

The portfolio is your opportunity to explain how you have engaged fully with the process of devising from the viewpoint of group member and designer. You will present the journey from the stimulus to your finished design. You need to:

- demonstrate your ability to work with your group to bring its artistic intentions to reality
- pinpoint specific examples of design choices that enhanced the meaning that was communicated to the audience.

LOOK HERE

Chapters 1 to 4 will guide you through the design process.

Pages 116–117 will help you to pin down your artistic intentions.

Pages 124–125 will help you to refine ideas in rehearsal and continue the collaboration.

FOCUS

Advice on avoiding or recovering from group-work problems.

ASSESSMENT CHECK

You are expected to work collaboratively to generate, develop and communicate ideas.

DESIGN TIP

Analise your collaborative involvement. Is it thorough and supportive?

KEEPING COMMUNICATION OPEN

WORKING POSITIVELY AS A GROUP

The importance of good communication

Teachers have to consider many things when they form groups for practical work. Not everyone will be happy with the resulting make-up of their group, but the ability to work collaboratively is a valuable skill needed here, and for life.

Most importantly, good communication is essential for creating good theatre.

TASK 5.2

As a group, share thoughts of examples in life of excellent communication. Be specific and try to assess what skills are being used.

For example, a particular teacher might be really effective at communicating their subject. This could be to do with their skills in bringing the subject to life, their enthusiasm, and the way they make students feel that their ideas are listened to.

Alternatively, you might think about pedestrian crossings, where clear visual and aural cues are given to pedestrians and drivers. Bumps near the edge of the pavement also help sight-impaired pedestrians. Excellent communication in terms of design!

Building a positive group environment

Negative dynamics are a common problem in group work, with a range of causes. The chart below offers some ideas for improving your group's ability to get along socially and make practical progress.

TASK 5.3

Use the points below to evaluate a recent group session. Ask yourself:

- What are my qualities as a group member?
- How could I improve my contribution to the group?
- Do I offer ideas and consider others' ideas too?

Have a clear objective for the session, for example to gather ideas of how the stimulus can be explored through drama.

Listen sensitively and carefully when others are speaking. Don't just wait for your turn to speak.

Try to be objective about difficulties. Focus on what has gone wrong rather than on an individual. Try to limit comments to those that help the objective of the meeting.

Highlight the positive things people say and do.

Take turns to speak. If necessary, have an object that can be held by the speaker, and pass it on frequently.

Encourage everyone to talk. Go around the circle every few minutes so that everyone has a chance to contribute. Keep it positive.

Ask a teacher for support early on if communication is not going well.

Always avoid blaming one person. Communication is a shared activity!

RESPONDING TO STIMULI

First thoughts

All drama devisers use stimuli to feed their theatre-making process. The exam board will supply four different pieces of stimulus for you and/or your teacher to choose from. These will take the form of:

- a quotation
- a picture
- a song
- a concept or statement.

Your teacher will also set you tasks to enable your group to explore the stimuli. This exploration will begin to fire individual and group responses in the form of:

- personal experiences
- experiences of people you know
- stories you have heard and read about
- social and cultural similarities and differences (such as the way people from different backgrounds might think about the stimulus.

To begin with, try to let your minds roam freely from your initial experience of the stimulus. You could use (and include in your portfolio):

- annotated copies of the stimuli
- mind maps and spider diagrams
- flow charts and tables.

FOCUS

Ways to think about different stimuli in your role as a group member and designer.

ASSESSMENT CHECK

Under AO1, you describe how you researched, created and developed your ideas in response to the chosen stimulus (in Stage 1 of your portfolio).

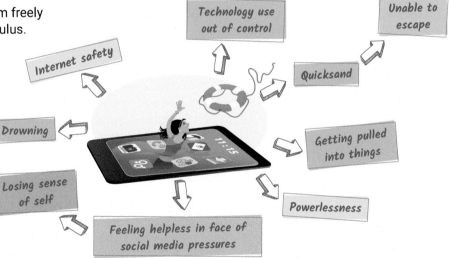

Ideas that excite

Once you start sharing ideas, take particular notice of those that excite you or other people in your group. These are the ones that are producing strong social and personal reactions. If they interest you, they are likely to interest your audience. Do remember, though, that ideas will change and develop as you begin to work with them creatively.

DESIGN TIP

Remember to chart all the stages of your design and devising work in detail.

TASK 5.4

Spend some time at home thinking about the stimulus and then report back to your group. Use a table like this to organise your ideas. (An example has been provided, using the image above.)

Stimulus: Cartoon of young person 'drowning' in smartphone	
Themes, messages, issues	**Ideas that come from the stimulus and themes**
• Internet safety. • Gaming as a distraction from the real world.	• Movement piece. • Sinister music or sound effects. • Monologues from people affected by too much gaming.

DESIGN TIP

At first, don't push your role as designer to the front of your mind. Respond to the stimulus's overall potential for drama instead.

FOCUS

How to pin down the aims and objectives of your devised drama.

ASSESSMENT CHECK

This process helps you to:

- communicate and realise your intentions
- consider the impact that you can make on an audience
- explore ideas that you want to communicate
- collaborate and come to decisions.

Make sure your discussions address the focus of AO1: 'Create and develop ideas to communicate meaning for theatrical performance.'

DESIGN TIP

Revisit your ideas board often while agreeing your artistic intentions. Update it by removing, adding and regrouping ideas.

AGREEING ON YOUR ARTISTIC INTENTIONS

What are artistic intentions in a devised piece?

When you perform or design from a playscript, the content (narrative, characters, setting and so on) are already in place. Your artistic intentions will be how you interpret that script for an audience.

In devised theatre, by contrast, your artistic or dramatic intentions relate to what you want to tell the audience. You might begin with a message or question that springs from your stimulus, for example:

- What can society do to avoid climate catastrophe?
- Why is a sense of community important?
- How can we use social media platforms more positively?

FOLLOWING WARM TRAILS

This metaphorical idea encourages you to trust your instincts when developing ideas. Look for signs that a particular route on the devising trail will lead you to an excellent devised piece. If an idea excites several members of the group, you are probably onto a good thing.

How can our group decide on its aims and objectives?

TASK 5.5

Work together to test some of the group's ideas through drama activities such as improvisations. Make notes on successful points that move you closer to agreeing your artistic intentions.

TASK 5.6

An ideas board is a useful way of bringing ideas together and specifying aims and objectives. More than just a list of ideas, look to include on your board (you could use a pin-board, whiteboard or a large sheet of cardboard):

- the stimulus, its title, or a description of it
- themes, messages and questions that arise from the stimulus
- descriptions, photographs or sketches of dramatic explorations you have found inspiring
- news headlines and articles, for example, that have prompted ideas
- images that have captured your imagination
- initial design ideas – keep that part of your brain firing!

Deciding on your artistic intentions

In addition to generating and sharing ideas, you need to analyse and evaluate this creative process. This will help you to make decisions and assess why they are the best choices.

Time will be limited. Settling on the aims and objectives for your piece should be a relatively quick aspect of the creative process. If your group starts to feel stuck, try the following task.

> **TASK 5.7**
>
> 1 One at a time, each member of the group takes one item from the ideas board and puts it on the floor or table.
> 2 Give yourselves two minutes to arrange the items in priority order. If there is indecision or argument, collect items for further review.
> 3 Study the result. Sensitively analyse and evaluate the group's decisions and confirm your artistic intentions.

Wording artistic intentions

Once you have agreed on what your artistic intentions are, try the following task as a way of writing them down.

> **TASK 5.8**
>
> 1 As a group, write a short paragraph that sums up the theme or message you want to share with your audience.
> 2 Highlight the most important key words.
> 3 Use these key words to write a brief, clear aim for your theatre piece.
>
> The following table provides a couple of examples.

The general idea (theme)	The clear artistic intentions	
Climate change is **threatening our world. We** can all do something to **help**, but it's not enough. **Governments** need to work together and **make big changes quickly**. Young people should be listened to – some of us have joined **protests** because we feel so strongly about **our future**.	Aim	To highlight climate change as a major global threat.
	Key messages	• Young people should be encouraged to protest. • Everyone should contribute. • Governments need to work together to tackle the problem urgently.
Social media sites are **useful** ways of staying in touch with friends and sharing ideas. But they can be **dangerous** because they allow **bullying** and extremism. They encourage people to **stay at home** rather than actually being with friends. There are important things to do to **stay safe online**. We want to share this with younger students.	Aim	To help Year 7 students get the best from social media.
	Key messages	• Avoid personal details – use privacy settings. • Don't get involved in bullying or discrimination: report it instead. • Stay in touch with friends and have fun, but **be** with people too.

ASSESSMENT CHECK

These tasks will help you to work collaboratively to generate, develop and communicate ideas.

LOOK HERE

Pages 124–125 will help you to maintain your creative intentions during rehearsals.

DESIGN TIP

Remember that you can adapt the wording of your intentions during the rehearsal process.

FOCUS

The use of a practitioner or genre to help communicate the meaning of your devised piece.

ASSESSMENT CHECK

Your response to the stimulus should demonstrate either the techniques of an influential practitioner or the characteristics of a genre.

PERFORMANCE STYLE

Genre and performance style

Exploring the methods of theatre practitioners or genres can enhance your work. The exam board requires you to choose a practitioner or a genre. You need to incorporate key features or techniques associated with the practitioner or genre to influence your own performance style and, importantly, to communicate meaning.

What makes an influential theatre practitioner?

As someone who makes theatrical experiences for others, you are a practitioner! Generally, however, we use the term to identify a person who makes a significant impact on audiences and other theatre makers through their distinctive approach to their art. Taking Konstantin **Stanislavski** as an example, this Russian director broke new ground in the world of acting through his naturalistic performances. He developed exercises and processes that encouraged actors to draw on their memories and experiences to create performances with the feeling of truth. Before this, acting was far more stylised and, many would argue, more superficial. The same can be said for design styles associated with Stanislavski. In keeping with the naturalistic movement, the fourth wall was put up, often in the form of a proscenium arch. Costume, lighting, sound and sets were designed to enhance the reality of the overall performance and produce a harmonious world on the stage.

Becoming a noteworthy theatre practitioner usually develops over time, and involves the creation of a very particular experience. Bertolt **Brecht** was driven by the desire to present political messages to his audience. Whereas Stanislavski sought to pull his audience into the world of the play and encourage them to suspend disbelief, Brecht wanted audiences to remain acutely aware that they were watching a play rather than reality. He developed alienation techniques which detached the audience. He wanted playgoers to analyse the action and be alert to the messages about social injustices contained in plays such as *The Caucasian Chalk Circle*. In terms of design, lighting was generally strong and from visible sources. Sets were minimal and involved items such as placards. Actors multi-roled, so costumes included representational items such as hats. Music and songs were often live on stage.

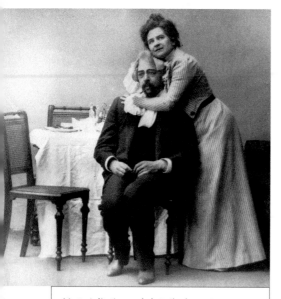

Naturalistic and detailed costume and set design in *The Seagull* (with Stanislavski and Olga Kipper)

In this production of Brecht's *The Caucasian Chalk Circle*, the hard, unpainted scaffolding of the set gives a cold, functional, industrial feel. This is complemented by the white light from the visible strip lights along with the stark blue wash and the basic white costumes. By contrast, the musician playing live on stage sits in a warmer spotlight and is given a softer, more colourful outfit. (Set by Nathan Burmeister, costumes by M'ck McKeage, lighting by Brittany Lazzarini-Pholi; Victorian College of the Arts, Melbourne.)

Using practioners' techniques in your work

You should aim to use between four and six techniques or characteristics of your chosen practitioner in your devised piece. If you are influenced by Steven **Berkoff**, for example, you might incorporate slow motion, direct address, ensemble work, minimalism and tableaux. Emma **Rice** might inspire the use of bold colours and modern music.

As a designer, you might develop ideas for different lighting states, sound effects, costumes or a minimalist set to enhance each technique and communicate meaning.

 DESIGN TIP

There are always design implications in the characteristics of particular practitioners. It is vital that you use them to create meaning within your devised piece.

TASK 5.9

1 Choose an influential practitioner whose work you are not yet very familiar with.

   Research their work. If possible, watch a video of their work in performance. List the techniques associated with them.

2 Using the theme of *loneliness* and a design option of your choice, write three bullet points about how you might incorporate the practitioner's style into a design. For example (using the theme of *family*):

Theme	Practitioner	Techniques/characteristics	Costume design ideas
Family	Emma Rice	• Ensemble work • Physical theatre • Circus tricks • Comedy • Music/songs	• Stretch fabric to enable movement • Net fabric to enhance circus characteristics • Humorous style for different family members.

Working with a genre to communicate meaning

In theatre terms, genre defines a type of theatre such as comedy or tragedy. Your exam board mentions Theatre in Education (TIE), physical theatre and musical theatre as examples of genres that you may consider for your devised piece. You are, however, free to choose any suitable genre.

To choose a genre, or practitioner, you need to consider which one will allow you to communicate your meaning and artistic intentions in a suitable and interesting way. For example:

- Dark comedy tackles serious themes, but presents them in an amusing way. This is often very successful in being thought-provoking for an audience without being heavy.

- Theatre in Education is well suited to communicating a topic to a target audience of young people.

- Physical theatre might be particularly suitable for a more expressive exploration of a certain theme.

Influential practitioner Emma Rice, at a Broadway party in 2010

Lin-Manuel Miranda's *Hamilton* is set in 18th-century New York, but is stylistically influenced by very modern musical genres such as rap and R&B.

The importance of design

Remember that designers play an important role in establishing genre and performance style. At the most basic level, for example, all design elements can communicate light and dark in some way. This could be through the choice of materials, colour, pitch, key and so on.

Most importantly, your examiner will look for a range of strong evidence that you have made appropriate creative decisions to affect the meaning of the piece as a whole. This might mean, for example, that you have spotted a weakness in how a theme is being presented and so introduce a design idea, such as a soundscape, lighting effect, prop or costume, that supports the intended meaning and is in keeping with your chosen genre or practitioner.

LOOK HERE

The case studies on pages 122–123 offer further examples of how design enhances meaning.

DESIGN TIP

Play to the strengths of your group when selecting the genre or practitioner. For example, a group whose performers have some singing and dancing ability, would make musical theatre a genre worth considering.

TASK 5.10

Work with your group to complete a table like this to summarise advantages and disadvantages – for you – of different genres and performance styles. (Examples have been included to start you off.)

Genre / practitioner	Strengths for our group	Challenges for our group
Physical theatre	• Suits our theme. • Some performers are very comfortable with this style. • Interesting for lighting – lots of scope for sfx.	• Not everyone has experience of this style. • Costume design might be limited? • Is it too difficult for our audience to 'read' our artistic intentions?
Stanislavski	• Suits naturalistic performance style we feel suits our theme best. • Challenges our skills productively. • Should engage our audience strongly.	• Might be expensive in terms of naturalistic costuming.

STRUCTURE, CHARACTER AND LANGUAGE

Structure

Structure in drama is best described as the shape of the performance or the way it is built. Some narrative examples are:

- linear
- cyclical
- episodic.

A structure can emerge from the development of your devising process, rather than being an instant decision made early on.

As a designer, you will need to consider how the structure of the piece will affect your design. Your design could even be required to enhance the structure. A linear narrative, for example, might need changes of costume to support the sense of time moving forward. A cyclical piece might be helped by repetition of specific lighting states that signal a return to a location or situation. Set designers also need to pay close attention to the structure of the piece: lengthy scene changes, for example, could totally disrupt a fast-moving, episodic piece.

Character

Although costume might be considered the most important design aspect for communicating character, characterisation should be supported in some way by all designers. For example, music can help to present a character's emotions in a scene, and lighting could sharpen our attention on a character through the use of intensity (brightness) or a follow spot. Multi-roling would require a costume designer to seriously consider the pace at which outfit changes can be made off stage (or even on stage if your practitioner is Brecht, for example).

Language

At first glance, language might not seem to have a great deal to do with design. If you think about it more closely, however, a character who speaks in formal language is likely to wear more formal clothing. Words and language could also be part of a set design. In sound design, song lyrics should be carefully chosen to suit the language that is used in the piece.

FOCUS
- Different ways in which a devised piece can be presented
- Coming to decisions about your own devised piece.

ASSESSMENT CHECK

You should analyse and evaluate your decisions about how your piece will be communicated. Always consider why choices are taken. This will help you towards AO4.

DESIGN TIP

Your choice of practitioner or genre will be of central importance when considering form and structure, in particular.

The crowd line up to scorn and taunt Christ (Finbar Lynch) as he carries his cross in Steven Berkoff's *Messiah – Scenes from a Crucifixion*.

Design case studies

The following case studies demonstrate different ways in which design supports style, structure, character and language.

CASE STUDY: CYBERBULLYING

Starting from the concept of bullying as a stimulus, a group of Year 10 students set about devising a TIE genre piece on the topic of cyberbullying. They aimed for an audience of Year 7 students, whom they saw as being particularly vulnerable.

The group researched statistics, watched anti-bullying videos and shared their own experiences. They then improvised a few scenarios. They realised that it was much easier to understand the effects of cyberbullying than the reasons why young people get drawn into it. This led to further research and new improvisations.

One of the group had opted for sound design and began work on diegetic and non-diegetic sounds.

As well as the diegetic sounds of phone buttons, ringtones and notifications, the designer developed two underscores of ambient sounds. These supported characterisation by reflecting the feelings of the victim and the main perpetrator. These emerging soundtracks were used in rehearsals, where they helped to shape the devised piece.

The structure became a cyclical story of the bully. Scenes looked at her younger life and how she gradually came to understand the misery of her victim. Sound effects were an integral part of the performance and in establishing and enhancing the genre.

CASE STUDY: LIES

A quotation from Yevgeny Yevtushenko's poem 'Lies' was adopted as a devised performance stimulus:

Yevgeny Yevtushenko

Lies

Telling lies to the young is wrong.

Proving to them that lies are true is wrong.

Telling them that God's in his heaven

and all's well with the world is wrong.

The young people know what you mean.

The young are people.

1 Work with your group to complete a table like this to summarise advantages and disadvantages – for you – of different genres and styles. (Examples have been included to start you off.)

2 You could complete similar tables to help you consider genre, style and structure.

Genre	Strengths for our group	Challenges for our group	Notes
Physical theatre	• Suits our non-naturalistic style. • Some performers feel very comfortable with this style. • Interesting for lighting – lots of scope for SFX.	• Not everyone has experience of this style. • Costume design might be limited? • Is it too difficult for our audience to 'read' our artistic intentions?	• Could mix physical theatre with docudrama. • Follow Frantic Assembly techniques.
Comedy	• Suits non-naturalistic style. • Adds audience appeal and interest.	• Can be difficult to accomplish successfully.	Communicates character.

CASE STUDY: BEAUTY AND THE BEAST

Using a picture as a stimulus, a small group devised a modern version of *Beauty and the Beast*, incorporating physical theatre. Their artistic intentions concentrated on the physical and emotional repercussions of substance abuse.

The only piece of set was a white wooden frame, the size of a doorframe. It was used to represent a door, a window, a picture frame and a cage. It was supported and moved by the performers, which made it very versatile.

Costumes were simple – mostly black – and stretchy to support the form and minimalist style.

The lighting designer made a highly significant contribution to characterisation and the physical theatre genre. A range of cover washes enhanced the atmosphere and body language in ensemble scenes. Transitions between lighting states were sometimes very slow to enhance changes in emotional states. At other times, he used snap transitions for moments of shock or sudden change. In addition, tight white spotlights were used during monologues.

The group shared ideas about young people being lied to by adults. They worked these ideas through improvisation into a powerful episodic drama influenced by Brecht.

They chose to differentiate between harmless pretences, such as the tooth fairy, and lies that could be damaging. Using a range of Brechtian techniques, including multi-roling, placards, a narrator and direct address, the scenes focused on politicians, family and other authority figures lying to young people and the effects of this.

In end-on staging, the set created levels and 'hidden' areas with a clever arrangement of existing stage **rostra blocks**. Two levels were placed upstage centre to increase the proximity of those in authority to young people. The spaces under the stage blocks created locations such as a bedroom. The set strongly supported the episodic narrative.

FOCUS

Working together to develop the devised piece.

ASSESSMENT CHECK

You should demonstrate your engagement with the process of collaboration, rehearsal and refinement. Keep in mind that you are working towards AO1: 'Create and develop ideas to communicate meaning for theatrical performance.'

SIGNPOST

Make sure you have tried Task 5.1 on page 113. Remember that it is a starting point. Your ideas will develop and change.

LOOK HERE

'Your design challenge' on pages 112–113, and the appropriate practical design chapter, will support you further.

USING REHEARSALS TO DEVELOP AND REFINE YOUR DESIGNS

Focus on your design specialism

As the performers start to rehearse, you will need to turn your attention to designing.

TASK 5.12

As a way of clarifying your thoughts, begin your own version of the following journal. Add to it as you go along to help your evaluation and portfolio.

Group details: 5 performers plus Lighting, Costume, Set: Total 8		
Artistic intentions	Notes on style, practitioner, genre, structure	Set design notes
To explore the importance of community, locally, nationally, internationally. • Gain a better awareness of what 'community' means. • Understand the value of being part of a community. • See what happens when communities are broken up or divided.	7 Oct Non-naturalistic social drama. Berkoff: • ensemble • exaggerated movement • direct address • tableaux • episodic.	7 Oct Use image or symbol (invented) on fabric – flag? Suggests togetherness – performers could use dramatically to connect, wrap, be a barrier? 12 Oct Circular – perform in the round? Create semi-circular shape using curved cyclorama – project onto it? 23 Oct Levels for dramatic interest? Small steps? Could show people helping others up? Sightlines? 25 Oct Colour – monochrome to allow for strong coloured lighting and give a neutral feel? Bursts of colour with the flag idea? Talk to Costume.

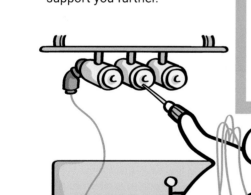

Remember your health and safety responsibilities, and ask for help!

Ongoing research

Your design work will progress quite rapidly as long as you 'feed' your creativity. This is continuous research, of which rehearsals are an important part. These ideas should keep you going.

> What inspiration do you find in the themes and messages of your artistic intentions?

> Keep an eye on the news. Are there topical examples of issues that relate to your artistic intentions?

> What do the characteristics of your chosen genre/practitioner suggest in terms of design?

> Are there other plays related to your artistic intentions? They could be useful for design ideas. For bullying, for example, you could look at *DNA* by Dennis Kelly or *The Terrible Fate of Humpty Dumpty* by David Calcutt.

> Be in rehearsals as much as possible. An improvised scene might lead you to a new underscore or different lighting effect.

TASK 5.13

Keep a detailed record of your research and response to rehearsals (use the table in Task 5.12) for your portfolio. Save images (or links to them). Keep in mind the 'how and why' of your design.

Developing your design alongside performers and other designers

It is critical that you collaborate with the rest of your group. This will be a balance between presenting your ideas and responding to ideas that others bring. Together, you need to arrive at a harmonious world on the stage. Below are some suggestions for working collaboratively during rehearsals:

ASSESSMENT CHECK

The research and rehearsal processes will help you to:

- develop and refine your ideas and those of the group
- respond to feedback.

It is essential that you collaborate in order to meet AO4: 'Analyse and evaluate your own work and the work of others.'

LOOK HERE

Use the guidance on page 114 to help with offering and receiving suggestions and making changes.

DESIGN TIP

You should write about the influence of your research in Stage 1 of your portfolio, and collaboration in Stage 3.

Keep returning to your artistic intentions.

Hold them at the front of your mind.

Spend time in rehearsals.

Notice what performers are doing.

Check that you are effectively using characteristics of your genre/practitioner.

Spend a few minutes before each rehearsal with any other designers.

Share plans supportively and check that all design elements are in harmony.

Feed performers with your developing design ideas.

Take in mood boards or design items as appropriate.

ASSESSMENT CHECK

Overcoming challenges shows that you can work collaboratively to generate, develop and communicate ideas.

Along with rehearsals, regular meetings should help you to use a range of effective techniques during the devising process.

PRODUCTION MEETINGS

AGENDA PERFORMANCE PROBLEMS
CHALLENGES PROGRESS DATES
COLLABORATION DESIGN ISSUES DEADLINES TIMESOURCE
PLAN COSTUME PRIORITY
TECHNICAL LIGHTING
COMMUNICATION EVALUATION SOUND SET
POSITIVITY COLLABORATE ANALYSIS
IMPORTANT CHECK STRATEGY SOLUTION

The design and performance elements of your group might often be working separately. You will need regular times to meet and check overall progress. The benefits of having regular meetings with a set agenda are:

- The agenda can be short and the meeting focused.
- All designers have a chance to give and get peer feedback.
- Deadlines and schedules can be set and checked.
- Issues can be raised and support organised.
- Notes from the meeting will help to keep your portfolio detailed and let you show progression.

As you are likely to be a small group without a director, having a representative from the performing group is a good idea. Minutes of the meeting can be shared with the rest of the group.

Agenda
- Progress report.
- Sharing of research and sketches etc (for each designer).
- Schedules and deadlines.
- Issues.
- Date of next meeting.

DESIGN TIP

File old agendas to help in compiling your portfolio.

Highlight and make notes on your agenda of what is discussed during the meeting. Include any changes to the piece that are being made and any actions you need to take. Use these notes as a checklist.

Just me?

If you are the only designer for your devised group, you should still have brief production meetings with the performers. Deadlines need to be met and it is in everyone's interests to maintain progress towards a harmonious performance.

If you need to, ask fellow group members to support with particular design elements. For example, could one or two performers operate some basic lighting or sound equipment for you when they are not on stage?

FINAL REHEARSALS

Now that your group's devised piece is nearly ready to be performed, it is time to check the effect of your work in full collaboration with the rest of the group.

Any production needs final technical and dress rehearsals before the actual performance. With a devised piece, it pays to put in an extra stage…

Pulling all the elements together

For a devised piece, you might work with visual and aural cues as much as with your script, and some of the performance might be polished improvisation. You will need to be extremely familiar with the piece if your production is going to reach the necessary level of harmony. The following task will help costume and sound designers, in particular, but could also raise valuable points for lighting and set.

TASK 5.14

Once the performers are able to do a run of the whole piece, you should watch it at least twice. Do it in costume and with the set, but without lights or sound. This allows you to concentrate on the action without having to operate light or sound.

Take detailed design notes in a table like this.

Moment in the piece	Event or line before the moment (*standby cue* for light or sound)	What should happen	Notes
Raising the flag above their heads	Performers move to top levels.	• Switch to sfx (2). • Costume cape should fall to the floor.	• Rehearse before the tech if possible. • Talk to performer.

Make sure you leave plenty of time for final rehearsals, and any last-minute design changes, in order to achieve a polished performance.

 FOCUS

How to run and use the key rehearsals in the final days before performance.

 ASSESSMENT CHECK

By the time of final rehearsals, you will have a range of theatrical skills and be able to apply them as a creative, effective, independent learner able to make informed choices in process and performance.

 LOOK HERE

Guidance on the technical and dress rehearsals in Chapters 1 to 4 will take you through the rehearsal process.

 DESIGN TIP

Complete the tasks in this chapter as you come to them. As you go along, record your decisions together with the reasons for making them.

NOTE

This chapter assumes that you are writing, rather than recording, your portfolio. If this is not the case, make detailed notes, spider diagrams and so on to support your final presentation.

FOCUS

- The start of the journey.
- How to approach it practically and record the process in your portfolio.

ASSESSMENT CHECK

AO1 asks you to create and develop ideas that communicate meaning.

SIGNPOST

Chapter 1 will support all your design work.

The following sections at the beginning of this chapter will help you to start the portfolio:

- Your design challenge
- Responding to stimuli
- Agreeing on your artistic intentions.

LIGHTING DESIGN FOR THE DEVISED PIECE

STAGE 1: RESPONSE TO THE STIMULUS

The early stages of documenting your work

This stage begins your process of documenting the practical creation and development of ideas, with a focus on the stimulus and your response to it. Your portfolio should provide carefully chosen evidence of how the stimulus kick-started this creative process for you as a designer and for the group as a whole. Discuss:

- how your ideas for the design developed from the stimulus
- the theme or message that emerged for the piece as a whole
- your research findings in response to the stimulus and how they influenced your design
- how mood boards, for example, influenced your design
- your personal contribution to the development of the piece in response to the stimulus.

Note that, as lighting designer, you should explain some of your early ideas, but you should also focus on your role as deviser and group member.

Initial ideas and research

Focus closely on the stimulus your group chose to work with. Include some detail in Stage 1 of the initial ideas, themes and settings you considered and the research you carried out individually and as a group.

TASK 5.15

1. Use the Stage 1 bullet points and the AO1 mark scheme to put the response on the following page into a band.
2. Share your thinking with a partner.
   - Why have you agreed or disagreed?
   - Pick out evidence from the example to justify your reasoning.
   - Can you come to an agreement and decide on a mark?
3. What advice would you give the writer to improve their work? (Have they made the best use of the number of words available)?

DESIGN TIP

See your lighting design and your portfolio as two parts of the same whole. They must be worked on at the same time. This could involve taking detailed notes, or writing the portfolio as you go along and then reviewing it at the end.

LOOK HERE

See page 111 for details of how to present your portfolio.

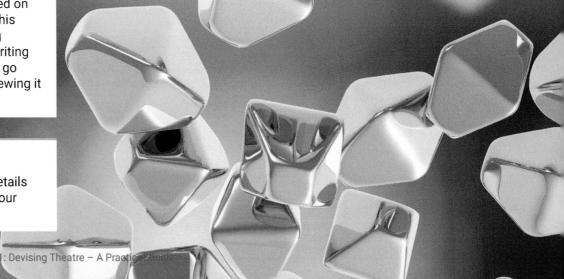

I was the lighting designer for our devised performance. Our stimulus was the song 'Titanium' by David Guetta and Sia. It is an urban dance track with a very energising feel. The lyrics are about strength and resilience.

One of the first things we did was some major research. We had the theme of strength and resilience from our stimulus, but needed to find out what was going to happen in the play. I suggested that we come back to the next lesson with examples.

Our exploration of inspirational strong young people was effective, as it threw up some very interesting characters including:

Malala Yousafzai, the Nobel Peace prize-winner who fought for girls to go to school in Pakistan.

Greta Thunberg, the Swedish teenager who campaigns about climate change.

Jesy Nelson, the singer from Little Mix who suffered cyberbullying and made a documentary to try to help others.

Musharaf Asghar, a student from the television series *Educating Yorkshire* who has a severe stammer, but learned to speak publicly with help from his teachers.

The Thai football team who were trapped in an underground cave for two weeks, but stayed positive.

Titanium is a silvery-grey metal that is strong and tough and doesn't corrode easily. In terms of lighting design, I immediately thought of hard-edged profile spots, high intensity and possibly gobos. The metal itself suggested bright, clean, sharp lighting. I researched different-coloured filters and found some, such as Deep Lavender and Electric Lilac, that would create the sense of drama I wanted. I tested these colours using par cans and profile spotlights, discovering that the electric lilac created a strong blast of colour which I went on to use in the movement pieces because they really defined the performers. The stimulus itself (the song) had the same kind of energy as the lighting, which worked well.

TASK 5.16

1 Look through the sections listed in the Signpost on page 128. Collect completed tasks and extra notes. Remind yourself of the Stage 1 bullet points (on page 111).

2 Begin by referring to the stimulus chosen by your group and what the initial responses were. You could include a briefly annotated copy.

3 Describe your group's artistic intentions, explaining what you want the audience to think and feel. What are your own artistic intentions as lighting designer?

4 Give details of your most important research and how it has influenced your lighting ideas and the devised piece itself.

5 Add any plans or mention lighting design ideas you had at this stage.

6 Read through your text to check that it covers all the bullet points and that the word count is about 250 words.

DESIGN TIP

Remember to:

- link your comments to the stimulus
- show how your research influenced your design
- give specific examples from your design and the piece as a whole.

LOOK HERE

These pages will be helpful:

- Performance style, pages 118–120
- Types of stage lantern, pages 18–19
- Understanding your lighting resources, pages 20–21.

FOCUS

How ideas from your practitioner/genre are incorporated into your lighting design.

ASSESSMENT CHECK

AO1 asks you to create and develop ideas that communicate meaning.

SIGNPOST

The following sections will be very helpful in making key decisions about your lighting and its development:

- Performance style, pages 118–120
- Angles, colour and intensity, pages 22–25
- Special effects in lighting, pages 26–27
- Research for lighting, page 29.

STAGE 2: THE INFLUENCE OF THE PRACTITIONER OR GENRE

This stage of your portfolio needs to remain process driven. In other words, you should chart significant moments in the development of your work in relation to your genre or practitioner. You must also explain particular features linked to your chosen practitioner or genre and how they have influenced or appeared in your design. You should explore:

- which practitioner/genre was chosen and why
- how you included features or characteristics of that practitioner/genre in your design (Focus on specific moments and features.)
- how the influence of your practitioner/genre helped to communicate meaning through your design. (Link a specific use of a feature of the practitioner/genre to how you are using it in the lighting design and the effect you hope this will have.)

It is very important that you describe moments from your piece that show precisely how your design uses the genre or practitioner to develop meaning in the piece as a whole. A word frame might help you:

In the scene where... I noticed..., so I decided to...

TASK 5.17

1. Look through the sections from Chapter 1 in the Signpost on the left. Keep the completed tasks and any extra notes handy.
2. Write a brief statement about which practitioner or genre you chose and how you came to settle on that choice.
3. Pick one moment from early on in rehearsals. It should, ideally, be a moment that can be seen in the final performance and which clearly shows the influence of the genre or practitioner. Write about the element of your lighting design that is marked by that moment. Include a photograph if possible.
4. Choose a later moment and repeat point 3. Make sure that you mention the impact you are hoping to have.
5. Add another moment if you wish and are within the word count (roughly 250 words).

TASK 5.18

1. Read the portfolio example on the following page and discuss it with a partner. Is this example better than that on page 129? Why?
2. Use the mark scheme to put the student response into a band. Do you agree with your partner?

TASK 5.19

Looking at your own work on practitioner/genre, are there any improvements you can make to Stage 2 of your portfolio?

Our chosen genre was Theatre in Education, as we wanted to encourage younger students to think about the importance of resilience in their own lives. The genre and theme suited the bold way I wanted to approach lighting, particularly as we were going to use a mixture of naturalism and non-naturalism in the piece.

Our target audience was Year 7 students. We decided to include audience participation in the form of hot-seating the character of a young eco-warrior. This wasn't easy to light. The audience - in the round - needed to be visible so that questions could be taken, but I didn't want to use the house lights, which would break the atmosphere on stage. 'Greta' needed to appear approachable for the audience to engage with her, so I lit the stage with warm, soft-edged profile spots using Pale Amber Gold (Lee 009). It seemed less intimidating to light all of the audience rather than pick out the hot seat. I used loosely focused fresnels in Wheat (Lee 763) and kept the intensity to around 30% so that the focus remained on the stage.

I designed the lighting with the aim of keeping the young audience interested throughout the piece. I didn't want to just 'light the space' or be repetitive. For example, I experimented with a number of coloured gels for a non-naturalistic monologue. It needed to have a lot of impact. The performer said that they found that the use of a cold, dramatic colour enhanced their ability to get into role. In the end, I opted for quite a strong gel (Electric Lilac) to produce a slightly mysterious, hard-edged profile spotlight.

DESIGN TIP

It is helpful to include lighting details, such as the names (and numbers) of colour filters. Many of these can be found online.

FOCUS

The development of your design throughout the rehearsal period.

ASSESSMENT CHECK

This stage of your portfolio continues your work towards AO1.

You need to demonstrate:

- effective application of design skills
- use of relevant techniques associated with the practitioner/ genre to realise artistic intentions
- your individual contribution to the performance through design.

SIGNPOST

Chapter 1 will guide you through the completion, rigging and plotting of your design.

STAGE 3: DEVELOPING AND REFINING YOUR LIGHTING DESIGN

The full wording for this stage of the portfolio is 'How ideas have been developed, amended and refined during the development of the devised piece.' It is very much about how you adapted your ideas in response to feedback or observations so that the meaning of the piece was made clearer.

You need to analyse the ways in which you worked through your creative ideas to arrive at a design that communicates meaning. You should discuss:

- how you used feedback to improve your ideas
- key moments that led to the refinement of your design and enhanced the meaning you wanted to communicate to the audience
- changes that you implemented towards the end of the process
- how technical or dress rehearsals helped you to refine your design.

TASK 5.20

1   The example below is for Stage 3 of a portfolio. Use the bullet points for this stage and the AO1 mark scheme to put it into a band.

2   Share your thinking with a partner.

- Why have you agreed or disagreed? Pick out evidence from the example to justify your reasoning.
- Can you come to an agreement and decide on a mark?

I found it easiest to develop my lighting on my own because I could work at my own pace. I have learned, however, that it is best to go to rehearsals often. This was obvious one day when the performers were working on a new movement piece to the stimulus song 'Titanium'. I developed and tested some ideas that I thought would add excitement to the scene involving AMLs. These lights worked with the rhythm of the song and threw changing colours onto the acting area. Feedback was good and the lighting increased the energy level for performers and audience.

I needed to design lighting states for a range of locations, including a cave, which proved to be an interesting challenge. I thought I could create atmosphere with a

Thai Navy Seals wear head-torches as they attempt to reach the trapped football team in June 2018.

low-intensity blue wash, but, in rehearsals it looked like an outdoor space. I tried altering the position of the fresnels and using soft-edged profiles in a deeper colour (Palace Blue) to create shadows, but it didn't create the mood I wanted.

One of the photographs of the Thai football boys showed them in a beam of light shone by rescuers. It also showed them using torches. I came up with a new plan that would have much more impact. I asked the performers to experiment with low-strength torches in their improvisation. Other than that, the acting area was completely dark. Now I was getting the effect we had been looking for.

Towards the end of the process, I noticed that the performers had decided to end the scene with the moment that the rescuers' lights hit them. For that, I used an AML in a cold colour (Hampshire Frost) that they could respond to as if in shock. I experimented with swiping the light upwards to 'catch' them suddenly. This was finalised in technical rehearsals.

The realisation of your lighting design

As a lighting designer, you should show an awareness and consideration of key elements associated with your design element. These could include:

- intensity
- focus
- angle
- special effects
- colour
- gobos
- types of lantern.

Your finished lighting design should be inventive and effective at every level. It should also sustain the interest of the audience and enhance the final production and its artistic intentions.

ASSESSMENT CHECK

Your teacher needs to know how your final design looks and the extent to which you actualised it on the stage.

TASK 5.21

Use the AO1 mark scheme and the bullet points for Stage 3 to write this section of your own portfolio.

TASK 5.22

Fill in your own version of the table below before you finalise your design.

My range of skills: How does my lighting design…	
…reflect my **artistic intentions** and those of my group?	Theme of inner strength and resilience enhanced by use of strong, motivating lighting states.
demonstrate **safe working practices**	• Electric cables taped down. • Focusing avoids dazzle for audience and performers. • Safety cables in use.
…enhance **mood** and **atmosphere**?	• Coloured gels. • Pace of transitions.
…show **inventiveness** and make an **impact** on the audience?	Wide range of special effects.
…incorporate **key features of genre/practitioner** to communicate meaning	• Practical effect involving torches used by performers. • Co-ordination on timing rehearsed with sound designer. • Continuous research in rehearsals.

Documenting your final design

Details of your final lighting design can be included in the portfolio.

You should provide some or all of the following:

- cue sheets
- a lantern schedule
- a lighting plot.

You should also supervise the rigging, focusing, programming (if applicable) and the operating of your design if you are not doing this yourself.

LOOK HERE

Pages 30–31 will help you with technical drawings and documents.

ASSESSMENT CHECK

Your portfolio is assessed for AO1 in this unit/component, so it is important to give in the best work possible.

DESIGN TIP

Look through the student-style examples for the other design elements in this chapter. They might inspire some new ideas.

REVIEWING AND EDITING YOUR PORTFOLIO

Your portfolio should cover:

- imaginative design ideas that you have created and developed in response to the stimulus
- ideas and techniques that communicate meaning effectively
- creative incorporation of characteristics linked to your chosen practitioner or genre
- a relevant individual contribution to the creation, development and refinement of your lighting design for the devised performance.

In achieving this, you should:

> Give a succinct range of specific examples and respond to all the bullet points for each section.

> Use this chapter and the mark scheme to guide each stage.

> Check that you have not drifted away from the point.

> Use different specific examples for each stage.

> Ensure you have charted the journey through the devising process.

> Know your best 'moments' and include them in your portfolio. What did you do? How did you do it? How did this communicate meaning in the final piece?

> Use the glossary at the end of Chapter 1. Can you include more subject-specific language?

> Keep to the limit of 900 words overall.

Editing

When you have completed your portfolio, proofread it and assess it against the relevant mark schemes.

Check that your word count is no more than 900 words, including annotations.

TIPS FOR REDUCING YOUR WORD COUNT

- Avoid repeating yourself. Which section does your point fit in best? Don't include it again elsewhere.
- Remove anything unnecessary. Don't waste words that won't gain marks.
- Give enough detail, but avoid waffling!
- See if some sentences could be made shorter by rephrasing.

TIPS FOR INCREASING YOUR WORD COUNT

- Repeat Task 5.19 on page 130.
- Can you add detailed annotations to your drawings?
- In Stage 1, add more details of your research.
- Check that you have included at least two specific examples in each of the three stages of the portfolio.
- Take feedback from an audience member. Include their comments, along with your own responses.

EVALUATING YOUR LIGHTING DESIGN

Until the performance has taken place, you will not be in a position to evaluate your design. You need to **analyse** (identify and investigate) and **evaluate** (assess the merit) of your design. You should analyse and evaluate:

- your design as it appeared in the final performance
- how your design skills contributed to the effectiveness of that performance
- your own contribution to the final performance, including how effectively you fulfilled your initial aims.

As long as you cover all of the bullet points for each stage, there is no need to deal with them one at a time. In fact, it might be better to apply all of them to a series of specific aspects and moments where your lighting design was successful or where it could have been improved.

Preparing for your evaluation

The evaluation is worth 15 marks, conducted under controlled conditions (like an exam) and you have 90 minutes to complete it. You should carefully prepare notes to guide you during your evaluation.

Your teachers and examiners are hoping to see detailed and thoughtful analysis and evaluation of less-successful aspects of your design as well as those you were pleased with. By reflecting on your creative design choices and asking yourself how effective they were, you will have the key to success. Recording these reflections in note form will enable you to be thorough and detailed when you come to write the evaluation itself.

Making notes

Preparing efficient and effective notes is a process that should not be rushed. If you can make your notes clear, you will have a blueprint for your evaluation and can be confident when you go into the supervised assessment. These tools should get you started:

- Photos of your lighting design. (These will be most useful if they show, say, a technical rehearsal with the lighting in use.)
- Your portfolio. (This can help you decide on aspects of the set and key moments when your design changed or enhanced meaning.)
- Your stimulus.
- Your artistic intentions for the lighting design and the piece as a whole.
- A video of the final performance.
- The three bullet points used in the evaluation question.
- Task 5.22 on page 133.

FOCUS

How to assess your own design in performance.

ASSESSMENT CHECK

Your evaluation should show how you have developed as a creative, effective, independent and reflective learner able to make informed choices in process and performance.

TASK 5.23

1. Once you have gathered these tools, pull out key aspects and moments that successfully (or not) communicated your artistic intentions. Be sure to consider how your set design worked in relation to other design elements, such as sound, and how the lighting contributed to the performance.

2. Make notes or a spider diagram for each aspect or moment in performance. These should cover all of the bullet points.

Identify/investigate – assess.

Practioner/genre.

Communicating artistic intentions – effect on audience.

DESIGN TIP

You might find it best to work in short bursts. Keep returning to your notes to add fresh thoughts and details.

Notice how the example below consists of detailed notes on the complexities of lighting theatre in the round, including genre, specific successful moments and a less successful moment.

Lighting in the round

Complex but successful:

* Avoided spillage
* Good use of resources.

TIE genre:

* Spotlight on narrator
* Warm lighting for hot-seat section (009/763 filters)
* Cool lighting for non-naturalistic monologues (Electric Lilac).

Health and safety:

* Avoid dazzling
* Careful use of safety equipment.

Movement scene:

* Intense, titanium-inspired colours and AMLs enhanced power of theme - exciting for audience.

Less successful:

* Intensity of lighting in school scene - brighter from some angles to pick out facial expressions clearly.

LOOK HERE

'Evaluating your lighting design' on page 39 will help you here.

DESIGN TIP

Use feedback from the audience, your teacher and other members of your group to help you pinpoint the moments and aspects to analyse and evaluate.

Refining your notes

Your aim should be to include all the successful and unsuccessful aspects of your lighting design. It is fine to include sketches and diagrams in your notes, but your finished bullet points must fit onto two sides of A4 paper. Your notes will be taken in at the end of the evaluation itself, so make sure that you have not included any prose (writing in full sentences/paragraphs).

When you are ready, the following task is good preparation for the supervised evaluation. You can repeat it as many times as you like.

TASK 5.24

1 Using only your notes, write your evaluation as if you are in the supervised assessment. You have 90 minutes, so be aware of the clock. If you finish early, try to add more detail. Consider using diagrams and annotated sketches to help communicate your design ideas.

2 Ask a teacher or classmate to put your evaluation into a band using the mark scheme. Hopefully, they will also give you some written or verbal feedback.

3 Use the mark scheme and the feedback to make improvements.

How do I use my notes in the assessment?

The main point is to have prepared your notes carefully in advance. If this has been achieved and you have refined your notes by updating them after every practice, you have the best chance of success in the exam.

If you created your notes well, you will be ready to both **analyse** and **evaluate**. It is crucial that you do not simply describe your lighting. You must also remember that you are writing about your lighting design in performance and **not** during its development (that was for the portfolio).

Am I analysing?

Using phrases that ensure you are identifying and investigating will increase your confidence. For example:

> One aspect of my design was… I used this idea because I wanted to communicate…
>
> > One aspect of my design was the use of AMLs. I used these because I wanted to communicate the speed and excitement of the movement scene…

> I had decided to… because…
>
> > I had decided to incorporate hand-held torches because they added a realistic atmosphere to the cave scene…

> In performance, [an aspect/moment] was particularly noticeable. This was because…
>
> > In performance, the moment when the sweeping lights of the rescuers caught the boys was particularly noticeable. The contrast between the low-intensity torchlight and the bright cold (Hampshire Frost) colour at high intensity made a great impact.

Am I evaluating?

Phrases containing judgement vocabulary will help you to evaluate. For example:

> The… was effective because…
>
> > The colour palette I used in my design was effective because it helped to create a variety of atmospheres. A clear example of this was when….

> … was successful/powerful because…
>
> > My use of a gobo was successful because it gave a strong visual representation of the natural world when the eco-warrior gave her monologue. This reinforced the importance of what she was fighting for through her strength and resilience.

> A moment that disappointed me was… I had intended… but… Another time I would…
>
> > A moment that disappointed me was the lack of intensity of light on the face of the child in the school scene. I had intended the gentle atmosphere, but his features couldn't be seen clearly. This was a crucial moment because the actor's facial expressions were so important. Another time I would change the intensity of the light using three-point lighting.

In the extract below, the student includes details about their lighting and how it communicated meaning.

> As we were in the round, I was glad that we had good equipment, including eight LED par cans and four AMLS, and a suitable rig. The height and position of the rig made it possible to avoid dazzling the audience or the performers. I also managed to avoid spilling light onto the audience by rigging and focusing precisely.
>
> I also had possibilities for variety in terms of colour and movement. My colour palette was effective because it could create different atmospheres. A clear example of this was in the movement piece which went with our stimulus 'Titanium'. The metal itself suggested bright, clean, sharp lighting and I used pale purples for a sense of drama, as well as evoking the metal itself. The strength of the colours mirrored the strength of the song and the performers' movements.
>
> One aspect of my design that worked particularly well in the round was the use of torches because the performers were able to control the lighting themselves (with my guidance). As they were sitting back to back in a group, the whole audience could see the atmospheric effect. The need for resilience in the dangerous situation was made more powerful through my lighting design.

FOCUS

- The start of the journey.
- How to approach it practically and record the process in your portfolio.

ASSESSMENT CHECK

AO1 asks you to create and develop ideas that communicate meaning.

SIGNPOST

Chapter 2 provides practical guidance for your sound design work and guides you through the entire process of designing, mixing, plotting and operating sound effects. Use it alongside the guidance at the beginning of this chapter.

DESIGN TIP

See your sound design and your portfolio as two parts of the same whole. They must be worked on at the same time. This could involve taking detailed notes or writing the portfolio as you go along and reviewing it at the end.

LOOK HERE

See page 111 for details of how to present your portfolio.

SOUND DESIGN FOR THE DEVISED PIECE

STAGE 1: RESPONSE TO THE STIMULUS

The early stages: your chosen stimulus

This stage begins your process of documenting the practical creation and development of ideas, with a focus on the stimulus and your response to it. Your portfolio should provide carefully chosen evidence of how the stimulus kick-started this creative process for you as a designer and for the group as a whole. Discuss:

- how your ideas for the design developed from the stimulus
- the theme or message that emerged for the piece as a whole
- your research findings in response to the stimulus and how they influenced your design
- how mood boards, for example, influenced your design
- your personal contribution to the development of the piece in response to the stimulus.

Note that, as sound designer, you should explain some of your early ideas, but you should also focus on your role as deviser and group member.

Initial ideas and research

Focus closely on the stimulus your group chose to work with. Include some detail in Stage 1 of the initial ideas, themes and settings you considered and the research you carried out individually and as a group.

TASK 5.25

1 Use the Stage 1 bullet points and the AO1 mark scheme to put the example answer below into a band.
2 Share your thinking with a partner.
    - Why have you agreed or disagreed?
    - Pick out evidence from the example to justify your reasoning.
    - Can you come to an agreement and decide on a mark?
3 What advice would you give the writer to improve their work? (Have they made the best use of the number of words available?)

I was the sound designer for our devised performance. Our stimulus was 'Nothing is ever really lost to us as long as we remember it', a quote from The Story Girl by Lucy Maud Montgomery.

We decided that we would devise our piece around memories and the idea that they can be joyful or painful; important to hold onto or impossible to forget.

One of the first things we did in responding to the stimulus was to get into pairs and improvise our earliest memories. We discovered that they were nearly all linked to strong emotions such as fear, pain or joy. This strengthened our focus on the link between emotion and memory.

I did some research on memory and found that 'emotionally charged events' are the most memorable. I learned about how memories are encoded, stored and retrieved by our brains. Work on these ideas started me thinking about sound effects such as a metronome or a clock ticking, and how special effects, such as reverb, could be used to distort a sound into something less recognisable.

I created a mood board:

I was inspired to use sound to highlight the importance of emotions in memory. This suggested quite an abstract performance piece. This challenging approach was picked up on by the group and our finished piece came to involve a mixture of styles and forms.

I have a great-grandparent with dementia and talked about how difficult it is because her memory loss is pretty bad. Sometimes, she doesn't even know who I am. At other times, she can remember things from when she was young, but not what she has done that day. A scene based on this appeared in our final piece with sound that I designed and created.

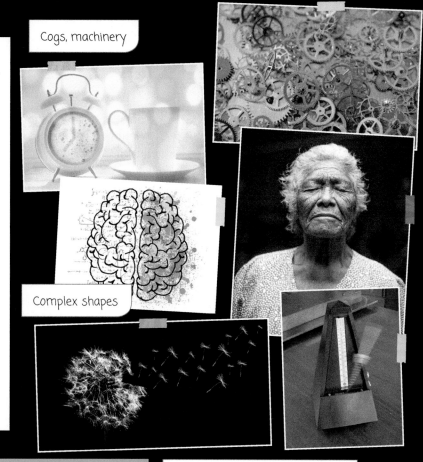

Cogs, machinery

Complex shapes

What does memory sound like?
- Laughter/tears?
- Regular/random?

TASK 5.26

1 Look through the sections in the Signpost on page 138. Collect completed tasks from Chapter 2 and any additional notes. Remind yourself of the Stage 1 key points (on page 111).

2 Begin by referring to the stimulus chosen by your group and what the initial responses were. You could include a briefly annotated copy.

3 Describe your group's artistic intentions, explaining what you want the audience to think and feel. What are your own artistic intentions as sound designer?

4 Give details of your most important research and how it influenced your sound design ideas. and the devised piece as a whole.

5 Add any ideas for sound design that you had at this early stage.

6 Read through your text to check that it covers all the bullet points and that the word count is about 250 words.

 LOOK HERE

'Introduction to sound design', pages 42–43, and 'Research for sound design', pages 46–47, will be helpful here.

TASK 5.27

Check your own Stage 1 text against the bullet points and the AO1 mark scheme. Can you make at least three improvements?

FOCUS

How ideas from your practitioner/genre are incorporated into your sound design.

ASSESSMENT CHECK

AO1 asks you to create and develop ideas that communicate meaning. You will be creating a design that contributes positively to the performance.

SIGNPOST

The following sections will be particularly helpful in making key decisions about your sound design:

- Research for sound design, pages 46–47 Sourcing, creating and mixing sounds, pages 48–51
- Special sound effects, pages 52–53
- Performance style, pages 118–120.

STAGE 2: THE INFLUENCE OF THE PRACTITIONER OR GENRE

This stage of your portfolio needs to remain process driven. In other words, you should chart significant moments in the development of your work in relation to your genre or practitioner. You must also explain particular features linked to your chosen practitioner or genre and how they have influenced or appeared in your design. You should explore:

- which practitioner/genre was chosen and why
- how you included features or characteristics of that practitioner/genre in your design (Focus on specific moments and features.)
- how the influence of your practitioner/genre helped to communicate meaning through your design. (Link a specific use of a feature of the practitioner/genre to how you are using it in the set design and the effect you hope this will have.)

It is very important that you describe moments from your piece that show precisely how your design uses the genre or practitioner to develop meaning in the piece as a whole. A word frame might help you:

In the scene where... I noticed..., so I decided to...

TASK 5.28

1   Look through the sections from Chapter 2 in the Signpost on the left. Keep the completed tasks and any extra notes handy.

2   Write a brief statement about which practitioner or genre you chose and how you came to settle on that choice.

3   Pick one moment from early on in rehearsals. It should, ideally, be a moment that can be seen in the final performance and which clearly shows the influence of the genre or practitioner. Write about the element of your sound design that is marked by that moment. Include a photograph if possible.

4   Choose a later moment and repeat point 3. Make sure that you mention the impact you are hoping to have.

5   Add another moment if you wish and are within the word count (roughly 250 words).

TASK 5.29

1   The extract on the following page is the second stage of the portfolio from pages 138–139. Use the bullet points for this stage and the AO1 mark scheme to put it into a band.

2   Share your thinking with a partner.

- Why have you agreed or disagreed? Pick out evidence from the example to justify your reasoning.
- Can you come to an agreement and decide on a mark?

We took Katie Mitchell as our practitioner because we wanted to challenge ourselves to create an ambitious piece. The performers were keen to create realism in their characters and the lighting designer and I wanted to stretch ourselves by using technology in an exciting way.

I included several non-diegetic soundscapes and underscores to enhance atmosphere and to support our artistic intentions. One of the first scenes I worked on was where the lady with dementia was with her great-grandson. I used the sound of children playing (from her distant memories) and added a slow metronome effect and a distorted drone sound to create some of the confusion the character was experiencing. This gave the kind of effect I associate with Katie Mitchell. I asked the performer playing the old lady if she could introduce the sound of a teaspoon going around and around inside a cup to bring sound design onto the stage. I wanted the audience to feel that the woman could hear the sounds that they could hear and that she was 'playing' along with them.

I also incorporated techniques I associate with Katie Mitchell when I designed the sound for the scene where a character remembers getting lost on a ship as a young child. We aimed to show how frightening memories are hard to shake off. For this scene it was important to suggest location and I used some diegetic sea and boat effects mixed with the recorded sound of people calling for her and the child crying. The sound worked alongside projections which were mainly grey waves.

A scene from Katie Mitchell's *Fräulein Julie*.

FOCUS

The development of your design throughout the rehearsal period.

ASSESSMENT CHECK

This stage of your portfolio continues your work towards AO1: 'Create and develop ideas to communicate meaning for performance.'

STAGE 3: DEVELOPING AND REFINING YOUR SOUND DESIGN

The full wording for this stage of the portfolio is 'How ideas have been developed, amended and refined during the development of the devised piece.' It is very much about how you adapted your ideas in response to feedback or observations so that the meaning of the piece was made clearer.

You need to analyse the ways in which you worked through your creative ideas to arrive at a design that communicates meaning. You should discuss:

- how you used feedback to improve your ideas
- key moments that led to the refinement of your design and enhanced the meaning you wanted to communicate to the audience
- changes that you implemented towards the end of the process
- how technical or dress rehearsals helped you to refine your design.

TASK 5.30

1 The example below is for Stage 3 of a portfolio. Use the bullet points for this stage and the AO1 mark scheme to put it into a band.

2 Share your thinking with a partner.
- Why have you agreed or disagreed? Pick out evidence from the example to justify your reasoning.
- Can you come to an agreement and decide on a mark?

TASK 5.31

Use the AO1 mark scheme and the bullet points for Stage 3 to write this stage for your own portfolio.

A good example of how everyone's work was developed through collaboration related to a scene where a woman is arranging flowers in a vase while remembering the time her first boyfriend bought her flowers. The aim of the scene was to show how memories can be triggered and that the woman might always think of her old boyfriend when she arranges flowers.

To begin with, I created the sound of the vase being filled with water and then snapping sounds as each stem was cut. When I first tried the sound effect in the rehearsal room, it sounded all wrong. It just didn't match the actions and was comical, which wasn't our intention. I brought a microphone in and held it very close to water as it was poured from a big jug into a small metal 'vase'. The actor spoke her lines as the action took place. I did a similar thing while the stems were being cut. This ended up in the final performance with one of the other actors, in blacks, holding the microphone.

Much later in the process, I refined the sound design for the dementia scene, as I wanted it to have more impact and definition. When recording the sound of children playing, I varied the volume so that it faded in and out continuously, from very quiet to about 40%. I also added reverb to the drone effect to increase atmosphere. Once I was happy with each effect, I experimented with mixing them together. I also played with the balance in terms of different volume levels. After the technical rehearsal, I changed speaker positions to create a sense of the sound coming from different directions.

I had also experimented with adding a piece of 1940s swing music, but it felt that there was too much going on, so I had removed it by the time of the actual performance.

The realisation of your sound design

As a sound designer, you should show an awareness and consideration of key elements associated with your design element. These could include:

- music
- sound effects
- live sounds
- recorded sounds
- volume and amplification
- reverb/echo
- sound sources and directions, including position on stage.

Your finished sound should be inventive and effective. It should sustain the audience's interest and enhance the production and its artistic intentions.

You will need to make your sound design reasonably complex to attain high marks. Ideally, go beyond the minimum requirements and:

- mix sounds to create a soundscape
- experiment with both live and recorded sound
- at least consider using special effects, such as echo and reverb
- remember the power of silence – don't use sound just for the sake of it
- consider the use of directional sound
- select music carefully, including pre-set and post-show music, and during scene transitions

If not doing them yourself, you should supervise the production of sound in terms of creating and recording, and operation during the performance.

ASSESSMENT CHECK

Your teacher needs to know how your final design looks and the extent to which you actualised it on the stage.

You need to demonstrate:

- effective application of design skills
- use of relevant techniques associated with the practitioner/genre to realise artistic intentions
- your individual contribution to the performance through design.

LOOK HERE

'How to document your sound design', pages 54–55, and 'Operating sound equipment', pages 60–61, will help you with the evidence.

TASK 5.32

Fill in your own version of this table before you finalise your design:

My range of skills: How does my sound design...	
...reflect my **artistic intentions** and those of my group?	• Memories are important, but some can be difficult to forget. • The metronome marking time. • Music evokes particular periods. • Soundscape raises questions around memory.
...demonstrate **safe working practices**?	• Sound levels checked. • Cables taped down.
...enhance **mood** and **atmosphere**?	Atmospheric effects and music enhance performance.
...show **inventiveness** and make an impact on the audience?	• Carefully chosen effects in addition to music. • Gradual volume changes/fades.
...show **collaboration** with performers and other designers?	• Close work with performers improved the piece. • Used sound effects during rehearsals. • Worked closely with lighting designer.
... incorporate **key features of genre/practitioner** to communicate meaning?	• Use of live microphone on stage. • Complex, layered sound alongside naturalistic acting style.

Documenting your final design

Your final sound design can be included in the portfolio with:

- cue sheets
- a sound plot.

FOCUS

Checking and improving your work.

ASSESSMENT CHECK

Your portfolio is assessed for AO1 in this unit/component, so it is important to give in the best work possible.

DESIGN TIP

Look through the student-style examples for the other design elements in this chapter. They might inspire some new ideas.

REVIEWING AND EDITING YOUR PORTFOLIO

Your portfolio should cover:

- imaginative design ideas that you have created and developed in response to the stimulus
- ideas and techniques that communicate meaning effectively
- creative incorporation of characteristics linked to your chosen practitioner or genre
- a relevant individual contribution to the creation, development and refinement of your sound design for the devised performance.

In achieving this, you should:

- Give a succinct range of specific examples and respond to all the bullet points for each section.

- Use this chapter and the mark scheme to guide each stage.

- Check that you have not drifted away from the key points.

- Use different specific examples for each stage.

- Ensure you have charted the journey through the devising process.

- Know your best 'moments' and include them in your portfolio. What did you do? How did you do it? How did this communicate meaning in the final piece?

- Use the glossary at the end of Chapter 2. Can you add more subject-specific language?

- Keep to the limit of 900 words overall.

Editing

When you have completed your portfolio, proofread it and assess it against the relevant mark schemes.

Check that your word count is no more than 900 words, including annotations.

TIPS FOR REDUCING YOUR WORD COUNT

- Avoid repeating yourself. Which section does your point fit in best? Don't include it again elsewhere.
- Remove anything unnecessary. Don't waste words that won't gain marks.
- Give enough detail, but avoid waffling!
- See if some sentences could be made shorter by rephrasing.

TIPS FOR INCREASING YOUR WORD COUNT

- Repeat Task 5.27 on page 139.
- Can you add detailed annotations to your drawings?
- In Stage 1, add more details of your research.
- Check that you have included at least two specific examples in each of the three stages of the portfolio.
- Take feedback from an audience member. Include their comments, along with your own responses.

EVALUATING YOUR SOUND DESIGN

Until the performance has taken place, you will not be in a position to evaluate your design. You need to **analyse** (identify and investigate) and **evaluate** (assess the merit) of your design. You should analyse and evaluate:

- your design as it appeared in the final performance
- how your design skills contributed to the effectiveness of that performance
- your own contribution to the final performance, including how effectively you fulfilled your initial aims.

As long as you cover all of the bullet points for each stage, there is no need to deal with them one at a time. In fact, it might be better to apply all of them to a series of specific aspects and moments where your set design was successful or where it could have been improved.

Preparing for your evaluation

The evaluation is worth 15 marks, conducted under controlled conditions (like an exam) and you have 90 minutes to complete it. You should carefully prepare notes to guide you during your evaluation.

Your teachers and examiners are hoping to see detailed and thoughtful analysis and evaluation of less-successful aspects of your design as well as those you were pleased with. By reflecting on your creative design choices and asking yourself how effective they were, you will have the key to success. Recording these reflections in note form will enable you to be thorough and detailed when you come to write the evaluation itself.

Making notes

Preparing efficient and effective notes is a process that should not be rushed. If you can make your notes clear, you will have a blueprint for your evaluation and can be confident when you go into the supervised assessment. These tools should get you started:

- Your portfolio. (This can help you decide on aspects of the set and key moments when your design changed or enhanced meaning.)
- Your stimulus.
- Cue sheets and sound plots.
- Your artistic intentions for the set design and the piece as a whole.
- A video of the final performance.
- The three bullet points used in the evaluation question.
- Task 5.32 on page 143.

FOCUS

How to assess your own design in performance.

ASSESSMENT CHECK

Your evaluation should show how you have developed as a creative, effective, independent and reflective learner able to make informed choices in process and performance.

TASK 5.33

1 Once you have gathered these tools, pull out key aspects and moments that successfully (or not) communicated your artistic intentions. Be sure to consider how your sound design worked in relation to other design elements, such as lighting, and how the sound influenced the performers.

2 Make notes or a spider diagram for each aspect or moment in performance. These should cover all of the bullet points.

Identify/investigate – assess.

Practioner/genre.

Communicating artistic intentions – effect on audience.

DESIGN TIP

You might find it best to work in short bursts. Keep returning to your notes to add fresh thoughts and details.

LOOK HERE

'Evaluating your sound design' on page 63 will help you here.

TASK 5.34

1 Using only your notes, write your evaluation as if you are in the supervised assessment. You have 90 minutes, so be aware of the clock. If you finish early, try to add more detail. Consider using diagrams and annotated sketches to help communicate your design ideas.

2 Ask a teacher or classmate to put your evaluation into a band using the mark scheme. Hopefully, they will also give you some written or verbal feedback.

3 Use the mark scheme and the feedback to make improvements to your notes.

DESIGN TIP

Use feedback from the audience, your teacher and other members of your group to help you pinpoint the moments and aspects to analyse and evaluate.

Notice how the student of the following example has created detailed notes on one moment of sound in performance, including practitioner and technical detail, as well as a less successful moment.

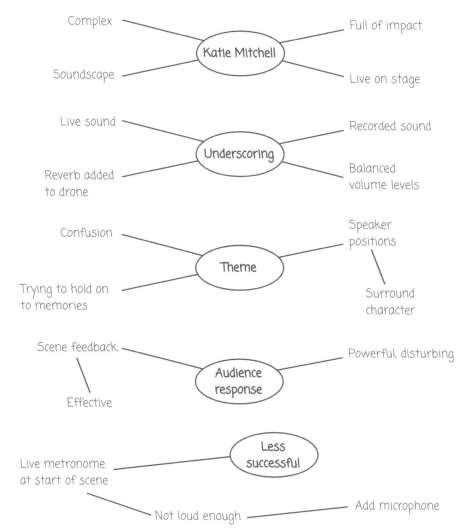

Refining your notes

Your aim should be to include all the successful and unsuccessful aspects of your set design. It is fine to include sketches and diagrams in your notes, but your finished bullet points must fit onto two sides of A4 paper. Your notes will be taken in at the end of the evaluation itself, so make sure that you have not included any prose (writing in full sentences/paragraphs).

When you are ready, Task 5.34, left, is good preparation for the supervised evaluation. You can repeat it as many times as you like.

How do I use my notes in the assessment?

The main point is to have prepared your notes carefully in advance. If this has been achieved and you have refined your notes by updating them after every practice, you have the best chance of success in the exam.

If you created your notes well, you will be ready to both **analyse** and **evaluate**. Your teacher will assess your writing with these two words at the front of their minds. It is crucial that you do not simply describe your sound. You must also remember that you are writing about your sound design in performance and **not** during its development (that was for the portfolio).

Am I analysing?

Using phrases that ensure you are identifying and investigating will increase your confidence. For example:

One aspect of my design was... I used this idea because I wanted to communicate...

> **One aspect of my design** was the use of AMLs. **I used these because** I wanted to communicate the speed and excitement of the movement scene...

I had decided to... because...

> **I had decided to** use underscoring because it added atmosphere and meaning during dialogue/monologues.

In performance, [an aspect/moment] was particularly noticeable. This was because...

> **In performance,** the moment when the little girl was lost on the ship was **particularly noticeable.** This was because I blended diegetic and non-diegetic sound powerfully.

Am I evaluating?

Phrases with judgement vocabulary will help you to evaluate, such as:

The... was effective because...

> The scene in which the onstage microphone amplified the sound of water was effective because it was unexpected and brought the audience closer to the memories of the character.

... was successful/powerful because...

> The soundscape in the dementia scene **was powerful because** it was so atmospheric.

A moment that disappointed me was... I had intended... but... Another time I would...

> A **moment that disappointed me** was the transition between the school scene and the dementia scene. **I had intended** to cross-fade the two tracks smoothly, **but** the volume for the second track was down, so there was an untidy gap. **Another time I would** practise more and run more checks during the performance.

In the extract below, the student includes detailed information about their sound design and how it communicated meaning to the audience.

> I received a lot of positive feedback after the performance. Audience members said the sound design was really powerful.
>
> An example was the scene about dementia. I was told that it was very moving because the soundscape evoked the strong feelings that the characters were experiencing. I was very pleased because we had set out to explore complex emotions and situations in that scene. I had decided to underscore the dialogue to add atmosphere and meaning. This was made up of the sound of children playing (from the character's distant memories) mixed with a drone track with reverb. The drone was eerie and the reverb added depth and fullness. The volume levels varied, with the drone sound becoming dominant when the memory became confused. This communicated my artistic intentions clearly. I also used a 1940s swing tune to take us into the scene, which helped locate the period of the woman's childhood. I had intended to cross-fade from the end of the previous track into the swing tune smoothly, but the volume was turned down, so there was an unwanted pause, which was frustrating. Another time, I would make careful checks during the performance.
>
> The way that sound worked alongside projection was an exciting element in the performance. In the scene where the girl is lost on the boat, the blending of the sea soundscape with the non-naturalistic sounds of her dad calling for her was quite chilling. The projection of the waves crashing worked really effectively with the sound because they gave a sense of how huge the ship and the sea seemed to the child.

FOCUS

- The start of the journey.
- How to approach it practically and record the process in your portfolio.

ASSESSMENT CHECK

AO1 asks you to create and develop ideas that communicate meaning.

SIGNPOST

These sections at the beginning of the chapter will be your resource for starting the portfolio:

- Your design challenge
- Responding to stimuli
- Agreeing on your artistic intentions.

Use them alongside the practical guidance in Chapter 3.

DESIGN TIP

See your set design and your portfolio as two parts of the same whole. They must be worked on at the same time. This could involve taking detailed notes, or writing the portfolio as you go along, then reviewing it at the end.

LOOK HERE

See page 111 for details of how to present your portfolio.

SET DESIGN FOR THE DEVISED PIECE

STAGE 1: RESPONSE TO THE STIMULUS

The early stages of documenting your work

This stage begins your process of documenting the practical creation and development of ideas, with a focus on the stimulus and your response to it. Your portfolio should provide carefully chosen evidence of how the stimulus kick-started this creative process for you as a designer and for the group as a whole. Discuss:

- how your ideas for the design developed from the stimulus
- the theme or message that emerged for the piece as a whole
- your research findings in response to the stimulus and how they influenced your design
- how mood boards, for example, influenced your design
- your personal contribution to the development of the piece in response to the stimulus.

Note that, as set designer, you should explain some of your early ideas, but you should also focus on your role as deviser and group member.

A set design sketch, with several levels, for *West Side* Story.

Initial ideas and research

Focus closely on the stimulus your group chose to work with. Include some detail in Stage 1 of the initial ideas, themes and settings you considered and the research you carried out individually and as a group.

TASK 5.35

The example below is the beginning of a set design portfolio.

1 Use the Stage 1 bullet points and the AO1 mark scheme for Unit/Component 1 to put the example answer into a band.

2 Share your thinking with a partner.
- Why have you agreed or disagreed? Pick out evidence from the example to justify your reasoning.
- Can you come to an agreement and decide on a mark?

3 What advice would you give the writer to improve their work?

DESIGN TIP

Remember to:
- directly link your comments to the stimulus
- show how your research influenced your design.
- give specific examples from your design and the piece as a whole.

Our chosen stimulus was a quotation from a poem called 'Lies' by the Russian poet Yevgeny Yevtushenko. It was written in 1952 and calls upon adults to tell young people the truth.

We discussed the stimulus and decided to create a piece about situations where young people are not told the truth and the problems that can cause. Humans have immense challenges to face, like climate change, that we need to talk about and understand.

We decided to share our experiences of lies. In my own case, for example, some serious information about my dad's health was kept from me for quite a long time. I understand why, but would have rather known. This example became a stimulus itself for one of the scenes in the finished piece.

I researched set designs to see how I could use levels in a modern way to represent power. For example, in our final piece a character was standing on one of the levels as she realised that the lie she had told to a child had been a mistake. She stepped down and sat on the floor next to the child. My set design helped to show her mood. This also fitted with our artistic intention of exploring the effect of withholding the truth from young people.

During the early stages, I had an idea of using bars or barriers of some kind, so I researched the roads and buildings around my house. I became interested in temporary fencing.

I discovered that I could borrow four of these barriers from a local plant hire firm. Four would make a square or a short alleyway. These design ideas fitted well with the stimulus, which suggests that lies create obstacles. In the final piece, the barriers were used in all of the scenes in a versatile way.

TASK 5.36

1 Look through the sections in the Signpost on page 148 and remind yourself of the Stage 1 bullet points. Collect notes and completed tasks.

2 Begin by referring to the stimulus and initial responses. You could include an annotated copy.

3 Describe your group's artistic intentions, explaining what you want the audience to think and feel. What are your own artistic intentions for the set?

4 Give details of your most important research and how it influenced your set design and the devised piece.

5 Add any sketches or mention set design ideas you had at this stage.

6 Read through your text to check that it covers all the key points and that the word count is about 250 words.

From 'Lies' by Yevgeny Yevtushenko
Telling lies to the young is wrong.
Proving to them that lies are true is wrong.
Telling them that God's in his heaven
and all's well with the world is wrong.
The young people know what you mean.
The young are people.

FOCUS

How ideas from your practitioner/genre are incorporated into your set design.

ASSESSMENT CHECK

AO1 asks you to create and develop ideas that communicate meaning. You will be creating a design that contributes positively to the performance.

SIGNPOST

The following sections will be particularly helpful in making key decisions about your set and its development.

- Two styles of set design, page 68
- Research for set design, page 69
- Understanding your resources, page 75
- Performance style, pages 118–120.

STAGE 2: THE INFLUENCE OF THE PRACTITIONER OR GENRE

This stage of your portfolio needs to remain process driven. In other words, you should chart significant moments in the development of your work in relation to your genre or practitioner. You must also explain particular features linked to your chosen practitioner or genre and how they have influenced or appeared in your design. You should explore:

- which practitioner/genre was chosen and why
- how you included features or characteristics of that practitioner/genre in your design (Focus on specific moments and features.)
- how the influence of your practitioner/genre helped to communicate meaning through your design. (Link a specific use of a feature of the practitioner/genre to how you are using it in the set design and the effect you hope this will have.)

It is very important that you describe moments from your piece that show precisely how your design uses the genre or practitioner to develop meaning in the piece as a whole. A word frame might help you:

In the scene where... I noticed..., so I decided to...

TASK 5.37

1. Look through the sections from Chapter 3 in the Signpost on the left. Keep the completed tasks and any extra notes handy.
2. Write a brief statement about which practitioner or genre you chose and how you came to settle on that choice.
3. Pick one moment from early on in rehearsals. It should, ideally, be a moment that can be seen in the final performance and which clearly shows the influence of the genre or practitioner. Write about the element of your set design that is marked by that moment. Include a photograph if possible.
4. Choose a later moment and repeat point 3. Make sure that you mention the impact you are hoping to have.
5. Add another moment if you wish and are within the word count (roughly 250 words).

TASK 5.38

1. Use the bullet points for this stage, plus the AO1 mark scheme to put the example on the following page into a band.
2. Share your thinking with a partner.
   - Why have you agreed or disagreed?
   - Pick out evidence from the example to justify your reasoning.
   - Can you come to an agreement and decide on a mark?

TASK 5.39

Check your own portfolio so far against the mark scheme. Can you make at least three improvements?

Our group chose Berthold Brecht as a practitioner. There was a strong message in our piece and we knew an episodic structure would suit the fact that we wanted a number of diverse scenes.

We chose end-on staging to suit Brecht's style and our performance space. Early in rehearsals I decided to use levels as I could see that this would enable the performers to show authority and use **proxemics** effectively. Two levels were placed upstage centre. I chose to use our existing stage blocks and not dress them at all. Brecht would have approved of this, I think, because it is a feature that is devoid of naturalism.

Later in rehearsals I found this image (below) from a Shakespeare production and thought the idea of pasting words and quotes onto a run of flats would be effective. Unlike this set, however, I decided to make the quotes like placards to use the influence of our practitioner and include a strong visual effect that supports our artistic intentions.

These are the quotes I chose to use as they are thought-provoking:

> O, what a tangled web we weave, when first we practise to deceive.
>
> *(Walter Scott, 'Marmion')*

> False face must hide what the false heart doth know.
>
> *(Shakespeare, Macbeth)*

> Integrity is the lifeblood of democracy. Deceit is a poison in its veins.
>
> *(Edward Kennedy)*

Each quote relates to lies and uses Brecht's idea of placards to communicate our theme to the audience. I hope it keeps our message in their minds throughout the piece.

DESIGN TIP

Note how this example uses all of the bullet points for this stage of the portfolio.

FOCUS

The development of your design throughout the rehearsal period.

ASSESSMENT CHECK

This stage of your portfolio continues your work towards AO1: 'Create and develop ideas to communicate meaning for performance.'

LOOK HERE

Chapter 3 will guide you through the completion and construction of your design for the performance.

STAGE 3: DEVELOPING AND REFINING YOUR SET DESIGN

The full wording for this stage of the portfolio is 'How ideas have been developed, amended and refined during the development of the devised piece.' It is very much about how you adapted your ideas in response to feedback or observations so that the meaning of the piece was made clearer.

You need to analyse how you worked through your creative ideas to arrive at a design that communicates meaning. You should discuss:

- how you used feedback to improve your ideas
- key moments that led to the refinement of your design and enhanced the meaning you wanted to communicate to the audience
- changes that you implemented towards the end of the process
- how technical or dress rehearsals helped you to refine your design.

TASK 5.40

1 The example below is for Stage 3 of a portfolio. Use the bullet points and the AO1 mark scheme to put it into a band.

2 Share your thinking with a partner.
- Why have you agreed or disagreed? Pick out evidence from the example to justify your reasoning.
- Can you come to an agreement and decide on a mark?

In rehearsals, I noticed that the performers were making all their entrances and exits from the sides of the stage. This was repetitive. I changed my design so that there were large gaps between the flats to use for access. I helped the actors to use three tables to represent the flats so they could start to work with the positions of entrances and exits. This refinement to my design changed the meaning of the piece enabling, at one point, the character of the young person who had not been told the truth about his father's serious illness (based on my experience) to stand in the 'doorway' and hear the truth. This would not have been as effective if he had stood at the edge of the stage.

The placards on the flats also changed as part of the design process. At first, I thought about writing on them with marker pens and spray paint. When I tested it out on cardboard, however, members of the group said that the writing wasn't easy to read. I discovered it would be better to paste on large photocopies of the quotes. I used a newspaper-style print. To begin with, I thought I would paint the flats white and have the lettering in black. In a production meeting with the lighting and costume designers, we decided that monochrome and red would be our colour palette. The monochrome aspects would be good for coloured lights and the costume designer was keen to use monochrome with red accents to suggest the danger of lies. The colour and newspaper-style placards would hopefully strengthen the impact of the quotations and have a powerful dramatic effect.

In terms of levels, I used stage blocks to create two small raised sections of different heights. To begin with, I thought these blocks would work best DSR and CSL because it would add variety. However, when I watched the technical rehearsal, I could see sightline problems, so I changed their positions to DSR and DSL.

TASK 5.41

Use the AO1 mark scheme and the bullet points for Stage 3 to write this stage for your own portfolio.

The realisation of your set design

As a set designer, you should show an awareness and consideration of key elements associated with your design element. These could include:

- choice of stage configuration (for example in the round)
- flooring
- backdrop/cyclorama
- props and set dressings
- furniture
- colour
- use of space
- entrances and exits
- sightlines.

Your finished set should be inventive and effective at every level. It should also sustain the interest of the audience and enhance the final production and its artistic intentions.

You only need to supervise the construction elements, but may benefit from being involved in some aspects of the build, such as painting.

TASK 5.42

Fill in your version of the following table before you construct your set.

My range of skills: How does my set design...	
...reflect my **artistic intentions** and those of my group?	• Theme of lies carried in quotes on flats. • Levels to suggest power and barriers (to truth).
...demonstrate **safe working practices**?	• Barriers light to lift. • Non-slip surfaces. • Flats securely weighted and fire retardant. • Height of levels not too great.
...enhance **mood** and **atmosphere**?	• Metal barriers suggest captivity. • Serious/harsh tone.
... incorporate **key features of genre/ practitioner** to communicate meaning and show **collaboration**?	• Levels and entrances between flats allow characters to eavesdrop. • Performers found practice items useful in rehearsal. • Co-ordinated colour with lighting and costume. • Combination of costume and set is safe.
...show **inventiveness** and make an **impact** on the audience?	• Powerful impact because set is uncluttered. • Symbolic and practical elements like the barriers, flats and levels. • Details help to communicate meaning. • Use of colour is engaging.

Documenting your final design

Your final set design can be included in the portfolio.

You should provide some or all of the following:

- drawings and/or photographs of the final design that was realised in the performance space, including props and set dressings
- sketches of earlier designs to illustrate the development of your ideas
- a ground plan of the performance space, including entrances and exits, audience positioning and any stage furniture
- photographs of your model box.

ASSESSMENT CHECK

Your teacher needs to know how your final design looks and the extent to which you actualised it on the stage. You need to demonstrate:

- effective application of design skills
- use of relevant techniques associated with the practitioner/ genre to realise artistic intentions
- your individual contribution to the performance through design.

LOOK HERE

'How to document your set design', pages 71–74, will help you with the technical drawings and model box.

DESIGN TIP

The ground plan needs to be drawn to scale, unlike the more artistic drawings.

FOCUS

Checking and improving your work.

ASSESSMENT CHECK

Your portfolio is assessed for AO1 in this unit/component, so it is important to give in the best work possible.

DESIGN TIP

Look through the student-style examples for the other design elements in this chapter. They might inspire some new ideas.

REVIEWING AND EDITING YOUR PORTFOLIO

Your portfolio should cover:

- imaginative design ideas that you have created and developed in response to the stimulus
- ideas and techniques that communicate meaning effectively
- creative incorporation of characteristics linked to your chosen practitioner or genre
- a relevant individual contribution to the creation, development and refinement of your set design for the devised performance.

In achieving this, you should:

> Give a succinct range of specific examples and respond to all the bullet points for each section.

> Use this chapter and the mark scheme to guide each stage.

> Check that you have not drifted away from the key points.

> Use different specific examples for each stage.

> Ensure you have charted the journey through the devising process.

> Know your best 'moments' and include them in your portfolio. What did you do? How did you do it? How did this communicate meaning in the final piece?

> Use the glossary at the end of Chapter 3. Can you include more subject-specific language?

> Keep to the limit of 900 words overall.

Editing

When you have completed your portfolio, proofread it and assess it against the relevant mark schemes.

Check that your word count is no more than 900 words, including annotations.

TIPS FOR REDUCING YOUR WORD COUNT

- Avoid repeating yourself. Which section does your point fit in best? Don't include it again elsewhere.
- Remove anything unnecessary. Don't waste words that won't gain marks.
- Give enough detail, but avoid waffling!
- See if some sentences could be made shorter by rephrasing.

TIPS FOR INCREASING YOUR WORD COUNT

- Repeat Task 5.39 on page 150.
- Can you add detailed annotations to your drawings?
- In Stage 1, add more details of your research.
- Check that you have included at least two specific examples in each of the three stages of the portfolio.
- Take feedback from an audience member. Include their comments, along with your own responses.

EVALUATING YOUR SET DESIGN

Until the performance has taken place, you will not be in a position to evaluate your design. You need to **analyse** (identify and investigate) and **evaluate** (assess the merit) of your design. You should analyse and evaluate:

- your design as it appeared in the final performance
- how your design skills contributed to the effectiveness of that performance
- your own contribution to the final performance, including how effectively you fulfilled your initial aims.

As long as you cover all of the bullet points for each stage, there is no need to deal with them one at a time. In fact, it might be better to apply all of them to a series of specific aspects and moments where your set design was successful or where it could have been improved.

Preparing for your evaluation

The evaluation is worth 15 marks, conducted under controlled conditions (like an exam) and you have 90 minutes to complete it. You should carefully prepare notes to guide you during your evaluation.

Your teachers and examiners are hoping to see detailed and thoughtful analysis and evaluation of less-successful aspects of your design as well as those you were pleased with. By reflecting on your creative design choices and asking yourself how effective they were, you will have the key to success. Recording these reflections in note form will enable you to be thorough and detailed when you come to write the evaluation itself.

Making notes

Preparing efficient and effective notes is a process that should not be rushed. If you can make your notes clear, you will have a blueprint for your evaluation and can be confident when you go into the supervised assessment. These tools should get you started:

- Photos of your set design. (These will be even more useful if they show, for example, the set in use in a technical rehearsal.)
- Your portfolio. (This can help you decide on aspects of the set and key moments when your design changed or enhanced meaning.)
- Your stimulus.
- Your artistic intentions for the set design and the piece as a whole.
- A video of the final performance.
- The three bullet points used in the evaluation question.
- Task 5.42 on page 153.

FOCUS

How to assess your own design in performance.

ASSESSMENT CHECK

Your evaluation should show how you have developed as a creative, effective, independent and reflective learner able to make informed choices in process and performance.

TASK 5.43

1 Once you have gathered these tools, pull out key aspects and moments that successfully (or not) communicated your artistic intentions. Be sure to consider how your set design worked in relation to other design elements, such as lighting, and how the set was used by the performers.

2 Make notes or a spider diagram for each aspect or moment in performance. These should cover all of the bullet points.

> Identify/investigate – assess.
>
> Practitioner/genre.
>
> Communicating artistic intentions – effect on audience.

Notice how the student of the following example has taken the set design aspect of painted placards and flats and added a good range of notes.

Brecht — Artistic intention 'Lies'

Successful under lights — Use of colour (Black/White/Red)

Stark — Alienation

Distance between three flats — Enabled effective/varied entrances

Child overhearing parent moment

Communicated emotion — Powerful

Flats/placards

Health and safety

Flats securely braced

Quality/size — Lettering — Less successful

What change needed?

DESIGN TIP

You might find it best to work in short bursts. Keep returning to your notes to add fresh thoughts and details.

LOOK HERE

'Evaluating your set design' on pages 80–81 will help you.

DESIGN TIP

Use feedback from the audience, your teacher and other members of your group to help you pinpoint the moments and aspects to analyse and evaluate.

Refining your notes

Your aim should be to include all the successful and unsuccessful aspects of your set design. It is fine to include sketches and diagrams in your notes, but your finished bullet points must fit onto two sides of A4 paper. Your notes will be taken in at the end of the evaluation itself, so make sure that you have not included any prose (writing in full sentences/paragraphs).

When you are ready, the following task is good preparation for the supervised evaluation. You can repeat it as many times as you like.

TASK 5.44

1   Using only your notes, write your evaluation as if you are in the supervised assessment. You have 90 minutes, so be aware of the clock. If you finish early, try to add more detail. Consider using diagrams and annotated sketches to help communicate your design ideas.

2   Ask a teacher or classmate to put your evaluation into a band using the mark scheme. Hopefully, they will also give you some written or verbal feedback.

3   Use the mark scheme and the feedback to make improvements.

How do I use my notes in the assessment?

The main point is to have prepared your notes carefully in advance. If this has been achieved and you have refined your notes by updating them after every practice, you have the best chance of success in the exam.

If you created your notes well, you will be ready to both **analyse** and **evaluate**. Your teacher will assess your writing with these two words at the front of their minds. It is crucial that you do not simply describe your set. You must also remember that you are writing about your set design in performance and **not** during its development (that was for the portfolio).

Am I analysing?

Using phrases that ensure you are identifying and investigating will increase your confidence. For example:

> One aspect of my design was... I used this idea because I wanted to communicate...
>
> > **One aspect of my design** was the use of levels. **I used this idea because** I wanted to communicate a sense of power and authority, which was an important part of my artistic intentions...
>
> I had decided to... because...
>
> > **I had decided to** paint placards onto the flats **because** they were a typical aspect of Brecht's stage designs that I felt...

> In performance, [an aspect/moment] was particularly noticeable. This was because...
>
> > **In performance,** the moment when the adult stepped down from the higher level and sat on the stage floor with the child **was particularly noticeable. This was because** the performers were able to make great use of the symbolism in an adult physically coming down to a child's level.

Am I evaluating?

Phrases with judgement vocabulary will help you to evaluate, such as:

> The... was effective because...
>
> > **The colour palette** I used in my design **was effective because** it helped the audience to focus on important moments. A clear example of this was when....
>
> ... was successful/powerful because...
>
> > My choice of flooring **was successful because,** it enabled the teacher character to create the loud footsteps which intimidated the child. I collaborated with the costume designer to create this powerful effect.
>
> A moment that disappointed me was... I had intended... but... Another time I would...
>
> > **A moment that disappointed me** occurred during the scene where the child confronts the mother. **I had intended** the audience to see the child's face before he came out from under the block, **but** the heads of the audience stopped many people from getting a clear view. **Another time I would** take much greater care to check sightlines.

In the extract below, the student gives brief details of the devised piece as a whole and then moves into analysis and evaluation.

> I was the set designer for our devised piece 'Lies'. Brecht's style and techniques influenced my work significantly. Our piece was episodic and grew from the stimulus of an extract from the poem by Yevteshenko. My artistic intentions were to use Brecht's alienation techniques in putting across the message of the performance: 'Telling lies to the young is wrong.'
>
> My set design was effective in creating a harmonious world in collaboration with the other designers and the performers. An example was when the lights turned red. As the set was mainly monochrome, the colour change had a powerful impact. The character was standing on a raised level in a white coat as she realised that the lie she had told to a child had been a mistake. She stepped down and sat on the stage floor. My set design helped to share her experience of her regret. This also fitted our artistic intention of exploring the effect of withholding the truth from young people.
>
> I set out to achieve a set that would support the episodic structure of our piece. I think I was particularly successful because of the speed with which the set could be rearranged, meaning that the flow of the performance was not interrupted. As the actors multi-roled in Brechtian style, the moving of items such as the barriers took place in full view of the audience. This became part of the spectacle.
>
> An aspect that disappointed me was the quality and size of the lettering on the flats. I had intended the text to have a big impact throughout the piece, but, in the final performance, it was ineffective in moments that took place under tightly focused spots. Another time, I would spend more time working with the lighting designer early in the design process.

FOCUS

- The start of the journey.
- How to approach it practically and record the process in your portfolio.

ASSESSMENT CHECK

AO1 asks you to create and develop ideas that communicate meaning.

SIGNPOST

Chapter 4 provides practical guidance for your costume design work and guides you through the process of designing, sourcing and creating costumes. Use it alongside the guidance at the beginning of this chapter.

DESIGN TIP

See your costume design and your portfolio as parts of the same whole. They must be worked on at the same time. This could involve taking detailed notes, or writing the portfolio as you go along and then reviewing it at the end.

COSTUME DESIGN FOR THE DEVISED PIECE

STAGE 1: RESPONSE TO THE STIMULUS

The early stages: your chosen stimulus

This stage begins your process of documenting the practical creation and development of ideas, with a focus on the stimulus and your response to it. Your portfolio should provide carefully chosen evidence of how the stimulus kick-started this creative process for you as a designer and for the group as a whole. Discuss:

- how your ideas for the design developed from the stimulus
- the theme or message that emerged for the piece as a whole
- your research findings in response to the stimulus and how they influenced your design
- how mood boards, for example, influenced your design
- your personal contribution to the development of the piece in response to the stimulus.

Note that, as costume designer, you should explain some of your early ideas, but you should also focus on your role as deviser and group member.

Initial ideas and research

Focus closely on the stimulus your group chose to work with. Include some detail in Stage 1 of the initial ideas, themes and settings you considered and the research you carried out individually and as a group.

A detail from a stimulus photograph that shows a range of circus performers, including acrobats and a ringmaster.

1 The example below is the start of a costume design portfolio. Use the Stage 1 bullet points and the AO1 mark scheme to put it into a band.

2 Share your thinking with a partner.
- Why have you agreed or disagreed? Pick out evidence from the example to justify your reasoning.
- Can you come to an agreement and decide on a mark?

3 What areas for improvement would you suggest?

TASK 5.46

What words and phrases could you add as a response to the stimulus photograph on page 158?

LOOK HERE

See page 111 for details of how to present your portfolio.

The stimulus we chose was a photograph of circus performers. They are balancing, juggling and presenting their skills. As a designer, I was inspired by the costumes' worn, slightly shabby appearance while also being colourful and richly textured.

I researched the history of circus costumes and discovered that performers used to make their own outfits from anything they could find. Our budget was small, so I decided to adapt and embellish reused garments as much as possible.

Our discussions gave me a sense of what was on show and what was being hidden. I suggested that each performer chose a character from the photograph and created a freeze-frame, which was thought-tracked by the rest of the group. We discovered that what they said and did was very different from what they were thinking. I know that this is something that many people do, so we took the theme of public v private. I think that most people have a public persona to some extent and, outside the circus setting, this idea had dramatic potential. Our artistic intentions were to create a piece with broad appeal that explored the difference between people's public and private 'faces'.

Three of the performers in our group do dance or gymnastics, which drew us to using these skills in the circus setting. I knew that my design would need to take this physicality into account.

We needed dialogue to communicate our theme and struck on the idea that conversation and thought-tracking or monologues could be interspersed with physical theatre. The characters were drawn from the photograph, and I chose to design for the Ring Mistress and the Acrobat.

TASK 5.47

1 Look through your work from Chapter 4. Collect completed tasks and any extra notes. Remind yourself of the Stage 1 key points.

2 Begin by referring to the stimulus chosen by your group and what the initial responses were. You could include a briefly annotated copy.

3 Describe your group's artistic intentions and what you want the audience to think and feel. What are your own artistic intentions, as costume designer?

5 Add any costume design ideas you had at this early stage.

4 Give details of your most important research and it influenced your costume design and the devised piece as a whole.

6 Read through your text to check that it covers the key points and the word count is about 300 words.

TASK 5.48

Check your own Stage 1 text against the AO1 mark scheme. Can you make at least three improvements?

LOOK HERE

'Introduction to costume design' on pages 84–85 might help with Task 5.47.

FOCUS

How ideas from your practitioner/genre are incorporated into your costume design.

ASSESSMENT CHECK

AO1 asks you to create and develop ideas that communicate meaning. You will be creating a design that contributes positively to the performance.

STAGE 2: THE INFLUENCE OF THE PRACTITIONER OR GENRE

This stage of your portfolio needs to remain process driven. In other words, you should chart significant moments in the development of your work in relation to your genre or practitioner. You must also explain particular features linked to your chosen practitioner or genre and how they have influenced or appeared in your design. You should explore:

- which practitioner/genre was chosen and why
- how you included features or characteristics of that practitioner/genre in your design (Focus on specific moments and features.)
- how the influence of your practitioner/genre helped to communicate meaning through your design. (Link a specific use of a feature of the practitioner/genre to how you are using it in the lighting design and the effect you hope this will have.)

It is very important that you describe moments from your piece that show precisely how your design uses the genre or practitioner to develop meaning in the piece as a whole. A word frame might help you:

In the scene where... I noticed..., so I decided to...

TASK 5.49

1. Look through the sections from Chapter 4 in the Signpost on the facing page. Keep the completed tasks and any extra notes handy.
2. Write a brief statement about which practitioner or genre you chose and how you came to settle on that choice.
3. Pick one moment from early on in rehearsals. It should, ideally, be a moment that can be seen in the final performance and which clearly shows the influence of the genre or practitioner. Write about the element of your costume design that is marked by that moment. Include a photograph if possible.
4. Choose a later moment and repeat point 3. Make sure that you mention the effect that you are hoping to have.
5. Add another moment if you wish and are within the word count (roughly 250 words).

TASK 5.50

The example on the following page is the second stage of the costume design portfolio from page 159.

1. Use the Stage 2 key points and the AO1 mark scheme to put it into a band.
2. Share your thinking with a partner.
   - Why have you agreed or disagreed? Pick out evidence from the example to justify your reasoning.
   - Can you come to an agreement and decide on a mark?

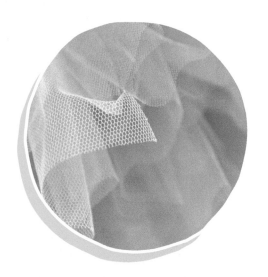

Emma Rice was the practitioner who most interested us. This was because she uses physical theatre as well as other styles and takes a joyful approach to telling stories. Her interest in circus tricks and acrobatics suited the stimulus too. Looking at the playful staging of Emma Rice's productions and the stimulus, I was drawn to an element of steam-punk meets circus apparel for my costume designs.

I chose to design one of my costumes for the Ring Mistress, partly based on the opportunity it gave me to introduce an element of tailoring, although I knew it would have to be loose enough to allow a full range of movement. The costume I decided on was a cherry-red coat from a charity shop, adapted with gold embellishments. I re-styled it with the help of a family friend. Under the coat, the actor wore lycra black leggings and a stretch T-shirt. Her make-up and hair were bold, with backcombing adding height to her hair. The colour palette of red, black and gold reflected the fun, impactful style that Emma Rice often favours. I wanted the audience to find the costumes powerful.

The other costume I designed was for the Acrobat. Having researched materials that would best suit a performer who moves very flexibly, I started to work on a Lycra bodysuit with accessories and removable garments on top. I needed the costumes to be easily adapted to suit the backstage scenes as well as the onstage ones. I felt that my designs would suit the flamboyant costume style I associate with Emma Rice.

SIGNPOST

The following sections will be helpful in making key decisions about your costumes and their development.

- Style: what we wear, and why, page 87
- Colour and fabric for the stage, pages 88–91
- Adapting costume items, page 96
- Hair and make-up, pages 98–99
- Performance style, pages 118–120.

Emma Rice's production of *Twelfth Night* at the Globe Theatre.

TASK 5.51

Check your own portfolio so far against the mark scheme. Can you make at least three improvements?

STAGE 3: DEVELOPING AND REFINING YOUR COSTUME DESIGN

The full wording for this stage of the portfolio is 'How ideas have been developed, amended and refined during the development of the devised piece.' It is very much about how you adapted your ideas in response to feedback or observations so that the meaning of the piece was made clearer.

You need to analyse the ways in which you worked through your creative ideas to arrive at a design that communicates meaning. You should discuss:

- how you used feedback to improve your ideas
- key moments that led to the refinement of your design and enhanced the meaning you wanted to communicate to the audience
- changes that you implemented towards the end of the process
- how technical or dress rehearsals helped you to refine your design.

TASK 5.52

1 The example below is for Stage 3 of a portfolio. Use the bullet points for this stage and the AO1 mark scheme to put it into a band.
2 Share your thinking with a partner.
   - Why have you agreed or disagreed?
   - Pick out evidence from the example to justify your reasoning.
   - Can you come to an agreement and decide on a mark?

The performer who played the Ring Mistress was less comfortable with physical theatre. I had noticed in one rehearsal that she was still for some of the time and looked slightly awkward. I spoke to her about developing her costume in a way which would work for our artistic intentions, her character and her confidence level. She found it very helpful being able to rehearse in elements of her costume. I adapted this, for example, by taking the lining out of the red coat to make it less bulky. I also gave her a black feather boa to use in the song 'The Show Must Go On', which was an eye-catching accessory for her to work with.

I also refined my design for the acrobat. I had started with a black-and-white striped leotard, which I teamed with red footless tights. Red ballet-net frills were added to the outer part of the hips. This looked effective but, during the first rehearsal under lights, I noticed that the costume didn't have the impact I had hoped for, so I added a stretch sequined bodice to add some sparkle. I was able to add a similarly stretchy fabric directly onto the leotard and sew it very securely. The improved costume seemed to work very well with the lighting, particularly in the acrobatic sequence where her movements were emphasised by the lilac lights. I added a glitter topcoat to her lips for a similar effect.

TASK 5.53

Use the AO1 mark scheme and the bullet points for Stage 3 to write this section for your own portfolio.

The realisation of your costume design

As a set designer, you should show an awareness and consideration of key elements associated with your design element. These could include:

- features, choice and use of materials/fabrics
- garments
- hairstyles and wigs
- make-up techniques, effects and colours
- accessories
- patterns
- textures.

Your finished costume design should be inventive and effective at every level. It should also sustain the interest of the audience and enhance the final production and its artistic intentions.

TASK 5.54

Fill in your version of the following table before you construct either of your final costumes.

My range of skills: How does my costume design…	
…reflect the **artistic intentions** of my group?	The theme of private and public identities is supported by layering costumes that can be changed quickly and easily.
…demonstrate **safe working practices**	• Avoid trailing items. • Ensure freedom of movement. • Non-slippery footwear.
…enhance **mood** and **atmosphere**?	Red in the jacket and the vividness of make-up enhance the circus element.
…show **inventiveness** and make an **impact** on the audience	Transforming the charity-shop jacket into a flattering ring mistress coat.
…show **collaboration** with performers and other designers?	• Co-ordinated use of colour palette with lighting designer.
…incorporate the **genre/ practitioner**?	• Flamboyant designs with bold colours and sparkle. • Fabric suitable for physical theatre.

Documenting your final design

Details of your final costume design can be included in the portfolio.

You should provide some or all of the following:

- photographs of your design at different stages, ideally including some being worn during rehearsals
- swatches and accessory samples (or photographs of them)
- sketches of costume and make-up, showing their design development.

You should also supervise the making of your design if you are not doing this yourself.

ASSESSMENT CHECK

Your teacher needs to know how far you actualised your design on the stage.

You need to demonstrate:

- effective application of design skills
- use of relevant techniques associated with the practitioner/ genre to realise artistic intentions
- your individual contribution to the performance through design.

LOOK HERE

'How to document your costume design', pages 100–101, will help you with the technical drawings.

DESIGN TIP

Make sure you annotate your drawings so that the details are clear.

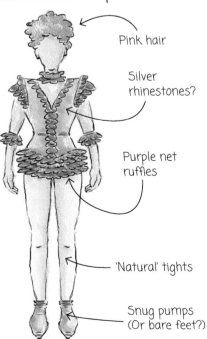

Acrobat / Trapeze Artist

Pink hair

Silver rhinestones?

Purple net ruffles

'Natural' tights

Snug pumps (Or bare feet?)

FOCUS

Checking and improving your work.

ASSESSMENT CHECK

Your portfolio is assessed for AO1 in this unit/component, so it is important to give in the best work possible.

DESIGN TIP

Look through the student-style examples for the other design elements in this chapter. They might inspire some new ideas.

REVIEWING AND EDITING YOUR PORTFOLIO

Your portfolio should cover:

- imaginative design ideas that you have created and developed in response to the stimulus
- ideas and techniques that communicate meaning effectively
- creative incorporation of characteristics linked to your chosen practitioner or genre
- a relevant individual contribution to the creation, development and refinement of your costume design for the devised performance.

In achieving this, you should:

> Give a succinct range of specific examples and respond to all the bullet points for each section.

> Use this chapter and the mark scheme to guide each stage.

> Check that you have not drifted away from the key points.

> Use different specific examples for each stage.

> Ensure you have charted the journey through the devising process.

> Know your best 'moments' and include them in your portfolio. What did you do? How did you do it? How did this communicate meaning in the final piece?

> Use the glossary at the end of Chapter 4. Can you include more subject-specific language?

> Keep to the limit of 900 words overall.

Editing

When you have completed your portfolio, proofread it and assess it against the relevant mark schemes.

Check that your word count is no more than 900 words, including annotations.

TIPS FOR REDUCING YOUR WORD COUNT

- Avoid repeating yourself. Which section does your point fit in best? Don't include it again elsewhere.
- Remove anything unnecessary. Don't waste words that won't gain marks.
- Give enough detail, but avoid waffling!
- See if some sentences could be made shorter by rephrasing.

TIPS FOR INCREASING YOUR WORD COUNT

- Repeat the Task 5.51 on page 161.
- Can you add detailed annotations to your drawings?
- In Stage 1, add more details of your research.
- Check that you have included at least two specific examples in each of the three stages of the portfolio.
- Take feedback from an audience member. Include their comments, along with your own responses.

EVALUATING YOUR COSTUME DESIGN

Until the performance has taken place, you will not be in a position to evaluate your design. You need to **analyse** (identify and investigate) and **evaluate** (assess the merit) of your design. You should analyse and evaluate:

- your design as it appeared in the final performance
- how your design skills contributed to the effectiveness of that performance
- your own contribution to the final performance, including how effectively you fulfilled your initial aims.

As long as you cover all of the bullet points for each stage, there is no need to deal with them one at a time. In fact, it might be better to apply all of them to a series of specific aspects and moments where your set design was successful or where it could have been improved.

Preparing for your evaluation

The evaluation is worth 15 marks, conducted under controlled conditions (like an exam) and you have 90 minutes to complete it. You should carefully prepare notes to guide you during your evaluation.

Your teachers and examiners are hoping to see detailed and thoughtful analysis and evaluation of less-successful aspects of your design as well as those you were pleased with. By reflecting on your creative design choices and asking yourself how effective they were, you will have the key to success. Recording these reflections in note form will enable you to be thorough and detailed when you come to write the evaluation itself.

Making notes

Preparing efficient and effective notes is a process that should not be rushed. If you can make your notes really clear, you will have a blueprint for your evaluation and can be confident when you go into the supervised assessment. These tools should get you started:

- Photos of your costume design. (These will be even more useful if they show the costume being worn in, say, a dress rehearsal.)
- Your portfolio. (This can help you decide on aspects of the set and key moments when your design changed or enhanced meaning.)
- Your stimulus.
- Your artistic intentions for the costume design and the piece as a whole.
- A video of the final performance.
- The three bullet points used in the evaluation question.
- Task 5.54 on page 163.

 FOCUS

How to assess your own design in performance.

ASSESSMENT CHECK

Your evaluation should show how you have developed as a creative, effective, independent and reflective learner able to make informed choices in process and performance.

TASK 5.55

1. Once you have gathered these tools, pull out key aspects and moments that successfully (or not) communicated your artistic intentions. Be sure to consider how your costume design worked in relation to other design elements, such as lighting, and how the costume benefitted the performers.
2. Make notes or a spider diagram for each aspect or moment in performance. These should cover all of the bullet points.

Identify/investigate – assess.

Practioner/genre.

Communicating artistic intentions – effect on audience.

DESIGN TIP

You might find it best to work in short bursts. Keep returning to your notes to add fresh thoughts and details.

Notice how the student for the following example has created detailed notes on one costume in performance, including practitioner influence, effective moments and a less successful moment.

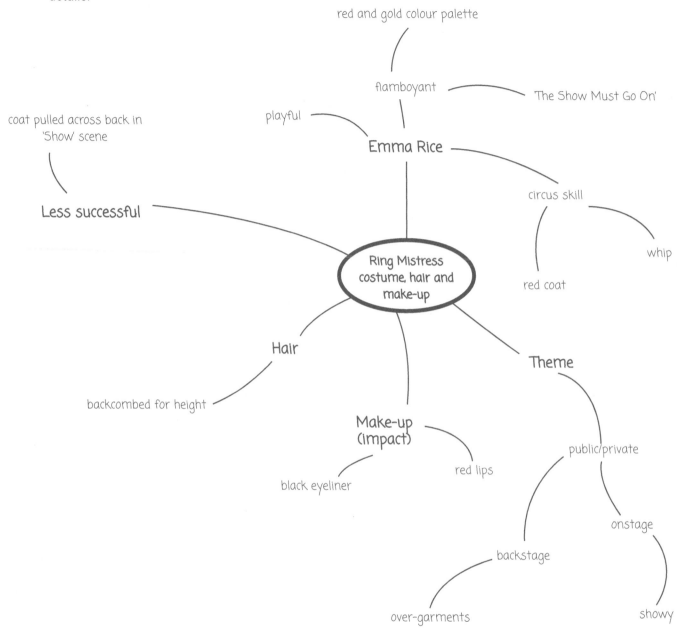

LOOK HERE

'Evaluating your costume design' on page 107 will help you here.

Refining your notes

Your aim should be to include all the successful and unsuccessful aspects of your costume design. It is fine to include sketches and diagrams in your notes, but your finished bullet points must fit onto two sides of A4 paper. Your notes will be taken in at the end of the writing time, so make sure that you have not included any prose (writing in full sentences and paragraphs).

When you are ready, the following task is good preparation for the supervised evaluation. You can repeat it as many times as you like.

DESIGN TIP

Use feedback from the audience, your teacher and other members of your group to help you pinpoint the moments and aspects to analyse and evaluate.

TASK 5.56

1   Using only your notes, write your evaluation as if you are in the supervised assessment. You have 90 minutes, so be aware of the clock. If you finish early, try to add more detail. Consider using diagrams and annotated sketches to help communicate your design ideas.

2   Ask a teacher or classmate to put your evaluation into a band using the mark scheme. Hopefully, they will also give you some written or verbal feedback.

3   Use the mark scheme and the feedback to make improvements.

How do I use my notes in the assessment?

The main point is to have prepared your notes carefully in advance. If this has been achieved and you have refined your notes by updating them after every practice, you have the best chance of success in the exam.

If you created your notes well, you will be ready to both **analyse** and **evaluate**. Your teacher will assess your writing with these two words at the forefront of their minds. It is crucial that you do not simply describe your costume. You must also remember that you are writing about your costume design in performance and **not** during its development (that was for the portfolio).

Am I analysing?

Using phrases that ensure you are identifying and investigating will increase your confidence. For example:

One aspect of my design was... I used this idea because I wanted to communicate...

> **One aspect of my design** was the monochrome colour base, contrasted with red and gold. **I used this** to communicate the on/off glamour of the circus...

I had decided to... because...

> **I had decided to** use very bold hair and make-up because they added definition to facial features...

In performance, [an aspect/moment] was particularly noticeable. This was because...

> **In performance**, the moment when the acrobat removed her dungarees **was particularly noticeable**. This highlighted the contrast between the plain, everyday, slightly scruffy garment with the circus outfit underneath and had significant impact.

Am I evaluating?

Phrases with judgement vocabulary will help you to evaluate, such as:

> ### The... was effective because...
>
> The **lycra bodysuit** for the acrobat was **effective because** it showed off her movements perfectly and allowed full flexibility.

> ### was successful/powerful because...
>
> The addition of a sequinned bodice for the acrobat **was powerful** because it sparkled brilliantly under the lights and was commented on positively in feedback.

> ### A moment that disappointed me was... I had intended... but... Another time I would...
>
> **An aspect that disappointed me** was the Acrobat's plaited hair. **I had intended** to weave ribbons through it. It would be covered with a woolly hat until she changed into her circus outfit, **but** I left myself short of time. The plait looked a bit untidy and some of the ribbon came loose. **Another time I would** allow enough time for all aspects of hair and make-up.

In the extract below, the student includes detailed information about their costume design and how it communicated meaning to the audience.

> Our audience told us that the piece was exciting and entertaining, which is exactly what we set out to achieve.
>
> One of the moments in the performance that was particularly effective involved the Ring Mistress. She really owned the stage. Her posture was upright and her gestures were broad and powerful. Her confidence in the scene and in the role in general was outstanding. She said that the costume had really helped her, and audience members commented on the strength of her character and the impact of her costume. I am prouder of that than of anything else. The removal of the bulky lining of the coat was successful in that the actor was able to move fluently in the physical theatre sequences. Restyling the coat to give it a short swallow-tail was highly effective. The tails were short enough not to be trodden on and added the formality I was looking for.
>
> In the backstage sections, the actor removed her coat and pulled on a broken-down red cardigan. I chose the colour for visual continuity; a constant reminder of her onstage role. The fact that the cardigan was roughly textured, pilled acrylic with stretched cuffs and a few holes was effective in supporting the character's offstage role. I used a cheese grater to raise the surface and produce the holes. I stretched the cuffs by pulling them while the garment was wet. The fact that it was second hand made it easier to produce the look that I wanted than if I had bought a new one. This aspect of costume design worked well in terms of incorporating the influences of Emma Rice and communicating our artistic intentions.
>
> The actor changed her posture when she wore the cardigan by rounding her shoulders and slouching a little, which emphasised the difference between her on- and offstage personality. I designed a hairstyle which she was able could flatten for the backstage sections. Again, this reinforced the differences in her personality.
>
> The overall visual effect of the performance was very strong and the offstage/onstage variations in the costumes supported our intentions very effectively.

UNIT/COMPONENT 2: PERFORMING THEATRE / PERFORMING FROM A TEXT

Chapter

6

FOCUS

How to approach the written account of your design.

SIGNPOST

Refer closely to the guidance and tasks in the relevant Practical Guide to Design at the beginning of this book.

LOOK HERE

See page 9 for how each design role should be applied in Unit/Component 2.

Explanation and guidance for the central concept of artistic intentions are given on pages 116–117.

DESIGN TIP

An example of an outline of artistic intentions can be found on your exam board website.

HOW YOUR DESIGN SKILLS WILL BE ASSESSED

Unit/Component 2 is assessed by a visiting examiner. For the scripted extracts, the examiner will look at two types of evidence of your design skills:

- your written outline of artistic intentions
- the design you produce for the performance.

The outline of artistic intentions

Your finished design will be seen or heard in the performance. In addition, you are required to provide information about how your design fits the artistic intentions of the scripted piece.

This written explanation is not assessed, but allows the examiner to see how well your designs in performance match the artistic intentions you set out with. Check this carefully. It should be approximately 150 words.

Including the information so briefly can be tricky, but you do need to cover these points:

- your design role
- how you aim to interpret the scene through your design
- how the text studied has been edited to create the final performance
- how that edit enables your own artistic intentions to be realised.

Editing the text for your performance

Together with your group, you will use sections from two ten-minute extracts to create your scene for performance. You need to:

- choose extracts that are key to understanding the full play
- take ideas for your design from the whole of both extracts
- edit the extracts so that your scenes work together sensibly
- create a design that works for the entire piece shown to the examiner
- create a design that complements the text and works harmoniously with the style of all performance and design elements
- shows consistency and/or progression in your design, to reflect, for example, a different time of day or a change in mood.

The minimum requirements are:

Four different cues using, for example:

- recorded sound effects
- effects used at source
- atmospheric sound effects
- specials.

Four different states using, for example, different:

- colours
- angles
- strengths
- specials.

- Set created for performance of one group
- Set dressed appropriately
- Props for the performance of chosen group.

One full costume, hair and make-up for one character.

The designs in performance

AO2 is the objective for the finished designs: 'Apply theatrical skills to realise artistic intentions in live performance.' Your designs should therefore demonstrate your knowledge about how to develop and create finished designs for the scenes.

The examiner will look very carefully for the way design is used during the performance. They will be assessing your ability to:

INTERPRET

the text creatively and believably, making your design a significant and harmonious part of the production.
Aim to create designs that inform the audience about the play. These designs should be in keeping with the work of other designers and enhance the artistic intentions of the piece.

PRODUCE

creative and engaging designs that match your written outline.
Check that your outline of artistic intentions accurately reflects the process that led to the finished designs. These designs should make a significant impact on the audience.

MAKE THE BEST USE

of the resources and time available.
Plan your time. Take up offers of help. Avoid putting anything that looks unfinished onto the stage.

UNDERSTAND AND APPLY

the technical aspects of your design.
Aim for the most professional-looking designs possible.

USE DESIGN

to amplify the mood, atmosphere, genre and style of the performance as a whole.
Think about being accurate to the period and fitting the style of the text, for example whether it is naturalistic or non-naturalistic. How does your design match the feel of the piece?

The performers in their muted period costumes are dominated by the back projection in this scene from *1984* at Nottingham Playhouse.

STEP ①

Working on your own with the script

As soon as you know that you are designing the lighting, start your independent work. This is likely to be at the same time as rehearsals begin.

Look at the script with the eyes of a lighting designer. Think about the genre, style, context and locations you will need to enhance. Your teacher should be able to tell you what the stage configuration will be.

1   Read the whole play (or a detailed summary). Use a table like the one below to note general points that could influence your design choices.

Play: *Sparkleshark* by Philip Ridley				
Genre: Social drama				
Staging configuration	**Location/s**	**Historical, social and cultural contexts**	**Themes/ messages**	**Style, moods and atmosphere**
In the round.	Rooftop of block of flats.	• Contemporary (modern day) • Youth culture.	• Friendship • Bullying.	• Mixture of naturalism and non-naturalism • Comedy • Fantasy.

2   Carefully read each extract as well as the edited scenes. Highlight and mark brief annotations on:

- locations – specific (such as a rooftop) and more general (city, for example), and whether they are interior or exterior
- weather/season and time of day
- shifts in mood and atmosphere
- the need for a special lighting state, such as colours for a fantasy scene
- any questions that crop up.

See the example on the following page.

3   Make more detailed notes from your table, above. Use your annotations to begin a chart like the following.

Locations	Interior/exterior	Time of day (or night)	Weather/season
• Street • Kitchen.	Forest (p27).		
Shifts in mood or atmosphere	**Special lighting state**	**Direct address or other non-naturalistic feature**	**Questions/ideas**
	Opening fridge (p5, l11).		

LIGHTING

'Hansel and Gretel' has the structure of a <u>nightmare</u>. A few domestic objects – buckets, a knife, a blanket, a plate, a jug, an axe – create both the <u>house</u> and the <u>forest</u> and appear in the <u>Witch's house</u>. The Mother also reappears, grotesque, as the Witch. A chorus of three is always present, and active. [...] The story is one of starvation, terror and catharsis. The rhythms of speech are taut and violent, containing the fearful tensions and, finally, joyous release of the drama.

House interior (1a)

Father It was no more than once upon a time when a poor woodcutter lived in a <u>small house</u> at the <u>edge of a huge, dark forest</u>. Now, the woodcutter lived with his wife and his two young children – a boy called Hansel and a little girl called Gretel. [...] <u>Night after hungry night</u>, he lay in bed next to his thin wife, and he worried so much that he tossed and he turned and he sighed and he mumbled and moaned and he just couldn't sleep at all. [...]   *Q Build*

Q Build up father

Is this a special, eg spot? Or is there other action here?

And as he fretted and sweated <u>in the darkness</u>, back came the bony voice of his wife; a voice as fierce as famine. [...]

   <u>*Outside. Bright light*</u>.   *Location 1b*

There was <u>bright, sparkling moonlight</u> outside and the <u>white pebbles</u> on the ground <u>shone like silver coins and precious jewels</u>. Hansel bent down and filled his empty pockets with as many pebbles as he could carry. [...]

   <u>*Inside*</u>.   *Location 1a returning*

'Don't worry, Gretel, you can go to sleep now. We'll be fine, I promise.' And he <u>got back into bed</u>.

Q Sunrise state

Mother At <u>dawn, before the sun had properly risen</u>, their mother came and woke the two children. [...]   *Q Location 2 - Forest*

Father Then the whole family <u>set off along the path to the forest</u>. [...]

Mother 'You stupid boy, that's not your kitten. It's just <u>the light of the morning sun glinting</u> on the chimney. Now come on.' [...]

   The family go <u>deeper into the dark heart of the forest</u>.   *Time passing*

Gretel The forest was <u>immense and gloomy</u>. [...]   *Darkening*

Hansel Hansel and Gretel collected a big pile of firewood and when it was <u>set alight</u> and the <u>flames were like burning tongues</u>, their mother said: *SFX*

Mother 'Now lie down by the fire and rest.'

Locations:

1) <u>House</u>   (a) <u>interior</u> - 2 spaces?
2) <u>Forest</u>   (b) <u>exterior</u> - night, bright
                          moonlight
3) <u>Witch's house</u>   *dawn*

* - <u>Fire</u> - They light it: Practical*
                     - Battery and bulb?
                     <u>OR</u> Staging - Footlights? Unit within set?

STEP ❷

The design brief meeting and rehearsals

Now that you have an understanding of the script and have started to think about lighting design, arrange a meeting with your group. Take your script and notebook and any lighting ideas you might already have. If you have a set, sound or costume designer, they should be there too.

You will not be able to finalise your lighting design until there is agreement on:

- the staging configuration (Is it in the round, traverse, end on?)
- a rough idea of the set design
- the style and setting of the performance (Is it naturalistic or stylised? Do you need to include a practical special such as a table lamp, for example? If so, what period does it need to reflect?)

⬭⬭ LOOK HERE

Details on making a mood board for lighting can be found on page 208.

During the meeting

1 Be ready to share your thoughts so far about lighting. Show any sketches or mood boards and invite feedback. Try to deal with any criticism positively: very few designers are likely to get it all right first time.

2 Listen carefully to others and give similar sensitive feedback.

3 Make sure you discuss the following questions.

- Do we have issues from Step 1 that can be covered in this meeting? If not, how and when can they be addressed?
- Are we beginning to move towards a shared artistic vision for the performance? What do we imagine it looks like?
- How will we communicate our ideas to each other? Can we create a resource bank for notes and images as we work independently? (This could be a shared folder on your school's intranet or a service such as Dropbox, which many professional theatres use.)
- What shall we work on before we next meet? What do we want to achieve by when?

4 Make detailed and well-organised notes of the discussions and any decisions made. You could put them under the heading 'Design Brief Meeting' in your notebook.

5 Agree on a date for the next design meeting.

STEP ③
Revisiting the script

This step is another stage you can complete independently. You should, however, be continuously checking in on rehearsals, as developments might influence your design. Similarly, other designers and the performers will benefit from your updates.

1 Add details to your script annotations and ideas tables, based on the design brief meeting. Your new knowledge of the staging and possible set design, for example, might allow you to think more clearly about locations, lighting states and colours. Similarly, shared artistic intentions might prompt you to consider moods to enhance at particular moments.

   Be clear on how your design can contribute to the artistic intentions. Have this at the front of your mind as you develop your ideas.

2 Sketch the acting area and mark areas with the positions for different locations. Break up your set into areas that you might want to light separately (rather than a general wash over the stage). Collaborate with the set designer to ensure that you know all the areas that need to be lit. These might include specific 'rooms', outdoor sites or a space that is used for monologues, for example.

   Once you have identified the areas to be lit separately, use them in different ways. For example, you could subtly highlight one area by increasing the intensity there. This will lead the audience's focus to, and encourage them to identify with, for example, the children who are listening on the other side of the door. Or, you could light just one area of the stage and leave the rest in darkness.

3 Are there special effects that need to be planned for? How could you to create moonlight, for example, or fire or bright sunlight? Do you need to plan a spotlight for a narrator or a monologue?

4 Create a key to use on your script that links to notes or sketches in your notebook. These could be asterisks, numbers or a letter Q, for example, to indicate a lighting change (see Step 1). An arrow down the side of a scene could show where you intend to build or decrease the intensity of a lighting state.

5 Carefully consider space, using it to its best potential interesting spatial interactions. For example, you could light an area in the auditorium to use for a monologue.

6 Continue to note down any questions that emerge.

7 Explore any additional equipment that might be needed and where it could come from.

ASSESSMENT CHECK

Check that you are on track with at least four different lighting states. You could use different:

- colours
- intensities
- angles
- specials.

LOOK HERE

See page 31 for a lighting plot for *Hansel and Gretel*.

'Understanding your lighting resources', pages 20–21, and 'Research for lighting', page 29, will be helpful here.

STEP 4

Confirming your final lighting design

For your lighting design to be agreed at the final design meeting, it needs to be at the final design stage itself. This means that you need to produce a well-presented design and be able to communicate your lighting ideas effectively.

Your design should complement the text and show consistency and/or progression. You might change a colour to reflect a different time of day, for example. Check that you have carefully considered how the editing for your scene is reflected in your lighting design.

Rehearsals will be well underway now. You should take your final design ideas into the rehearsal room and check that there are no new developments that affect you. An extra lighting state might be needed if the performers have introduced a visual flashback, for example. You should still have time to include this in your design.

1 Revisit the tasks on pages 20–21 before you finalise your lighting design on paper. Now is also the time to look back at 'Research for lighting', page 29. What additional items, such as colour gels or gobos, are included in your design?

2 If you are thinking of using special effects, experiment with the equipment to create them. Test their practicality and impact before committing them to the final design.

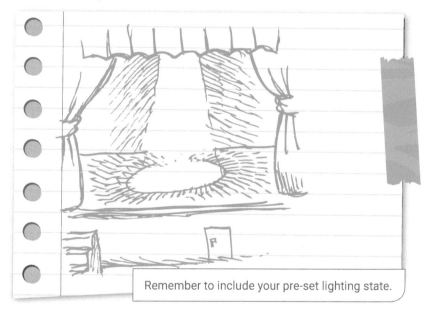

Remember to include your pre-set lighting state.

3 Check with the other designers that all the designs are compatible, both artistically and in terms of keeping performers and audience safe. Complete the checklist below.

Scene:					
Period, mood, style and genre?	Supports dramatic intentions?	Compatible with set design?	Compatible with costume?	Any notes on use of space and health and safety	Notes on special effects, colour, types of lantern, etc.
Y/N	Y/N	Y/N	Y/N		

STEP ⑤

The final design meeting

Hold a last design meeting. In professional theatre, the stage manager, production manager and other specialists would also be present.

This is the meeting where everything is agreed, including budgets. As a designer, you should not buy or make anything final, or start putting special effects together, until the design has been signed off.

1   Bring the finished plans for your design to be signed off. The documentation could include a rigging diagram, sketch of acting area(s) with lighting locations marked, your annotated script, plus any notes. Through discussion, confirm the final designs.

In terms of collaboration, this is the final chance to check that your designs harmonise with other designers' work. You need to complement set, costume and sound.

2   Don't be afraid to ask questions and raise concerns. It is vital that you leave this meeting ready to realise your design.

 DESIGN TIP

Help your group to envision the world of the stage. Make sure that you bring with you enough detail about your design, including, for example, gobos that you want to use.

3   Complete a table like this one during or straight after the meeting. (An example has been started for you.)

Extract:		
Agreed lighting design (including changes)	**Agreed budget**	**Notes**
All fine, but add an extra special effect for the monologue.		

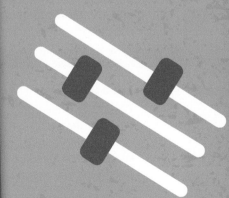

STEP 6
The completed lighting design

Clever use of lighting creates an oversized shadow and a sinister atmosphere in this scene from *The Woman in Black*.

Finally, you can set up your lighting ready for the performance.

You will supervise the rigging and focusing, so be sure to arrange suitable times for these tasks with your human resources.

Preparation

The last thing you want is to get to the day of rigging and focusing only to discover that something is missing. This checklist should help.

- ○ Rigging diagrams – checked and accurate.
- ○ If some lanterns are already rigged, do I know which ones are to be moved and where to?
- ○ Lanterns clean and ready to be rigged.
- ○ Sufficient cables in place or ready to be attached.
- ○ Safety equipment ready (eg, heat-resistant gloves and security cables).
- ○ Performance space booked/reserved for rigging.
- ○ Ladders or scaffolding tower located and booked in.
- ○ Lighting desk/board ready for focusing process.

Actualising

1 Make sure you know the date of the technical rehearsal. Have your lighting design operable and tested in good time.

2 Check that all lanterns are rigged and focused in good time and that your plan and cue sheet are finished and clear.

3 Once your lighting is rigged and focused, allow plenty of time for the operation of your lighting cues to be practised.

LOOK HERE

Refer to Chapter 1 for guidance on rigging, plotting and operating and for getting the best from rehearsals.

DESIGN TIP

Remember to evaluate your design at each stage. How successfully is it matching your intentions in terms of concept, interpretation and communication of meaning?

DESIGN TIP

Check carefully that your written outline shows how your design matches the artistic intentions you set out with.

SIX STEPS TO SOUND DESIGN FOR THE SCRIPTED PERFORMANCE

STEP ❶

Working on your own with the script

As soon as you know that you are designing sound, start your independent work. This is likely to be at the same time as rehearsals begin.

Look at the script through the eyes of a sound designer. This means thinking about the genre, style, context and locations you will need to enhance. Your teacher should tell you what the stage configuration will be.

1   Read the whole play (or a detailed summary). As you go through, use a table like the one below to note general points that could influence your sound design decisions. (An example has been suggested.)

Play: *Romeo and Juliet* by William Shakespeare				
Genre: Tragedy				
Staging configuration	**Location/s**	**Historical, social and cultural contexts**	**Themes/ messages**	**Style, moods and atmosphere**
End on.	• Grand house: bedroom, balcony • Street.	• Modern-day setting. • Race: Capulets are white; Montagues black.	• Love • Romance • Grief/ sorrow • Racial tension.	• Naturalistic • Romance • Violence • Tragedy.

2   Carefully read each extract and the edited scene/s. Highlight and mark brief annotations on:

-   locations, and whether they are interior or exterior
-   key moments where music or a sound effect is important
-   weather/season and time of day
-   shifts in mood and atmosphere
-   a specified requirement for a sound cue
-   any questions that crop up.

3   Make more detailed notes from your initial table, above. Use your annotations to begin a chart like the following. (Some examples for *Hansel and Gretel* have been given for guidance.)

Locations	Interior/exterior	Time of day (or night)	Weather/season
House in the woods.	Forest (p27).	Moonlight.	Gloomy.
Shifts in mood or atmosphere	**Sound effect**	**Direct address or other non-naturalistic feature**	**Questions/ideas**
The flames were like burning tongues.	Owl.	Father narrates at the start of the scene.	Is a soundscape appropriate? Lots of scope for non-diegetic sound.

FOCUS

-   The sound design process from page to stage.
-   How to interpret the script, analyse and evaluate as you experiment with different designs, select aspects that are most successful and realise your designs.

ASSESSMENT CHECK

Your design work for Component 2 will demonstrate your ability to contribute as an individual to a theatrical performance as you develop a range of theatrical skills and apply them to create performances.

SIGNPOST

Chapter 2 will help you with your practical work.

DESIGN TIP

It is your sound **design** that is assessed. Although you are expected to operate the sound equipment when possible, this is not part of the assessment.

SOUND

Period? Victorian?   Style?

'Hansel and Gretel' has the structure of a nightmare. A few domestic objects – buckets, a knife, a blanket, a plate, a jug, an axe – create both the house and the forest and appear in the Witch's house. The Mother also reappears, grotesque, as the Witch. A chorus of three is always present, and active. [...] The story is one of starvation, terror and catharsis. The rhythms of speech are taut and violent, containing the fearful tensions and, finally, joyous release of the drama.

Reflect in sound design

Diegetic: Forest - Owl
- Wind in trees
- Creaking
- Creatures - birds?
- Dripping brook?
- Blazing fire
- 'Wild beasts'

Non-diegetic:
Discordant music in minor key - wind instruments - falling.
Soundscape:
- Hunger, despair
- Creaking - samples

Soundscape before lights up

Father It was no more than once upon a time when a poor woodcutter lived in a small house at the edge of a huge, dark forest. Now, the woodcutter lived with his wife and his two young children – a boy called Hansel and a little girl called Gretel. [...] Night after hungry night, he lay in bed next to his thin wife, and he worried so much that he tossed and he turned and he sighed and he mumbled and moaned and he just couldn't sleep at all. [...]

Creaking

Owl

And as he fretted and sweated in the darkness, back came the bony voice of his wife; a voice as fierce as famine. [...]

Soundscape

Father 'No, no, wife, I can't do that. How could I have the heart to leave young Hansel and Gretel in the forest? The wild beasts would soon sniff them out and eat them alive.' [...]

And when their father and mother had finally gone to sleep, Hansel got up, put on his coat, opened the back door, and crept out into the midnight hour.

Outside. Bright light.   Location

There was bright, sparkling moonlight outside and the white pebbles on the ground shone like silver coins and precious jewels. Hansel bent down and filled his empty pockets with as many pebbles as he could carry.

Inside. [...]

Mother At dawn, before the sun had properly risen, their mother came and woke the two children. [...]

The family go deeper into the dark heart of the forest.   Volume

Gretel The forest was immense and gloomy. [...]

Hansel Hansel and Gretel collected a big pile of firewood and when it was set alight and the flames were like burning tongues, their mother said: Fire SFX

Mother 'Now lie down by the fire and rest.'

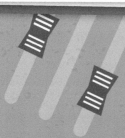

STEP ②

The design brief meeting and rehearsals

Now that you have an understanding of the script and have some set design ideas, arrange a meeting with your group. Take your script and notebook and any ideas for sound that you might already have. If you have a set, lighting or costume designer, they should be there too.

You will not be able to finalise your designs until there is agreement on:

- the staging configuration (Is it in the round, traverse, end on?)
- the style and setting of the performance (Is it naturalistic or stylised?)
- whether it is set in a particular time period that music should reflect (Music you choose for a modern interpretation of *Romeo and Juliet*, for example, would be very different from a 16th-century version.)

During the meeting

1 Share your thoughts so far about sound design. Play any effects or pieces of music you have found, and invite feedback. Try to deal with any criticism positively: very few designers are likely to get it all right first time.

2 Listen carefully to others and give similar sensitive feedback.

3 Make sure you discuss the following questions.

- Do we have issues from Step 1 that can be covered in this meeting? If not, how and when can they be addressed?
- Are we beginning to move towards a shared artistic vision for the performance? What do we imagine it looks like?
- How will we communicate our ideas to each other? Can we create a resource bank for our notes and images as we work independently? (This could be a shared folder on your school's intranet or a service such as Dropbox, which many professional theatres use.)
- What shall we work on before we next meet? What do we want to achieve by when?

4 Make detailed and well-organised notes of the discussions and any decisions made. You could put them under the heading 'Design Brief Meeting' in your notebook.

5 Agree on a date for the next design meeting.

DESIGN TIP

In professional theatre, a white-card meeting might be held once the set designer has constructed a simple 3D version of the set in paper or card. Alternatively, there might be 2D sketches of the set and possibly some costume sketches.

LOOK HERE

Details on making a mood board for sound are on page 218.

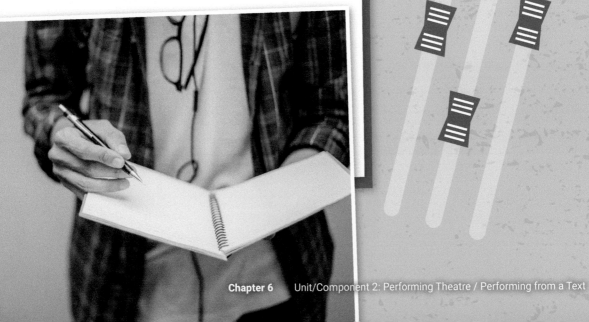

STEP ③
Revisiting the script

This step is another stage you can complete independently. You should, however, be continuously checking in on rehearsals, as developments might influence your design. Similarly, other designers and the performers will benefit from your updates.

1 Add details to your script annotations and ideas tables, based on what you learned at the design brief meeting. Your new knowledge of the style of the production might allow you to think more clearly about, for example, non-naturalistic soundscapes. Similarly, shared artistic intentions for the performance might prompt you to consider moods that you would like to enhance at particular moments.

   Be clear on how your designs could enhance your artistic intentions. Have this at the front of your mind as you develop your ideas.

2 Are there special effects that need to be planned for? How could you use sound to create the sense of night-time in a forest, for example?

3 Create a key to use on your script that links to notes or sketches in your notebook. These could be asterisks or numbers or a letter Q, for example, to indicate a change in sound. An arrow down the side of a scene could show where you intend to build or decrease the volume of an effect.

4 Think carefully about the space and where, for example, to best place your speakers to create the best sound quality for the audience.

5 Continue to note down any questions that emerge.

STEP ④

Confirming your final sound design

For your sound design to be agreed at the final design meeting, it needs to be at the final design stage itself. This means that you need to produce well-presented designs and are able to communicate your sound ideas.

Your design should complement the text and show consistency and/or progression. You might, for example, modify sound settings to reflect a change of mood. Check that you have carefully considered how the editing for your scene is reflected in your sound design.

Rehearsals will be well underway now. You should take your final design ideas, including any sounds you have produced, into the rehearsal room and check that there are no new developments that affect you. For example, you might need an additional piece of underscoring to enhance a moment of tension. You still have time to include this in your design.

1. Revisit the tasks in 'Sourcing, creating and mixing sounds', pages 48–50, before you finalise the sound design on paper. Now would also be a good time to check that you have all the resources you need to put your effects together. Have you made your music choices, for instance? Do you know what will play as the audience come in and leave the performance space?

2. If you are thinking of using special effects, such as reverb or echo, use 'Special sound effects' on pages 52–53 to guide you. Experiment with building the effects that you want. Test their practicality, suitability and impact before committing them to the final design.

3. Check with the other designers that all the designs are suitable, both artistically and in terms of keeping performers and audience safe. Complete the checklist below.

Extract:			
Period, mood, style and genre?	Compatible with other design elements?	Contributes to artistic intentions?	Safety notes and use of space, speaker positions
Y/N	Y/N	Y/N	
Y/N	Y/N	Y/N	

ASSESSMENT CHECK

In reviewing and selecting your designs, you are developing good habits for AO4. You are also applying design skills to enhance the intended effects.

DESIGN TIP

AO4 is tested in the written exam, but this step will give you excellent practice in the key skills of analysis and evaluation.

LOOK HERE

You might find these sections useful at this point:

- Research for sound design, pages 46–47
- How to document your sound design, pages 54–55
- Positioning sound equipment, pages 56–57.

DESIGN TIP

Help your group to understand the style of your effects and music by having some available to play.

STEP 5

The final design meeting

Hold a last design meeting. In professional theatre, the stage manager, production manager and other specialists would also be present.

This is the meeting where everything is agreed, including budgets. As a designer, you should not buy or make anything final, or start putting special effects together, until the design have been signed off.

1. Bring the finished plans for your design to be signed off. The documentation could include a rough cue sheet, sketch of acting area(s) with locations of speakers marked, your annotated script, plus any notes. Through discussion, confirm the final design.

In terms of collaboration, this is the final chance to check that your design harmonises with the other designers' work. Lighting in particular needs to complement your design.

2. Don't be afraid to ask questions and raise concerns. It is vital that you leave this meeting ready to realise your design.

3. Complete a table like the following during or straight after the meeting.

Scene:		
Agreed design (including changes)	Agreed budget	Notes
	£20	Start playing our music from 32 secs into track

STEP 6
The completed sound design

SIGNPOST
Work first through 'Plotting the sound design' (pages 58–59).

DESIGN TIP
Remember to evaluate your design at each stage. How successfully is it matching your intentions in terms of concept, interpretation and communication of meaning?

DESIGN TIP
Check carefully that your written outline shows how your design matches the artistic intentions you set out with.

Finally, you can finish setting up and mixing your sounds ready for the performance.

Preparation
Once you have all your effects and music saved in a folder on a laptop or organised for other playback devices, you need to plot them.

Plotting
Plotting is the crucial stage where you get your cues in order and create the cue sheet.

An example cue sheet is given below. The cue sheet is an essential guide for whoever operates the sound for your production, whether or not you do this yourself. It gives the source, order, length and volume of each sound.

Extract 1						
Sound cue sheet: Hansel and Gretel						
Cue no and page no	Cue signal	Sound	Playback device (if more than one)	Level (dB)	Transition	Notes and timings
1 Pre-set	House open	Play music	CD player	-10		Pre-set from time house is open Visual cue
2 p1	Visual: actors walk on	Music off		All out	Fade out	Over 10 seconds (in time with lighting)
3 p3	'Come over here!'	Soundscape 1	Laptop	+6	Fade up	Over 5 seconds gradual fade

Make sure that you know the date of the technical rehearsal. Have your sound design plotted and practised in good time.

Once your sounds are set, allow plenty of time for whoever is operating the sound to practise your sound cues.

LOOK HERE
The notes on page 62 will help you to make use of rehearsals.

TO SET DESIGN FOR THE SCRIPTED PERFORMANCE

FOCUS

- The process of set design from page to stage.
- How to interpret, analyse and evaluate as you experiment, select and then realise your designs as a completed set.

ASSESSMENT CHECK

Your design work for Component 2 will demonstrate your ability to contribute as an individual to a theatrical performance as you develop a range of theatrical skills and apply them to create performances.

SIGNPOST

Chapter 3 is designed to help you with every aspect of your practical work.

DESIGN TIP

It is your set **design** that is assessed. Although students are expected to construct the set when possible, this is not part of the assessment.

STEP ❶

Working on your own with the script

As soon as you know that you are designing the set, start your independent work. This is likely to be at the same time as rehearsals begin.

A non-naturalistic set design for Uchenna Dance's *Hansel and Gretel*. It is a very modern style that uses bold, primary colours, geometric shapes and click-together panels that recall children's building toys. This also makes the set versatile, as items can be put together differently to represent, for example, both the forest and the cottage.

Look at the script through the eyes of a set designer. This means thinking about the genre, style, context and locations you will need to enhance. Your teacher should tell you what the stage configuration will be.

1   Read the whole play (or a detailed summary). Use a table like the one below to note general points that could influence your set design decisions. (An example has been suggested.)

Play: *Alice* by Lorna Wade				
Genre: Black comedy				
Staging configuration	**Location/s**	**Historical, social and cultural contexts**	**Themes/ messages**	**Style, moods and atmosphere**
Proscenium arch.	• Wonderland • Alice's living room • Alice's attic.	Contemporary (modern day).	• Family • Growing up • Dealing with grief.	• Fantasy and realism • Mixture of naturalism and non-naturalism • Comic moments.

2   Carefully read each scene. Highlight and mark brief annotations on:

-   locations – specific (such as an attic) and more general (Wonderland, for example)
-   key events and moments of action where an item of set is important
-   the economic and social situation of characters
-   special settings, including levels (these might be given in the script)
-   any questions that crop up.

3   Ask your teacher what style of production is most likely: this will affect the style of your set. You might be dealing with a highly naturalistic style, for example. From that information, what images pop into your head as you read? Draw some sketches to capture your ideas.

If you have time, make white-card models of your favourite designs.

4   Make more detailed notes from your table, above. These might include the page and line number from the script, or a quotation.

DESIGN TIP

Remember that there must be a separate design for each extract, if you are the set designer for both.

SET DESIGN

Style: → Abstract?
→ Naturalistic?

p13: Are there beds in the cottage?

Keep these?
Scenery

'Hansel and Gretel' has the structure of a nightmare. A few domestic objects – buckets, a knife, a blanket, a plate, a jug, an axe – create both the house and the forest and appear in the Witch's house. The Mother also reappears, grotesque, as the Witch. A chorus of three is always present, and active. [...] The story is one of starvation, terror and catharsis. The rhythms of speech are taut and violent, containing the fearful tensions and, finally, joyous release of the drama.

Location: in house   Silhouette?

Father It was no more than once upon a time when a poor woodcutter lived in a small house at the edge of a huge, dark forest. Now, the woodcutter lived with his wife and his two young children – a boy called Hansel and a little girl called Gretel. [...] Night after hungry night, he lay in bed next to his thin wife, and he worried so much that he tossed and he turned and he sighed and he mumbled and moaned and he just couldn't sleep at all. [...]

Bed?
Boxes?

Levels?

Where?
Bedroom?

And as he fretted and sweated in the darkness, back came the bony voice of his wife; a voice as fierce as famine. [...]

Hansel Now, Hansel and Gretel had been so hungry that night that they hadn't been able to sleep either, and they'd heard every cruel word of their mother's terrible plan.

Gretel Gretel cried bitter salt tears, and said to Hansel: 'Now we're finished.'

Hansel 'Don't cry, Gretel. Don't be sad. I'll think of a way to save us.'

And when their father and mother had finally gone to sleep, Hansel got up, put on his coat, opened the back door, and crept out into the midnight hour.

Level?

Location Outside. Bright light.

There was bright, sparkling moonlight outside and the white pebbles on the ground shone like silver coins and precious jewels. Hansel bent down and filled his empty pockets with as many pebbles as he could carry. [...]

Literal?

Along the path. Hansel keeps stopping and turning back. [...]

Spaced-out pebbles he collects?

The family go deeper into the dark heart of the forest.

Gretel The forest was immense and gloomy. [...]

Hansel Hansel and Gretel collected a big pile of firewood and when it was set alight and the flames were like burning tongues, their mother said:

Props?

Scattered?

Mother 'Now lie down by the fire and rest.'

How do we create:
- forest
- house
- interior/exterior?
Revolving flats?
Composite?

Forest could be: imaginary
- hung fabric
- brooms/twigs
- flats
- scenery
- actors?

Flooring:
- Wooden, neutral – house and forest?
- Rush mats?
- Vinyl?

DESIGN TIP

In professional theatre, a white-card meeting might be held once the set designer has constructed a simple 3D version of the set in paper or card. Alternatively, there might be 2D sketches of the set and possibly some costume sketches.

STEP ❷

The design brief meeting and rehearsals

Now that you have an understanding of the script and have some set design ideas, arrange a meeting with your group. Take your script and notebook and any sketches and models you have. If you have a costume, sound or lighting designer, they should be there too. Other designers (particularly lighting) won't get far with their work until they have some clarity about the set.

You will not be able to fix your design until there is agreement on the style of the production. This will tell you whether you are aiming for a representative set, or a naturalistic one that seeks to fully create the illusion of reality.

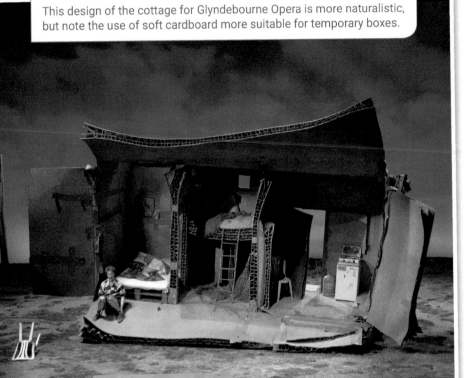

This design of the cottage for Glyndebourne Opera is more naturalistic, but note the use of soft cardboard more suitable for temporary boxes.

- Is it set in a particular time period?
- If there is to be a forest, for example, will there be literal representations of trees or something much simpler, such as strips of fabric hanging from the rigging? Might trees be depicted by actors, or simply imagined by the actors and audience?
- Will there be a composite set or will the stage be divided into locations?
- Will buildings and rooms be physically on stage in some form? Will there be stage furniture? What form might it take?

During the meeting

1. Share your thoughts so far about set design. Show any sketches or models and invite feedback. Try to deal with any criticism positively: very few designers are likely to get it all right first time.

2. Listen carefully to others and give similar sensitive feedback.

3. Make sure you discuss the following questions:

   - Do we have issues from Step 1 that can be covered in this meeting? If not, how and when can they be addressed?
   - Are we beginning to move towards a shared artistic vision for the performance? What do we imagine it looks like?
   - How will we communicate our ideas to each other? Can we create a resource bank for notes and images as we work independently? (This could be a shared folder on your school's intranet or a service such as Dropbox, which many professional theatres use.)
   - What shall we work on before we next meet? What do we want to achieve and by when?

4. Make detailed and well-organised notes of the discussions and any decisions made. You could put them under the heading 'Design Brief Meeting' in your notebook.

5. Agree on a date for the next design meeting.

LOOK HERE

'Two styles of set design' on page 68 and 'Understanding your resources' on page 75 will be helpful at this point.

STEP ③

Revisiting the script

This step is another stage you can complete independently. You should, however, be continuously checking in on rehearsals, as there could be developments that will influence your design. Similarly, other designers and the performers will benefit from your updates.

1. Add details to your script annotations and ideas table, based on what you learned at the design brief meeting.

   Be clear on how your set design can enhance your artistic intentions. Have this at the front of your mind as you develop your ideas.

2. Make any alterations to your draft designs as required. For example, does your colour palette need to change to fit in with the overall mood, or costume and lighting designs?

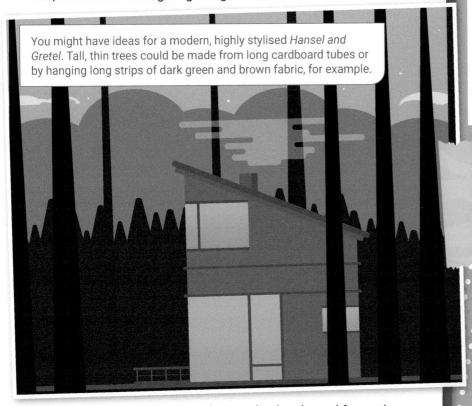

You might have ideas for a modern, highly stylised *Hansel and Gretel*. Tall, thin trees could be made from long cardboard tubes or by hanging long strips of dark green and brown fabric, for example.

Are there special considerations that need to be planned for, such as interaction with furniture? An outdoor fire, for example, is required in Carol Ann Duffy and Tim Supple's version of *Hansel and Gretel*. You would need to work closely with the lighting designer to achieve something workable.

3. Carefully consider space. Your design needs to use the available space to its best potential. This includes leaving plenty of space for the actors to perform in, checking audience sightlines and making the set work well in terms of interesting spatial interactions through the use of levels, for example. Think about what set dressings and props will enhance your design.

4. Continue to note down any questions that emerge.

5. Explore what materials you need and where you might find them.

ASSESSMENT CHECK

Check that you are on track to meet the minimum requirements of an appropriately dressed set, with props.

DESIGN TIP

Props might include set dressings (such as soft furnishings) and all items that cannot be classified as scenery, electrics or wardrobe.

Props handled by actors are known as **hand props**.

Props that are kept in an actor's costume (such as a phone in a pocket) are known as **personal props**.

LOOK HERE

'Research for set design' on page 69 will be helpful here.

STEP 4

Confirming your final set design

For your set to be agreed at the final design meeting, it needs to be at the final design stage itself. This means that you need to produce well-presented designs and are able to communicate your set design ideas.

Your design should complement the text and show consistency and/or progression. You might, for example, alter small details of the set to indicate the passing of time. Check that you have carefully considered how the editing for your scene is reflected in your design.

Rehearsals will be well underway now. You should take your final design ideas into the rehearsal room and check that there are now new developments that affect you. For example, a character might need somewhere to hide on stage. You still have time to include this in your design.

1   Complete ground plans and sketches for the scene. While you do not have to make model boxes, you might find that they help you to examine how workable your set design is. Whoever constructs your set will also find them invaluable.

2   Check with the other designers that the artistic intentions are being met and that lighting and costume, in particular, will work safely and effectively with your set. Complete the checklist below.

Extract:					
Period, mood, style and genre?	Practicalities including furniture and health and safety?	Supports artistic intentions?	Good use of space?	Compatible with other design elements?	Approximate costings
Y/N	Y/N	Y/N	Y/N	Y/N	

3   Check with your human resources that your design is achievable in terms of construction and sourcing. For example, is there time to build the platform you want to put into your design? You need to be ready to build once your design is given the go-ahead.

STEP ⑤

The final design meeting

Hold a last design meeting. In professional theatre, the stage manager, production manager and other specialists would also be present.

This is the meeting where everything is agreed, including budgets. You should not buy or make anything final until the design has been signed off.

1   Bring the finished plans for your design to be signed off. The documentation could include the ground plan, marked with entrances and exits, your annotated script plus any notes and models you have made. Through discussion, confirm the final design.

    In terms of collaboration, this is the final chance to check that your design harmonises with the other designers' work. Lighting and costume in particular have to complement your design.

2   It is essential that the actors can move freely around the stage and set. This is a health and safety issue. You are also creating a theatrical world. The actors cannot inhabit this if they are unable to function properly or maintain their characters fully.

3   Don't be afraid to ask questions and raise concerns. It is vital that you leave this meeting ready to realise your design.

4   Complete a table like the following one during or straight after the meeting. (An example has been started for you.)

DESIGN TIP

Check carefully that your written outline shows how your design matches the artistic intentions you set out with.

Extract:		
Agreed set design (including changes)	**Agreed budget**	**Notes**
• Use sketch and model box. • Change colour palette.	£50	Sketch shows new palette: replace blue tones with amber ones.

STEP ⑥

The completed set design

Finally, you can construct your set ready for the performance.

Preparation and construction

You will need to work very closely with the people building your set and helping you with materials, tools and equipment. Supervising the construction might involve basic assistance while things are being made or more actively helping to paint flats and so on.

Answer the questions below to help you produce your set in good time.

- Are items (including furniture and props) that need to be borrowed or bought being sourced in good time?
- What is the date of the technical rehearsal?
- Has health and safety been taken into account, including entrances and exits?
- When will the set be put into the performance area?
- Are there any issues with items that need to be built, such as the late arrival of materials ordered for a platform? (If so, chase them up.)
- Are there additional set dressings to be sourced?

LOOK HERE

Follow the guidance on page 77 for health and safety procedures.

FOCUS

- The process of costume design from page to stage.
- How to interpret, analyse and evaluate as you experiment, select and then realise your design.

SIX STEPS TO COSTUME DESIGN FOR THE SCRIPTED PERFORMANCE

ASSESSMENT CHECK

Your design work for Component 2 will demonstrate your ability to contribute as an individual to a theatrical performance as you develop a range of theatrical skills and apply them to create performances.

SIGNPOST

Chapter 4 is designed to help you with every aspect of your practical costume work.

DESIGN TIP

It is your costume **design** that is assessed. You are expected to assemble the costume if possible, but this is not part of the assessment.

STEP ①

Working on your own with the script

As soon as you know that you are designing a costume for each extract, start your independent work. This is likely to be at the same time as the performers begin rehearsals.

Look at the script through the eyes of a costume designer. This means thinking about genre, styles, contexts and locations. Your teacher should be able to tell you what the stage configuration will be.

1. Read the whole play (or a detailed summary). Use a table like the one below to note general points that could influence your costume decisions. (An example has been suggested.)

Play: *Dracula* by Bram Stoker/David Calcutt				
Genre: Horror				
Main characters	**Location/s**	**Historical, social and cultural contexts**	**Themes/ messages**	**Style, moods and atmosphere**
• Dracula • Jonathan • Mina • Lucy • Van Helsing	• Whitby • Dracula's castle.	• End of 19th century • Vampire stories.	• Fear • Love • The supernatural.	• Mainly naturalistic • Suspense • Horror.

2. Carefully read each scene. Highlight and mark brief annotations on:

- locations – specific (such as the living room in a wealthy Victorian home) and more general (north-east coast of England, for example)
- weather and time of year and time of day, as this will influence what a character would wear
- the economic and social situations of characters
- personality aspects that might affect characters' choice of clothing
- a stated requirement for a special feature (pocket, bag, hat and so on)
- any questions that crop up.

See the example on the following page.

3. Make detailed notes from your table and then annotated sketches of possible designs. Your notes should take the form of the page and line number or quotation from the script and then your note. For example:

p14: 'Hansel got up, put on his coat... filled his empty pockets with as many pebbles as he could carry...' Does he have nightwear, or is he in everyday clothes? Coat with big pockets could be a handed-down jacket from his father?

COSTUME

Style? - Germanic?
Period? - Victorian? Modern?
Times of famine, hunger, starvation
Freedom of movement

'Hansel and Gretel' has the structure of a nightmare. A few domestic objects – buckets, a knife, a blanket, a plate, a jug, an axe – create both the house and the forest and appear in the Witch's house. The Mother also reappears, grotesque, as the Witch. A chorus of three is always present, and active. [...] The story is one of starvation, terror and catharsis. The rhythms of speech are taut and violent, containing the fearful tensions and, finally, joyous release of the drama.

Woodcutter: Poor; works outdoors - manual
Outer clothes: Boots? Waistcoat? Belt? Pouch?
Nightwear?
Wife: Thin: angular silhouette - a hard woman
Hansel: 8? Coat: Threadbare - with pockets - size?
Gretel: 6 or 7? Apron with pocket - size?

Father It was no more than once upon a time when a poor woodcutter lived in a small house at the edge of a huge, dark forest. Now, the woodcutter lived with his wife and his two young children – a boy called Hansel and a little girl called Gretel. It was hard enough for him to feed them all at the best of times – but these were the worst of times; times of famine and hunger and starvation. [...]

Night after hungry night, he lay in bed next to his thin wife, and he worried so much that he tossed and he turned and he sighed and he mumbled and moaned and he just couldn't sleep at all. [...]

Hansel Now, Hansel and Gretel had been so hungry that night that they hadn't been able to sleep either, and they'd heard every cruel word of their mother's terrible plan. [...]

And when their father and mother had finally gone to sleep, Hansel got up, put on his coat, opened the back door, and crept out into the midnight hour. [...]

Hansel bent down and filled his empty pockets with as many pebbles as he could carry. [...]

Mother Then she gave each of them a miserable mouthful of bread: 'There's your lunch; think yourselves lucky, and don't eat it all at once, because there's nothing else.'

Gretel Gretel put the bread in her apron pocket, because Hansel's pockets were crammed with pebbles.

Father Then the whole family set off along the path to the forest.

Where does the bread come from?

STEP 2

The design brief meeting and rehearsals

Now that you have an understanding of the script and have some costume ideas, arrange a meeting with your group. Take your script and notebook and any costume sketches you have. If you have a set, sound or lighting designer, they should be there too. A costume designer needs to consider potential movement restrictions of the set, for example.

You will not be able to develop your costume design until you know:

- the style and setting of the performance (Is it naturalistic or stylised? Is it set in a particular time period? Do you need to create a typical early 20th century gown, or are you setting the scene in modern times?)
- which character(s) you will design for.

Your choice should give you plenty of scope for creativity and impact. It should allow you to contribute to characterisation and meaning. It must also set you a sufficient challenge. If you design costumes for both extracts, you might want to make the two designs quite different from each other.

Rough sketches for a contemporary costume design for *Hansel and Gretel*.

THE WITCH

During the meeting

1. Share your thoughts so far about costumes. Show any sketches or mood boards and invite feedback. Try to deal with any criticism positively: very few designers are likely to get it all right first time.

2. Listen carefully to others and give similar sensitive feedback.

3. Make sure you discuss the following questions.
   - Do we have issues from Step 1 that can be covered in this meeting? If not, how and when can they be addressed?
   - Are we beginning to move towards a shared artistic vision for the performance? What do we imagine it looks like?
   - How will we communicate our ideas to each other? Can we create a resource bank that we can put notes and images in as we work independently? (This could be a shared folder on your centre's intranet or a service such as Dropbox, which many professional theatres use.)
   - What shall we work on before we next meet? What do we want to achieve by when?

4. Make detailed and well-organised notes of the discussions and any decisions made. You could put them under the heading 'Design Brief Meeting' in your notebook.

5. Agree on a date for the next design meeting.

STEP ③

Revisiting the script

This step is another stage you can complete independently. You should, however, be continuously checking in on rehearsals, as there could be developments that will influence your design. Similarly, other designers and the performers will benefit from updates on your thinking.

1. Add details to your script annotations and ideas table, based on what you learned at the design brief meeting. Your new knowledge of the agreed style and historical period, for example, will allow you to develop your costume ideas.

   Similarly, shared artistic intentions for the performance might prompt you to consider enhancing atmosphere with a particular aspect of costume design. This could come from colour, shape and fabric choices.

   Be clear on how your design can contribute to the artistic intentions. Make sure your costume design is clearly influenced by these intentions.

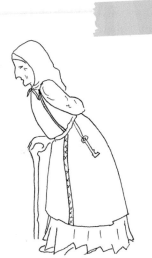 

More traditional versions of the Witch and the Mother.

2. Sketch a number of versions for your initial costume design.

3. Are there special considerations, such as pockets, masks or wigs, that need to be planned for? For pockets, for example, you will need to know what they will hold so that you can make them the correct size. Make sure details like this are included in your preliminary sketches, along with footwear, headgear, accessories and make-up as appropriate.

4. Carefully check the script for points where costumes might need to be changed. (These are often signposted in stage directions.)

5. Ensure you are aware of the acting space. This could mean you need to shorten hemlines to make steps easier. Alternatively, it could mean adding lots of detail to the back of a dress if the audience will see it frequently.

   It is essential that the actors can move freely around the stage and set. This is a safety issue. You are also creating a world where the characters can live and breathe. The actors cannot inhabit a theatrical world if they are unable to function properly or maintain their characters fully.

6. Continue to note down any questions that emerge.

7. Explore additional fabrics or accessories that might be needed and where they could come from.

ASSESSMENT CHECK

During this review of the script, you will be working on AO2: 'Apply theatrical skills to realise artistic intentions in live performance.'

STEP 4

Confirming your final costume design

For your costume designs to be agreed at the final design meeting, they need to be at final design stage themselves.

This doesn't mean that you need to be a great artist, but you do need to produce well-presented designs and communicate your costume design ideas.

Your design should complement the text and show consistency and/or progression. For example, a full costume change might not be necessary, but the addition of an item to show a change in circumstance or time might well be appropriate. Check that you have carefully considered how the editing for your scene is reflected in your design.

Rehearsals will be well underway now. You should take your final design ideas into the rehearsal room and check that there are no new developments that affect you. Perhaps a character needs an additional garment such as a cloak to hide something under. You still have time to include this in your design.

1   If you have a number of designs that you like, try to bring it down to two. Just one is ideal. Completing the table below should help you to decide which costume is the most effective. Remember that your design needs to contribute to meeting the artistic intentions of the whole group.

Check with the other designers that colour palettes work together and that the costumes are appropriate to the proposed set and lighting. You must also keep performers safe.

Extract:					
Period, mood, style and genre?	Compatible with other design elements?	Suits social and economic background?	Suits personality/ character?	Suitable for the space and actor's comfort and safety?	Approximate costings, including accessories and make-up
Y/N	Y/N	Y/N	Y/N	Y/N	

2   Annotate your chosen sketch to help explain colour, fabric texture and finish.

3   Even if you will not be making your garment from scratch, it is useful to apply swatches to the design. These will help your fellow group members to see the 'look' you are aiming for.

THE WITCH

RED CONTACT LENSES TO BE WORN.

OFF CENTRE FASTENING ON COAT →

SAME WOOL SKIRT AS MOTHER →

KEY FOR LOCKING UP CHILDREN

LEG OF MUTTON SLEEVES →

OVERALL LOOK OF CLOTHES TO BE WELL WORN

Wool Skirt →

FLORAL FABRIC FOR THE HEAD SCARF

MOTHER

STEP 5

The final design meeting

Hold a last design meeting. In professional theatre, the stage manager, production manager and other specialists would also be present.

This is the meeting where everything is agreed, including budgets. As a designer, you should not buy or make anything until the design has been signed off.

1. Bring your finished design to be signed off. If you still have alternatives to be decided on, bring them for your colleagues to consider. Through discussion, confirm the final design.

   In terms of collaboration, this is the final chance to check that your design harmonises with the other designers' work. Set and lighting in particular have to complement your design.

2. Check that there have been no changes to the set or the amount of physicality used by the actor, as this could mean having to change aspects of your costume design.

3. Don't be afraid to ask questions and raise concerns. It is vital that you leave this meeting ready to realise your designs.

4. Complete a table like this one during or straight after the meeting. (An example has been started for you.)

Extract:

Agreed costume design (including changes)	Agreed budget	Notes
As final drawings – design approved.	£20	Need to find cheaper fabric for cape.

DESIGN TIP

Help your group members to envision the world of the stage by making sure that you show the detail of your designs. As well as your designs, bring notes, fabric swatches and images of garments, hairstyles and make-up.

DESIGN TIP

Gather everything you need in one place and know where it all is! Add to your selection as you go along, including tools, accessories and make-up materials.

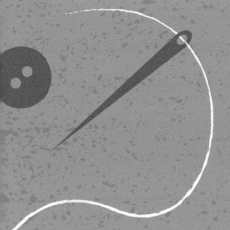

DESIGN TIP

Remember to evaluate your design at each stage. How successfully does it contribute to characterisation, meaning and atmosphere? Does it match the artistic intentions you set out in your written outline?

LOOK HERE

The guidance on page 106 will help you with using rehearsals.

STEP 6
The completed costume design

Finally, you can make your costumes for the performance.

Preparation

Use your designs and budget to complete the following table. (Some examples have been included to guide you.)

Extract:			
Character:			
Actor:			
Costume item	**Source**	**Estimated cost**	**Completed**
Skirt	Alter existing one	none	
Apron	Charity shop?	£3	
Shoes	Actor's own	none	✓
Belt – with keys	Make	£2	
Make-up	Actor's and mine	none	✓
Hair – no wig: just styling		none	More practice

Actualising

1. Refer to Chapter 4 for help with sourcing, making, adapting and fitting. Remember that you need to supervise any making and alterations if you are not doing these yourself. Try to allow time for the actor to wear the costume in rehearsal to check that it works well for them in practice.

2. As you complete items of costume, add to or amend the table above.

3. Make sure you know the date of the technical rehearsal. You will need to have your costumes made and fitted in good time.

UNIT/COMPONENT 3: INTERPRETING THEATRE

Chapter 7

FOCUS

- Preparing for the written exam.
- Understanding what the examiner is looking for.

INTRODUCTION TO DESIGN IN THE WRITTEN EXAM

The written exam requires every student to have a detailed understanding of **all** aspects of theatre included in the GCSE Drama course. In Section B, you will be able to choose whether you focus on a performance or design aspect of the live show you saw. In Section A, there will be no choice and you will have to write about performing and designing in relation to your set text.

Masks help to characterise the Moon and the Sun in this movement performance.

Studying and analysing drama

How should I think about my writing in the exam?

For Section A, it would be useful to imagine that you are a team member (sound designer for one question perhaps, and actor for another) giving an explanation for your set text.

Imagine that you are staging a performance as part of a real team that works creatively to make the best choices to communicate ideas to the audience. This should help your written response have detail and depth.

Similarly, you watch the work of the creative team in the live performance you watch for Section B, and analyse and evaluate the impact of their work. Again, it helps to remember that these are people who made lots of choices throughout the process of getting the production on the stage. Did they make good decisions? How did these impact on you as a member of the audience?

What must I be able to do?

You need to have and demonstrate:

- a thorough and extensive knowledge of the set text you are studying and of the live performance you have seen
- knowledge of all the creative aspects of staging a theatre production, including the various roles of the people who put together a performance
- knowledge and experience of creating a piece of theatre, which will help to make your writing clear
- the ability to comment meaningfully and confidently about how the extract **could** be staged and about how the performance you saw **was** staged.

DESIGN TIP

Remember that a harmonious world is skilfully and collectively created by every person involved in a production. Understanding this is the key to success here.

LOOK HERE

The Practical Guide to Design chapters at the beginning of this book will give you valuable experience in how different theatrical elements can create impact and convey meaning.

Using your practical experience, knowledge and understanding

To succeed in the written exam, it is essential to prepare for it throughout your course.

Different roles and elements in drama

The four main theatre elements for production and design are set, lighting, costume and sound, but you might be asked more specifically about, for example, props and stage furniture or staging. These might overlap with other design elements, for example:

- Staging might include the use of set on a specific type of stage.
- Props and stage furniture might form part of a set design.
- Personal props, such as a phone, pen or spectacles, might form part of the costume design for certain characters.

The Curious Incident of the Dog in the Night-Time at the Gielgud Theatre.

- Do more than simply take part in drama lessons. Step back and really think about what is happening. Keep a project notebook to record your thoughts. You could have separate sections for performance and the different design elements.
- Use the knowledge and experience that you have gained to examine all elements of drama.
- Take an interest in all the elements of drama. For example, talk to the performers if you are the costume or lighting designer, and so on.
- Keep a glossary of technical terms you come across and try to use them in lessons and in your writing so that they become really familiar.
- Carry out as many tasks as you can from the Practical Guide to Design chapters at the beginning of this book.

TASK 7.1

Start a drama journal or scrapbook and add to it every week. Use the ideas above and include sketches, images and mood boards to keep yourself interested. (Search on Pinterest for some useful examples.)

Take inspiration from the fact that your journal will be invaluable when it comes to revising for your exam and the mock exams you take during your course.

Your experience from the whole course will help you

It would be a mistake to think of the exam as a big new element that takes place at the end of your course. Instead, try to think of it as an opportunity to show what you have learned over the years you have studied and been interested in drama.

Director Gerry Mulgrew of Communicado Theatre, on the set of *The Government Inspector* at Aberystwyth Arts Centre.

Local Hero at Edinburgh Lyceum.

Recognising artistic intentions and practical processes

Professional theatre makers are skilled in their fields. Similarly, you have developed your own knowledge and skills in a range of disciplines during your Drama course. You might have focused on acting and have learned a great deal about voice, movement and characterisation. Alternatively, you might have developed your skills as a designer, or studied both design and performance.

Either way, the devised and scripted performances you work on involve all of your group aiming to communicate a common artistic intention. If you work practically on lighting, sound, costume or set, you will have an opportunity to use those skills and knowledge very productively in the written exam. If not, you can develop your knowledge of the design elements by doing some design work as part of your exam preparation.

The portfolio is a major piece of written work for your devised theatre piece for Unit/Component 1. For Unit/Component 3, you are again writing from a very practical viewpoint:

- How would **I** perform or design an extract from my set play?
- How would **I** create impact for my audience within this crafted world?
- How do the performers and designers of live performances I have seen use their skills to create impact?

Sharing your skills and knowledge of design in the written exam

You will not know the exact questions or the extract you will be given in the written exam. You will, however, know the **kind** of questions to expect. The examiners are not trying to catch you out.

You simply need to use and develop the skills and knowledge you have already achieved and prepare carefully for these written tasks.

You have developed your own knowledge and skills in a range of disciplines, such as costume and set design, during the course. If you have worked practically on lighting, sound, costume or set, you will be able to use those skills and knowledge very productively in the written exam. You will need to prepare thoroughly, however, in order to apply them to the set text.

Even if you have not opted for design in Units/Components 1 and 2, you will have appreciated the use of costume, lights, set and sound. This might have been in performances you have been part of as well as ones you have seen.

You are unlikely to be an expert at every performance and design discipline. You should, however, have sufficient knowledge and specialist vocabulary to make insightful comments about techniques and designs and how they enhance the artistic intentions of a scene or moment.

You will be asked to explain, interpret, analyse and evaluate design from the perspective of an audience member, a designer and as a director.

TASK 7.2

Ask yourself how confident you are in your drama skills and knowledge. Complete your own version of this table.

DESIGN TIP

Revisit and update the table in Task 7.2 at regular intervals.

Drama skill	Good / OK / Not so good	Strengths and weaknesses
Costume design	🙂	✓ Helped to create my own costume for devised piece. + Need to know more technical terms to analyse costume for live production seen.
Set design	🙂	✓ Designed set for scripted piece and can make a model box and ground plan. + Need to create design for set text and analyse set for live production seen.
Lighting design	😠	✓ Know how effective lighting can be. + Need to understand different types of lantern and technical terms. + Explore lighting design for set text and live production seen.
Sound design	🙂	✓ Have explored sound design for set text and analysed sound for live production seen. + Make notes for live production and consider sound for set text.
Performance	🙂	✓ Acted in some pieces and understand about voice and movement. + I've focused on lighting recently and need to remind myself of technical terms.

This design by Kirk Bookman for *An Inspector Calls* separates certain characters and areas of the stage, bathing the Birling family in an eerie blue light. (Maltz Jupiter Theatre.)

ASSESSMENT CHECK

These questions in the exam assess AO3: 'Demonstrate knowledge and understanding of how theatre is developed and performed.'

TASK 7.3

1 Choose a design option that you are less familiar with.

2 Pick an extract from your set play that has plenty of scope for that design role.

3 • For **lighting** or **sound**, think about the locations, period and atmosphere you could create.

• For **lighting**, put together a mood board using the guidance in Chapter 1.

• For **sound**, jot down some diegetic and non-diegetic sound effects that you would like to hear, perhaps with some music choices.

• For **set** or **costume**, draw sketches to interpret the extract in an exciting way.

LOOK HERE

Revisit 'Stage configurations' on pages 12–14 to renew your knowledge of the benefits and challenges of different theatrical spaces.

DESIGN TIP

To help you remember right and left and up and down on stage, imagine you are an actor centre stage, facing the audience. Downstage right, for example, is on your right, down towards the audience.

PREPARING FOR THE EXAM

When revising for the design questions in the exam:

• use the specialist language glossaries in this book when you are writing – including notes and annotations – or reviewing your writing

• study your set play in detail and annotate it with design ideas that spring to mind or that you notice in the stage directions

• consider how you would stage your set text in different configurations

• make notes using specialist language about all the design options for the live performance you are writing about

• develop your ability to **interpret**, **analyse** and **evaluate**.

• make use of any design experience you have gained outside your course, such as in amateur theatre or further reading.

Section A: The study of one performance text

Here, you need to be able to imagine your set text on the stage. You will be assessed on the extent of your **knowledge** of the extract and the play as a whole and how that interacts with your **understanding** of how it could be staged. These **critical judgements** will also be used in Section B when you write about a live performance.

You will be working with the guidance of your teacher on a particular text for this section of the exam, where you will be given an extract of the play along with a series of questions about how you would perform and stage it.

This involves the key skills of interpretation and analysis. The two concepts are closely linked as it is your close study and knowledge (**analysis**) that will lead you to put forward choices (**interpretation**) of aspects of the play.

You will need to answer all the questions relating to your set text. There will be a mixture of performing and design-focused questions. The questions about design in this section could be on any design element and some will be worth more marks. You will be able to take a clean copy (with no annotations) of your set text into the exam.

In addition to staging configurations, knowledge of stage positioning will help you envisage and describe the text on stage, in appropriate vocabulary.

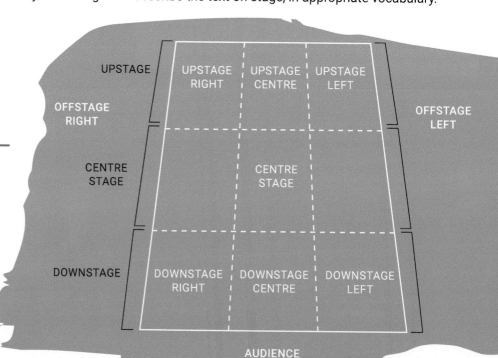

Section B: Live theatre review

In this section of the written exam, you will answer one question from a choice of two about a show you have seen. (This cannot be a performance of your set play.)

You will be able to choose between a performance question and a design question based on a specified design option. This question carries 15 marks.

Why should I consider answering optional design questions?

If you have enjoyed working practically on one or more design elements for Units/Components 1 or 2, the written exam gives you the opportunity to show what you have learned. Even if you have not been assessed on a design element, you might feel knowledgeable and interested enough to do the necessary preparation to write about design in the exam. Remember that that you must have some design knowledge to answer questions in Section A. You might also benefit from the opportunity to include sketches or diagrams that can be annotated. This allows you to convey knowledge, creativity and understanding with fewer words.

DNA set design.

Blue Stockings costume.

Developing your ability to answer questions on design

The most important point when approaching an exam question is to make sure that you answer the question fully. Check that you understand what you are being asked to do. If there are bullet points, make sure you cover all of them in your answer.

In Section A, the examiners want you to show knowledge and understanding. You need to use detailed examples, interpretations and clear explanations. In Section B, you need to analyse and evaluate. Again, you need to be detailed and focused. For both, it is important to have a good amount of drama terminology that you can use confidently. Chapters 1 to 4 and the glossaries in this book will help you.

ASSESSMENT CHECK

This question tests your ability to 'analyse and evaluate the work of others' for AO4.

DESIGN TIP

Visit your exam board's website for details of the mark schemes.

TASK 7.4

1. Work in your group to re-create, roughly, how the stage looked for a scene you all remember clearly or that your teacher suggests. Lay out the staging configuration and use levels, objects and furniture items to stand in for pieces of set.

2. On your 'stage', create a freeze-frame for a key moment in the scene.

3. Take it in turns to 'come out' of the freeze-frame and describe the costumes, sound and lighting for that moment.

4. If possible, photograph the freeze-frame you created to refer to when revising. You could also take notes.

FOCUS

Explaining your lighting design ideas.

ASSESSMENT CHECK

In Section A, you should demonstrate 'knowledge and understanding of how theatre is developed and performed' (AO3).

DESIGN TIP

- Answer every aspect of the question carefully and stay focused on the question.
- Give reasons for your ideas.
- Talk about production styles.
- Explain how your choice of colour communicates meaning.
- Be creative.

A real location that you know or see could inspire your lighting design.

LIGHTING DESIGN FOR THE SET TEXT (SECTION A)

Revising lighting for your set text

TASK 7.5

1 Research and make notes on the social, historic, political and economic contexts of the text. You need to know when it was first performed and in what stage configuration.

DNA, for example, was written in 2008 and first staged by the National Theatre using a minimal set with complex lighting and projections. The play is said (by the playwright Dennis Kelly) to have been inspired by feelings at the time in Britain, specifically, fear of terrorism and the sense that young people were becoming wild and dangerous. It was an era when 'youths' were demonised by the press and various laws were passed in an attempt to 'control' them.

By showing such an extreme example of youth violence in *DNA*, Kelly could be saying that people's fears are getting out of control. He is also asking the question 'Is it ever right to sacrifice the individual for the good of the group?'

2 Use your research to complete your own version of the table below. (Examples have been given using *DNA*.)

	How lighting could communicate meaning, theme, context and atmosphere
Settings: • Street • Field • Wood	• Lighting and projection will be important in the creation of location, time of day. • Gobos could create the leafy effect of the wood.
Themes: • Violence • Bullying • Power • Morality	• Red gels could enhance themes like violence and bullying. • **Uplighting** could create menacing shadows and suggest power.
Context: Britain in the 2000s	• LEDs could be used on stage for a modern look. • Tungsten street lights?
Mood/atmosphere: • Dark • Moments of humour • Fear	• Shadows could be created to add dark drama. • Brighter, warmer lighting would help the atmosphere during moments of humour. • Torches as practical effects could be very atmospheric.

Thinking as a lighting designer for your set text

You will not know in advance what extract you will be given, but you will know which play it will be from. Ask yourself the following questions:

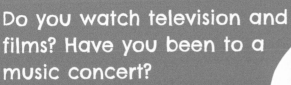

Do you watch television and films? Have you been to a music concert?

If yes, you will be able to harness your subconscious knowledge of how lighting can be used creatively.

Next time you go to a gig or watch a film, notice where the designer has gone beyond the use naturalistic lighting. Try to concentrate on the mood or meaning being enhanced. This might mean watching out for the use of colour, angle and pace of lighting transitions. Alternatively, it might simply mean noticing how bright or dim the lighting is, or how dramatic shadows are being produced.

To start you off, can you think of three ways you could explore the text? Anything that helps you to become familiar with the text on the page and in performance is worth spending time on. The best way to revise, however, is to create lighting designs yourself.

- Working with your design practically will make it memorable when it comes to the written exam.
- If you are new to lighting, you will gain practical knowledge and technical language that could be useful in the exam and in real life.
- It is also fun!

A student production of *DNA* at the Technical University of Berlin. The warm colour and high intensity of the spotlight on Adam suggests sunlight. This contrasts starkly with the very low intensity and cold colours on the rest of the gang, indicating the darkness of their behaviour.

DESIGN TIP

There is a useful interview with *DNA* designer Simon Daw and clips from his video ideas boards in the Resources section of his website: https://simondaw.com.

Why is it useful to create a lighting design for the set text?

LOOK HERE

'Introduction to lighting design' on pages 16–17 will develop your thinking.

DESIGN TIP

Using specialist design language is one of the most important things you can learn to do.

What early decisions about lighting need to be made?

Once you are familiar with the whole play, ask yourself:

Will non-naturalistic lighting work with the production style?

What do I want to communicate to the audience?

How else can I enhance the artistic intentions and mood and atmosphere? Gobos? Colour?

Are special effects needed?

Creating a mood board

Mood boards help a designer to think about style, atmosphere, colour and artistic intentions in terms of impact and meaning. They could be digital or produced on paper or card.

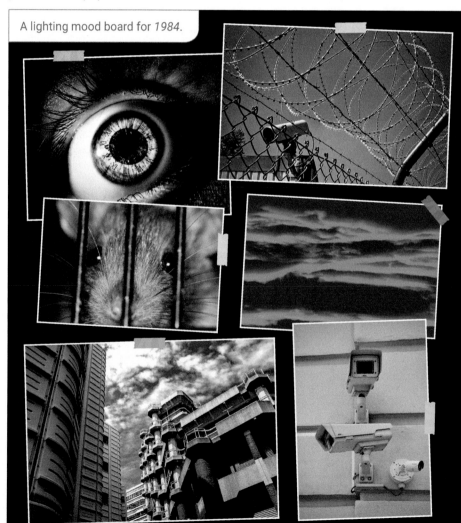

A lighting mood board for *1984*.

TASK 7.6

With a partner, discuss what lighting effects the creator of this mood board might produce.

1 To begin your own mood board, quickly think of ten adjectives for your text. Words for *1984* might include: *oppressive, frightening, violent, rebellious*.

2 Gather images that match your adjectives in some way.

3 Move on to think about suitable nouns, such as *surveillance, desk lamp, rat, diary,* and gather images for them with the same 'feel' as those for your adjectives.

4 Now think about how to organise these images onto the page. They could overlap or be grouped in ways that inspire you.

5 You could also add pictures or actual items showing colours and textures, such as red, glass and metal bars.

6 With a partner, discuss lighting effects suggested by your mood board.

Careful lighting that considers colour, intensity and use of shadow creates atmosphere. Here, this is enhanced with a smoke effect.

Planning and documenting your lighting design

TASK 7.8

1 After reading the play, begin a version of this table with factual, stylistic and atmospheric clues that could influence lighting choices.

Stage configuration:			
Location/s	Historical setting	Style, genre and atmosphere	Time of day, season, weather

2 Taking your mood board and the table above as a guide, begin to make some decisions about your design (as much as you can so far).

- What will the stage configuration be? Where will the audience sit?
- How will locations be suggested?
- What are the main moods and atmospheres?
- How might you fit in with the colour palette of set and costume?

If you decide to complete your lighting design, you could create the documentation that would allow it to be operated during a performance.

TASK 7.9

1 Select a section of your set text that offers plenty of opportunities for interesting lighting and transitions.

2 Make a list of the lighting effects that you want to create.

3 Read sections in Chapter 1 to help you make notes about how you could create those effects.

TASK 7.10

1 Have a go at creating a cue sheet and lighting plot for your chosen extract.

2 If you can, work with actors to perform the extract, so that you can operate some lighting yourself.

LOOK HERE

'Angles, colour and intensity', pages 22–25, and 'Research for lighting', page 29, provide inspiration and advice on achieving lighting effects.

'Types of stage lantern', pages 18–20, will help you with technical language.

Exam practice

You need to practise how you will respond in the written exam itself. If you have prepared well, it should not be too daunting.

A potential risk in any exam is running out of time. You need to be ready to write confidently and fairly rapidly as soon as you have understood the question. Completing the tasks in this section will put you in the best possible position.

The following task encourages you to think about possible lighting designs for your play and how they might communicate meaning. The format might be different from the exam questions, but is useful for any type of question from Section A. Try it for the full range of staging configurations and you will be expertly prepared.

TASK 7.11

Describe two lighting effects you would use in your chosen extract. Give reasons for your ideas, including the meaning you wish to communicate. You could consider:

- your choice of stage configuration and audience position
- use of colour, angles and intensity
- potential use of special effects, gobos and projections.

Working with an example answer

TASK 7.12

1 Highlight and check your understanding of the key words in this question:

> With reference to one key extract in the play, explain how you would light a stage production of *100*.
>
> In your answer refer to:
> - audience position
> - production style
> - atmosphere
> - special effects
>   (including the use of colour)   [15 marks]

2 Label the example answer on the following page with:

   F – Focus on the question

   Ex – Supporting example

   T – Appropriate technical language

   U – Understanding and knowledge of lighting in the performance.

3 Use the mark scheme to decide on a band and then a mark out of 15.

The following response is about Ketu's memory in *100*.

I would use lighting in this extract to add atmosphere, suggest location and to support the actors with the effects they create with their voices and movements. The production style is minimalist and I would use an expressive, atmospheric style of lighting to support this.

At the start of the extract, I would flood the stage with warm colours such as Chrome Orange (Lee 179) and Deep Amber (Lee 104) to help create the African location of Ketu's memory. I would slowly fade the lights up (over 5 seconds) to an intensity of around 70%. This bright lighting would create the atmosphere of hot sunshine. I would also use fresnels, with no colour filters, to light Ketu and the other performers. The light will need to come from the front to illuminate the performers clearly as the audience are facing an end-on stage. Some white light will be needed for visibility, as the use of only yellows and oranges would be too dark. I would also use two overlapping gobos of tightly formed leaves to suggest the rainforest at the start of the extract, but, rather than use green or blue filters, I would use white light to cut through the yellows and oranges. This would be purposefully non-naturalistic as lighting supports the narrative for this very short sequence.

The gobos would snap out when Ketu says, 'Life in my village was not easy...' The intensity of the orange lighting would slowly be reduced to around 40% in preparation for the lighting effect for 'Ketu follows the course of the sun's shadow over a day.'

To support the narrative and follow an expressive style, I would use a sequence of five spotlights to create the effect of the sun moving from east to west in an arc. Two profile spotlights would be in the wings, around knee height, at SL and SR. I would use Deep Amber filters and an intensity of around 50% to represent the sun lower in the sky. The three other spots would be located at equal distances along the back bar, where I would use a deeper orange colour and higher intensity to suggest the sun's brightness. Ideally using manual faders for control, I would create a kind of time-lapse effect by overlapped crossfading from SL to SR over a 7-second period, timed to coincide with Ketu making the arc with his stick. These lanterns would be focused to the side and over the top of Ketu with a white spot from the front shining on his head and shoulders. It would be tightly focused so that his features can be seen clearly.

DESIGN TIP

You might find it helpful to memorise a few filter colours that would be suitable for your set text.

Lee Filters colour temperature set of gels.

TASK 7.13

Test yourself.

1 Choose an extract from your set text of around 80 lines.

2 Have a go at the question in Task 7.26 under exam conditions. Allow yourself no more than 20 minutes.

3 Get feedback, if possible, and use it ti improve your writing.

ASSESSMENT CHECK

Section B assesses AO4: 'Analyse and evaluate your own work and the work of others.'

LOOK HERE

Pages 135–137 will help you understand what *analyse* and *evaluate* mean and how to write about them.

DESIGN TIP

The way lighting worked with sound and set or contributed to atmosphere and context would be valuable information to include in your exam.

TASK 7.14

1 Study any notes about lighting that you made after seeing the performance.

2 Draw a quick sketch of the set and mark lighting effects.

3 Annotate it with details of the lighting that created impact or otherwise contributed to meaning and mood. What do you remember about the lighting, and why?

4 Discuss the lighting with classmates. Pooling your memories will help you to recall the experience.

ANALYSING AND EVALUATING LIGHTING IN LIVE THEATRE (SECTION B)

In this part of the exam, you might be asked to give a detailed analysis and evaluation of the lighting design in a performance you have seen. You should justify your opinions with well-chosen examples. You are also aiming to use technical language.

You will need to:

- refer to **two** scenes or moments
- **evaluate** rather than describe (use judgements using words like *powerful, impact, exciting, confusing*)
- give your **personal** response (*I felt… I thought… I was moved by… because…*).

Preparation for a lighting design question

The tasks and student examples on these pages help you to:

- analyse and evaluate the use of set to communicate meaning to the audience, including reference to the **style** of the production
- analyse and evaluate your own response to the lighting as an audience member.
- use detailed and focused examples from **both** chosen scenes/moments.

Research and discussion

Look in the show programme, theatre marketing material and online for information about the lighting designer. Major productions and tours often have images, information and reviews online. Photographs in particular will help to remind you of details of the lighting and how they complemented other elements of the performance.

Remember that you were a member of the audience. The exam will ask you to comment on the impact lighting had on the audience. Share your different responses with your classmates, but aim to write about your own viewpoints in the exam. You are expected to make a critical evaluation.

Production style

Production style might be difficult to get your head around. Think about words such as:

- **Naturalistic** – Does the lighting aim to create a realistic effect? How?
- **Non-naturalistic** – Does the lighting use special effects or colours that you would not expect to see in that location?
- **Atmospheric** – Is lighting used to heighten mood or atmosphere? How?

Even if you find it hard to put a name to the overall production style, you can refer to aspects of the lighting design and link them to one of the production styles above, or another, such as **Brechtian**, **symbolic** or **abstract**. The important thing is to refer to production style in some detail.

Also consider how lighting combines with other design elements such as sound and set, as this might affect the overall style of the production.

Evaluation as a skill

TASK 7.15

Read page 39 carefully and complete Task 1.18, using examples from the live performance. Remember that you are evaluating someone else's lighting design, rather than your own.

SIGNPOST

'Evaluating your lighting design' on page 39 gives guidance on evaluative writing about lighting.

Lighting design evaluation

The exam question will ask you about a design element in two moments or scenes, but it will not specify which moments to write about. So, evaluate those that stood out for you as examples of effective lighting. Ideally, they will be contrasting moments to give you the opportunity to write about a greater range and avoid repetition.

TASK 7.16

1 If you can, find a copy of the script for the live performance you are writing about. Browse through it until you find two moments where you remember lighting having an impact on you.

2 Try to remember why the lighting had an impact. Consider transitions between lighting states.

3 Write at least two paragraphs of critical judgement, which include:
- subject-specific language, such as *intensity, transitions, colour gels, automated lights*, and so on
- how lighting enhanced style and helped to create settings
- how lighting changed the look of the set and the effect that had on atmosphere and meaning
- evaluation supported by detailed examples, such as, *The use of… was powerful because… and I was impressed by… because it made me feel/think…*

4 Swap your writing with someone else's for feedback.

Note the effective use of lighting in *Anything Goes* (at the Ahmanson Theatre, Los Angeles). What is the effect of putting lights behind the portholes? The couple downstage are lit from the front. How does their appearance differ from the couples on the platforms?

Working with an example answer

The mark scheme is a valuable tool when you are preparing for the exam. In the tasks below, you can use it to assess a sample answer and then practise one of your own.

TASK 7.17

1 Highlight the key words in the following example question:

> Analyse and evaluate how lighting was used in two key scenes to add atmosphere and communicate meaning to the audience. In your answer, refer to:
>
> - the production style
> - how lighting was used to add atmosphere and communicate meaning
> - your response to the performance as an audience member. [15 marks]

2 Now check your understanding of the key words.

3 Annotate the example answer on the facing page. Look for:

F – Focus on the question, including production style

Ex – Example to support argument or point

T – Appropriate technical language

U – Understanding and knowledge of lighting design in relation to the performance

E – Evaluation in terms of how successful the lighting was.

4 Use the AO4 mark scheme to decide on a band and a mark out of 15.

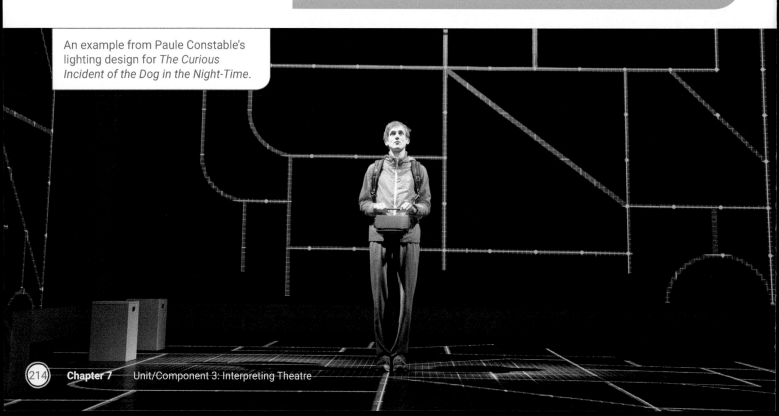

An example from Paule Constable's lighting design for *The Curious Incident of the Dog in the Night-Time*.

I saw *The Curious Incident of the Dog in the Night-Time* at the Lowry in Salford.

The lighting designer, Paule Constable, worked closely with the set designer to make the visual aspects of the play highly technical in terms of production style. She created something that I found magical.

The lighting works very closely with the set, which is basically a box. It represents Christopher's brain. How Christopher's brain works is one of the main themes in the play. In this way, lighting is a key element to communicating meaning.

The lighting for the scene where Christopher is describing his 'dream come true' of being an astronaut communicated his love and knowledge about space in a really atmospheric way. Low-intensity midnight blue washes flooded Christopher as he was 'flown' by the ensemble. It made me feel that he was really floating in space. For this high-tech production style, pixelated 'stars' and video projections of galaxies swirled around Christopher and around us. The floor and the three sides of the box are made of something that can be pixelated, so lighting happened alongside the images that appeared on all of the surfaces. I felt as though I was looking into a box full of moving images and light.

The bright, stark white against the deep blue was mesmerising. Christopher was largely lit from above, which cast the ensemble who were flying him into shadow. Lighting transitions for this scene were fades rather than snaps to hold the atmosphere of drifting in space. When I thought back on it later, I was very impressed by how all the complex lighting effects were co-ordinated to take me into Christopher's head (in space). In a highly technical piece like this, the collaboration between the production staff and the performers must be key to gaining the overall effect.

The lighting contributed to the pace of the show, which suggested the speed of Christopher's brain. Nearly all the lighting was cold white to reflect Christopher's mathematical, clean and ordered brain functions. Slower, more reflective scenes used special lighting effects for a different atmosphere, such as when Christopher's mum appears for the first time as a memory. Although Christopher is shown in the usual white spotlight, his mother is bathed in a warmer, straw-coloured, softly focused spotlight. This helped me to understand Christopher's warm memories of his mother. Location was communicated well too. The scene is set on a beach and the shallow cubes that make the sides of the acting area are flooded with blue light to represent the sea.

TASK 7.18

Test yourself.

1 Based on the live performance you have chosen, answer the question in Task 7.17 on the previous page.

   Use the AO4 mark scheme and other tasks to guide you. Try to work under exam conditions, giving yourself 25 minutes.

2 If possible, ask another student or your teacher to mark your answer. Can you make improvements based on their comments?

DESIGN TIP

Include as much detail as possible in your answers. Highlight your evaluative judgements by using terms such as 'effective' and 'powerful impact'.

ASSESSMENT CHECK

In Section A, you should demonstrate 'knowledge and understanding of how theatre is developed and performed' (AO3).

SOUND DESIGN FOR THE SET TEXT (SECTION A)

Revising sound design in your set text

TASK 7.19

1 Research and make notes on the social and historical contexts of the text. You need to know when it was first performed and in what stage configuration.

2 Use your research to complete your own version of the table below. (Examples have been given using *100*.)

	How sound design could communicate meaning
Time and location: • The void • Memory locations, such as African village, motorbike race, a park.	• Naturalistic soundscapes and underscoring. • Ambient drone sounds for the void.
Themes: • Death and dying • Re-evaluating life • Memories.	• Music in major and minor keys will help to draw together themes and moods at specific moments. • Non-naturalistic soundscapes and underscoring for void scenes.
Context: First performed at the Edinburgh Festival in 2002.	• The original production confined the use of sound to that made by the performers on stage. But, sound could be live and recorded.
Genre/style/atmosphere • Blending of reality and fantasy • The magic of theatre.	• Live sound effects created by the actors. • Atmospheric diegetic and non-diegetic sounds.

DESIGN TIP

• Answer every aspect of the question carefully and stay focused on the question.

• Give reasons for your ideas.

• Talk about production styles.

• Explain how your choice of sound communicates meaning.

• Be creative.

• Be able to write about your set text in any stage configuration.

100 is characteristically minimal in its production style, particularly set and costume. That could mean, however, that sound is particularly important in communicating meaning. In productions such as this, live sounds performed by the actors were used to great effect. What sounds, if any, would you use in this scene?

Thinking as a sound designer for your set text

You will not know in advance what extract you will be given, but you will know which play it will be from. Ask yourself the following questions:

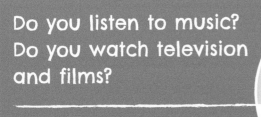

Do you listen to music? Do you watch television and films?

If yes, you will be able to harness your knowledge of how sound can be used creatively.

Next time you listen to music or watch something that has interesting soundconcentrate on the meaning and atmosphere being enhanced. Listen out for diegetic and non-diegetic sounds in a film or identify the dominant emotion or mood in a piece of music.

To start you off, can you think of three ways you could explore the text? This should you to become more familiar with the text. The best way to revise, however, is to create sound designs yourself.

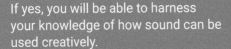

Why is it useful to create sound design for the set text?

- Working practically will make your design memorable for the exam.
- If you are new to sound design, you will gain practical knowledge and subject-specific language that will be useful in the exam and in real life.
- It is also fun!

What early decisions about sound need to be made?

Once you are familiar with the whole play, ask yourself:

Will non-diegetic sound work with the chosen style of the production?
(A purely diegetic and naturalistic design would only include the sounds that the actors would hear.)

What period of time is the production set in?

DESIGN TIP

Using specialist design language is one of the most important things you can learn to do.

LOOK HERE

'Introduction to sound design' on pages 42–43 will develop your thinking.

DESIGN TIP

The use of underscoring and soundscapes adds an extra dimension to sound design.

Creating a mood board

Mood boards help a designer to think about style, atmosphere, sound and artistic intentions in terms of impact and meaning. They could be digital or produced on paper or card.

A sound mood board for *100*.

TASK 7.21

1 To begin your own mood board, quickly think of ten adjectives for your set text. Words for *100* might include: *exciting, thoughtful, strong, intimidating*, and so on.

2 Gather images that match your adjectives in some way.

3 Think about suitable nouns, such as *tube train, motorbike, forest*, and gather images with the same 'feel' as for the adjectives.

4 Think about how to organise these images. They could overlap or be grouped in ways that inspire you.

5 You could also add pictures or items showing colours and textures, such as leaves, glass/mirror (for water) and metal.

6 Ask a partner what sounds your mood board suggests.

TASK 7.23

1 Select a section of your text that offers opportunities for interesting sounds and music.

2 List the sound effects and type of music you think would add the right atmosphere.

3 Make notes on how to find and cue those effects.

4 Set up a computer folder for your effects and music.

5 Play your design to your classmates. Use their feedback to evaluate your work.

TASK 7.20

With a partner, discuss what sound effects the creator of this mood board might produce.

Planning and documenting your sound design

TASK 7.22

1 After reading the whole play, begin a table with factual, stylistic and atmospheric clues that could influence sound design.

Locations	Historical period	Style, genre and atmosphere	Sounds required by the script/stage directions

2 Taking your mood board and the table above as a guide, begin to make some decisions about your design (as much as you can so far).

- What will the stage configuration be? Where will the audience sit? (This effects where you will place your speakers.)
- How will locations be suggested?
- How will the time period of the play be indicated?
- What are the main moods and atmospheres?
- How much non-diegetic sound might you want?
- Do you need your sounds to fit in with changes in lighting?

Exam practice

You need to practise how to respond in the written exam. If you have prepared well, it should not be too daunting.

A potential risk in any exam is running out of time. You need to be ready to write confidently and fairly rapidly as soon as you have understood the question and decided which design option to write about. Completing the tasks in this section will put you in the best possible position.

Task 7.25, below, encourages you to think about possible lighting designs for your play and how they might communicate meaning. The format might be different from the exam questions, but is useful for any type of question from Section A. Try it for the full range of staging configurations and you will be expertly prepared.

TASK 7.25

Describe two sound effects you would use in the play. Give reasons for your ideas, including the meaning and atmosphere you wish to communicate. You could consider:

- audience position
- diegetic and non-diegetic sound
- recorded and live sound
- special effects
- music
- volume and transitions.

TASK 7.24

1 Try creating a source sheet and cue sheet for an extract.

2 If you can, work with actors to perform the extract, so that you can operate the sound yourself.

 LOOK HERE

'How to document your sound design' on pages 54–55 has advice on creating a source sheet and a cue sheet.

 LOOK HERE

A sample cue sheet is available on the *Designing Drama* product page at illuminatepublishing.com.

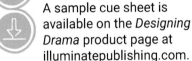

Working with an example answer

TASK 7.26

1 Highlight and make sure you understand the key words in this question:

> With reference to one key extract in the play, explain how you would use sound in a production of *1984*. In your answer, refer to:
>
> - audience position
> - production style
> - atmosphere. [15 marks]

2 Label the example answer on the following page with:

F – Focus on the three points in the question

Ex – Supporting example

T – Appropriate technical language

U – Understanding and knowledge of sound design in relation to the performance.

3 Use the mark scheme to decide on a band and then a mark out of 15.

Test yourself.

1 Choose an extract from your set text of around 80 lines.

2 Have a go at answering the question in Task 7.26 under exam conditions. Allow yourself no more than 20 minutes.

Use the AO3 mark scheme to guide you.

I would use sound design to help the audience's journey through the section where Julia and Winston are captured.

Silence is an important aspect of sound design, but there is a stage direction about halfway through the play that says 'The first real silence in the play', which suggests that sound is generally a constant background to the action. Of course, much of this is the dialogue on stage. I would, however, use this idea with recorded sound to enhance the oppressive and frightening atmosphere of the play. The production style is minimal in terms of set, with much use of technology, suggesting non-naturalism and a Brechtian style. I would contribute to this through the use of diegetic (klaxons, train whistles and so on) and non-diegetic sounds (drones and hums). A thrust stage would enable me to surround the audience with speakers to enhance the claustrophobic feel of the play.

At the start of my chosen extract, I would include a rare moment of absolute silence to intensify the moment of closeness in Winston's and Julia's relationship. This would be juxtaposed with a very loud recording of 'You are the dead', which would intensify the shock of it for the audience. The words would be a recording of O'Brien's voice, with reverb added as a special effect. I would use the 'ring' reverb to give the sound a metallic quality, in keeping with the stage direction. I would also equalise the sound, taking out the lower register and enhancing the middle and upper register, with the aim of a tinny, train-announcer kind of tone. This effect would be used for all of the 'Voice' announcements in this section.

The 'almighty crash' of the men in uniform entering the room would be achieved through a combination of carefully chosen effects mixed and played at very high volume. Julia's scream needs to be terrifying and is described as a 'howl'. I would achieve this effect by distorting the actor's voice through the use of feedback.

What sound effects and music – if any – might be suitable for this early scene from *1984*?

ANALYSING AND EVALUATING SOUND IN LIVE THEATRE (SECTION B)

In this part of the exam, you might be asked to give a detailed analysis and evaluation of the sound design in a performance you have seen. You should justify your opinions with well-chosen examples. You are also aiming to use technical language.

You will need to:

- refer to **two** scenes or moments
- **evaluate** rather than describe (use judgements using words like *powerful, impact, exciting, confusing*)
- give your **personal** response (*I felt... I thought... I was moved by... because...*).

Preparation for a sound design question

The tasks and student examples on these pages help you to:

- analyse and evaluate the use of sound to communicate meaning to the audience, including reference to the **style** of the production
- analyse and evaluate your own response to the sound as an audience member.
- use detailed and focused examples from **both** chosen scenes/moments.

Research and discussion

Look in the show programme, theatre marketing material and online for information about the sound designer to add to your exam notes. Major productions and tours often have images, information and reviews online. Photographs in particular will help to remind you of details of the sound and how it complemented other elements of the performance, although these cannot be included in your notes. You might also be able to find interviews with sound designers.

Remember that you were a member of the audience. The exam will ask you to comment on the impact sound had on the audience. Share your different responses with your classmates, but aim to write about your own viewpoints in the exam. You are expected to make a critical evaluation.

ASSESSMENT CHECK

Section B assesses AO4: Analyse and evaluate your own work and the work of others.

Christopher Shutt with his Tony Award for his sound design in *War Horse*.

LOOK HERE

Pages 145–147 will help you understand what *analyse* and *evaluate* mean and how to write about them.

TASK 7.28

1 Study any notes about the sound design that you made after seeing the performance.
2 Make some simple sketches based on your notes and images you find.
3 Annotate them with details of sound and music that created impact or otherwise contributed to meaning and mood. What do you remember about the sound, and why?
4 Discuss the sound with classmates. Pooling your memories will help you to recall the experience.

DESIGN TIP

The way sound worked with lighting or contributed to atmosphere and context would be valuable information to include.

SIGNPOST

'Evaluating your sound design' on page 63 gives guidance on evaluative writing about sound.

Production style

Production style might be difficult to get your head around. Think about words such as:

- **Naturalistic** – Does the sound aim to create a realistic effect? How?
- **Non-naturalistic** – Does the sound use non-diegetic sounds like drones and other special effects?
- **Minimalistic** – Is sound design used very sparingly to create a strong impact when it's used? Is silence important?
- **Atmospheric** – Does soundscape or underscoring heighten mood or atmosphere? How?

Even if you find it hard to put a name to the overall production style, you can refer to aspects of the set design and link them to one of the production styles above, or another, such as **symbolic** or **abstract**. The important thing is to refer to production style in some detail.

Also consider how the sound combines with other design elements, such as lighting, as this might affect the overall style of the production.

Evaluation as a skill
Sound design evaluation

The exam question will ask you about a specific design element in two moments or scenes, but it will not specify which moments to write about. So, evaluate the moments that stood out for you as examples of how sound was used effectively. Ideally, they will be contrasting moments to give you the opportunity to write about a greater range and avoid repetition.

TASK 7.29

1 If you can, find a copy of the script for the live performance you are writing about. Browse through it until you find a section where you remember sound having an impact on you.

2 Try to remember the sound at key points in this section. These could be as a single moment or a whole scene or more. Consider soundscapes and the mixing of sound effects as well as the use of music.

3 Write at least two paragraphs of critical judgement, which include:
   - subject-specific language, such as *volume levels*, *soundscape*, *live*, *recorded*, and so on
   - how sound contributed to the style of the production
   - atmosphere or meaning that sound enhanced for the audience
   - evaluations supported by details, such as, *The use of... was powerful because... and I was impressed by... because it made me feel/think...*

4 Swap your writing with someone else's for feedback. You could use the bullet points above as a checklist.

Working with an example answer

The mark scheme is a valuable tool when you are preparing for the exam. In the following tasks, you can use it to assess a sample answer and then practise one of your own.

Joey faces down the tank in *War Horse*.

DESIGN TIP

Include as much detail as possible in your answers. Highlight your evaluative judgements by using terms such as 'effective' and 'powerful impact'.

DESIGN TIP

When you feel ready to practise under exam conditions, give yourself a maximum of 25 minutes to complete your answer.

In this touching scene from *War Horse,* the young foal Joey is helped to graze by three animators.

I saw War Horse at the National Theatre. Christopher Shutt's sound design uses both live and recorded sound to enhance meaning and atmosphere. The production style was minimalist in terms of physical set, but very rich in its powerful use of projection, puppetry, costume, lighting and sound. The play came over as very realistic in terms of how it made me feel, even though I was looking at quite a non-naturalistic style. Sound was hugely important in creating this effect.

One of the sound design highlights is an excellent example of how all the elements came together to conjure up the period, location and atmosphere of the First World War battlefields. It was the moment when the tank comes onto the stage. It was shocking in terms of its scale and impact. The performers operating the tank wore special speakers. Realistic recorded sounds of a tank engine were amplified from these at a very loud volume, which gave me, in the audience, an incredible and overwhelming sense of the horror that the horse and the characters must have felt. Further speakers were placed at the sides of the stage and all around the auditorium, which intensified the sound on stage, pulling me powerfully into the action. The added recorded sound of heavy artillery played at very high volume made the experience really frightening.

Another scene which had a lot of impact in terms of sound created a totally different atmosphere. It was when Albert is building his relationship with Joey early in the play. Live sound effects were used when the performers used their voices to create the sounds of Joey. His snorting, whinnying and so on were synchronised with the puppeteers' movements. Recorded sounds could have been used, but the live sounds had more life and power. The three puppeteers had separate radio microphones, and then the sound was mixed and transmitted live as one sound by the sound engineer. I think this contributed significantly to my sense of the horse being alive. I also felt that these important moments between Albert and Joey were carefully crafted by the sound designer to create the tenderness of their relationship. Much of this effect came from the fact that the sounds the 'horse' made were gentle and at a relatively low volume to match the tone of Albert's voice. Diegetic sound was also introduced in the form of the sounds of rural birds, which was mixed with music at moments to help create the context of the scene. This was important as the stage itself was quite bare.

TASK 7.31

Test yourself.

1 Based on the live performance you have chosen, answer the question in Task 7.30.

   Use the AO4 mark scheme and other tasks in this chapter to guide you.

2 If possible, ask another student or your teacher to mark your answer. Can you use their comments to improve it?

SET DESIGN FOR THE SET TEXT (SECTION A)

Revising set design for your set text

TASK 7.32

1 Research and make notes on the social, historic, political and economic contexts of the text. You need to know when it was first performed and in what stage configuration.

2 Use your research to complete your own version of the table below. (Examples have been given using *Romeo and Juliet*.)

	How set design could communicate meaning, theme, context and atmosphere
Setting (time and location): A hot summer in Verona.	• Modern-day Italian-style scenery and props.
Themes: • Love • Fate • Family • Women's position/role.	• Symbolic items such as giant dice for fate – also used to create levels. • Projections of Venice or Verona landmarks.
Context: • Elizabethan era • First performed 1597 on a thrust stage.	• Balcony?
Mood/atmosphere	• Symbolic use of red to suggest danger as well as love/romance.

Thinking as a set designer for your set text

You will not know in advance what extract you will be given, but you will know which play it will be from.

To start you off, can you think of three ways you could explore the text? Anything that helps you to become familiar with the text on the page and in performance is worth spending time on. The best way to revise, however, is to create set designs yourself.

What do you think the set should look like?

Once you are familiar with the whole play, begin to imagine how the set might look.

It is often useful to study the original designs for the play. The designer will have had an excellent understanding of the playwright and director's artistic intentions and the circumstances of its production. *DNA* is a good example of a very particular design that used projections to suggest the various locations. You will want to put your own creativity to the test, however. How could you suggest a variety of locations in a different way?

FOCUS

Explaining your set design ideas.

ASSESSMENT CHECK

In Section A, you should demonstrate 'knowledge and understanding of how theatre is developed and performed' (AO3).

DESIGN TIP

Using specialist design language is one of the most important things you can learn to do.

LOOK HERE

See pages 12–14 and 204 for reminders of stage configurations and positioning.

DESIGN TIP

• Answer every aspect of the question carefully and stay focused on the question.
• Give reasons for your ideas.
• Talk about production styles.
• Explain how your choice of colour communicates meaning.
• Be creative.
• Be able to write about your set text in any stage configuration.

DESIGN TIP

There is an interesting conversation with designer Simon Daw in the Resources section at https://simondaw.com. You can also see his video mood boards and model boxes for the original production of *DNA*.

A set design mood board for *DNA*.

Creating a mood board

Mood boards help a designer to think about style and atmosphere and artistic intentions in terms of impact and meaning. They could be digital or produced on paper or card.

TASK 7.33

1   To begin your own mood board, quickly think of ten adjectives for your set text. Words for *DNA* might include *sharp, tangled, cold, grey.*

2   Gather images that match your adjectives in some way.

3   Move on to think about suitable nouns, such as *street, wood, teenager,* and gather images for them with the same 'feel' as those for your adjectives.

4   Now think about how to organise these images onto the page. They could overlap or be grouped in ways that inspire you.

5   You could also add pictures or actual items showing colours and textures, such as rope or wire.

Planning your set design

TASK 7.34

1   After you have read the whole play, begin your own version of this table with factual, stylistic and atmospheric clues that could influence set design choices.

Stage configuration:			
Historical period	**Locations/s**	**Genre and style**	**Atmosphere/s**

2   Taking your mood board and the table above as a guide, make some decisions about your design (as much as you can so far).

- What will the stage configuration be? Where will the audience sit?
- Will the set be permanent, changed for different scenes, or composite (all locations on stage at the same time)?
- How will locations be suggested?
- Will your set be naturalistic or abstract?
- What colour palette would you use?
- What textures and materials would work well (for instance, smooth and shiny metal or rough and earthy untreated wood)?
- What should be on the floor of the acting area?

This version of *DNA* at Queen's Theatre, Hornchurch, takes a simple, stark, but naturalistic, approach to set design, for a thrust stage.

DESIGN TIP

Deciding on your stage configuration (end on, in the round, and so on) is a vital early step.

Documenting your set design

LOOK HERE
There is another example of a set design sketch on page 71.

Why is it useful to document a set design that is unlikely to be constructed?

- Ground plans and sketches in your answer will show your skills and present an extremely clear idea of your design. These are often quicker to produce than a detailed description.
- You can annotate your drawing, which will be quicker than writing in prose.
- A model box that you might make during revision would allow you to explore how practical your design is. You can move things around and see how it would look.
- Working with your design practically will make it memorable when it comes to the written exam.
- If you are new to set design, you will gain practical knowledge and subject-specific language that could be useful in the exam and in real life.
- It is also fun!

DESIGN TIP
If you create a ground plan, you could base it on these approximate sizes:
- end on: 5 x 3 metres
- in the round: 4 x 4 metres
- traverse: 3 or 4 metres wide.

DESIGN TIP
You don't need to build your set design, but you could construct a simple one if you are rehearsing sections of the text in lessons.

> This labelled sketch of a set for *Blood Brothers* provides a lot of information in a few words!

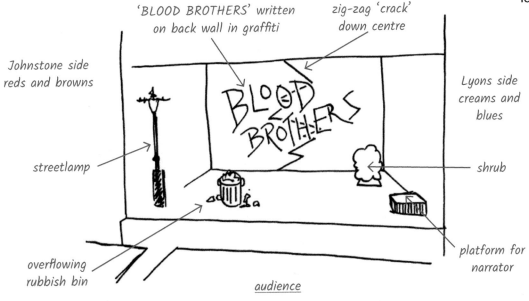

'BLOOD BROTHERS' written on back wall in graffiti

zig-zag 'crack' down centre

Johnstone side reds and browns

Lyons side creams and blues

streetlamp

shrub

overflowing rubbish bin

platform for narrator

audience

TASK 7.35

1 Draw some rough sketches of possible designs for your set text and decide which works best. You could work in pencil or add colour and annotations, if you wish.
2 When you have a sketch that you are happy with, follow the instructions on pages 71–72 to create a ground plan.
3 It is useful to create a 3D model, using the guidance on pages 73–74.

Exam practice

You need to practise how you will respond in the written exam itself. If you have prepared well, it should not be too daunting.

A potential risk in any exam is running out of time. You need to be ready to write confidently and fairly rapidly as soon as you have understood the question. Completing the tasks in this section will put you in the best possible position.

The following task encourages you to think about possible lighting designs for your play and how they might communicate meaning. The format might be different from the exam questions, but is useful for any type of question from Section A. Try it for the full range of staging configurations and you will be expertly prepared.

TASK 7.36

This task is designed to make you think about possible set designs for your set text and how they might communicate meaning. Although the format of this task may well be different to any question that appears in the written exam, it is good preparation for any type of question that appears in Section A.

Make a simple sketch of a suitable set design for an extract of your set text. Annotate it with brief explanations of your design and the effect you want different elements to have on your audience.

You should consider:
- Your choice of stage configuration and audience position
- Use of colour and materials
- Set dressings / props
- Communicating meaning

TASK 7.37

1 Highlight the key words in the following example question:

> With reference to **one** key extract in the play, explain how you would use an **end on** stage configuration for a production of DNA.
>
> In your answer, refer to:
> - audience position
> - production style
> - atmosphere
> - set and props (including the use of colour).
>
> [15 marks]

2 Now check your understanding of the key words, using a glossary if necessary.

3 Label the example answer on the following page with:

F – Focus on the question

Ex – Supporting example

T – Appropriate technical language

U – Understanding and knowledge of set design skill in relation to the performance.

4 Then use the AO3 mark scheme to decide on a band and then a mark out of 15.

DESIGN TIP

Try to use appropriate technical terms. Using them to annotate a sketch or ground plan could save you time.

TASK 7.38

Test yourself.

1 Choose an extract from your set text of around 80 lines. Answer the question in Task 7.37, staging your extract **in the round**.

DNA was first staged in 2007 in an end on configuration. I am also using end on staging and a representative style for the section in Part 3 where Adam has reappeared and the group are trying to decide what to do about it. I would use set design to enhance the fragmenting of the gang in this extract. I would also use it to show how some characters, such as Adam and Brian, are closer to being 'natural' human beings than the others.

The main elements of my set design are four three-sided flats, each mounted on a trolley with brakes. The DSL trolley is on a 20cm raised platform to help the performers show status, for example when Phil is taking the situation in hand, saying 'Everything is going to be fine.'

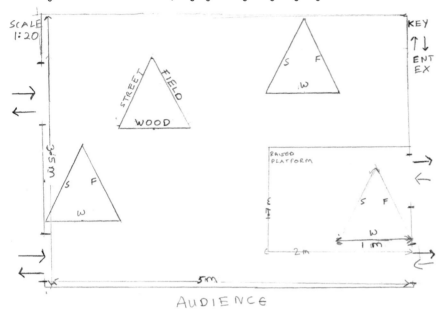

This ground plan (configured for the extract) helps to make the set design clearer.

The positioning of the flats that represent the woods is intended to build tension in an already tense scene: they enable characters to emerge and disappear through the 'trees'. One moment where this would have an impact is when 'Brian takes Adam off'. Brian could lead Adam behind the CSR flat. A moment later, Adam could reappear and step towards the group only for Brian to pull him away again. The audience would see the two boys making their way slowly between two or three of the flats, extending their exit. This should enhance the audience's sense that this is a tense and pivotal moment. Leah's line 'What's going on?' would not be given until everyone was sure that the two boys had gone. The tension from the prolonged silence would communicate itself to the audience.

I would collaborate with the lighting designer to use a gobo to create a dappled effect on the stage floor, which would be painted dull gun-metal grey. This neutral colour could work for all three locations in the play and be pale enough to use with coloured lighting. The actor playing Adam could also take real elements, such as twigs, from the nearest flat and smell them or pretend to eat insects from them. This would certainly help the audience's understanding that he is animalistic now. Phil would have a carrier bag filled with empty wrappers and a packet of Starbursts. Later in the scene, he will empty it out onto the floor. The Starbursts, left scattered on the floor, will remind the audience of Phil and Leah's abandoned friendship.

The untreated plywood flats that represent the wood would be roughly painted and textured to suggest trees. A base layer of forest-green matte paint would be painted with leaves in sombre autumn colours, such as deep orange and faded yellow. Pieces of open-weave hessian would be randomly fixed to the flats so that twigs and small pieces of foliage could be attached.

ANALYSING AND EVALUATING SET DESIGN IN LIVE THEATRE (SECTION B)

In this part of the exam, you might be asked to give a detailed analysis and evaluation of the set design in a performance you have seen. You should justify your opinions with well-chosen examples. You are also aiming to use technical language. You will need to:

- refer to **two** scenes or moments
- **evaluate** rather than describe (use judgements using words like *powerful, impact, exciting, confusing*)
- give your **personal** response (*I felt... I thought... I was moved by... because...*).

Preparation for a set design question

The tasks and student examples on these pages help you to:

- analyse and evaluate the use of set to communicate meaning to the audience, including reference to the **style** of the production
- analyse and evaluate your own response to the set as an audience member.
- use detailed and focused examples from **both** chosen scenes/moments.

Research and discussion

Look in the show programme, marketing material and online for information about the set designer. Major productions often have images, information and reviews online. These will remind you of details in the set and how they complemented other elements of the performance.

Remember that you were a member of the audience. The exam will ask you about the impact design had on the audience. Share your responses with your classmates, but make your own critical evaluation in the exam.

TASK 7.39

1 Study any notes about the set that you made after seeing the show.
2 Make some simple sketches based on your notes and images you find.
3 Annotate them with details of the set that created impact or conveyed meaning and mood. What do you remember about the set, and why?
4 Discuss the set with your classmates. Pooling your memories is valid and will help you to recall the experience of the production.

Production style

Production style might be difficult to get your head around. Think about:

- **Naturalistic** – Does the set aim to create a realistic effect? How?
- **Non-naturalistic** – Does the set use symbolic or representational features rather than scenery that looks like the real thing?
- **Minimalistic** – Is scenery, furniture and set dressing used very sparingly? Why might that decision have been taken?

Even if you find it hard to name the overall production style, you can link aspects of the set to one of the production styles above, or another, such as **atmospheric**, **symbolic** or **realistic**, or to a practitioner such as Katie Mitchell or Bertholt Brecht. The important thing is to discuss production style in detail.

Evaluation as a skill

SIGNPOST

'Evaluating your set design' on pages 80–81 gives guidance on evaluative writing about sets.

TASK 7.40

1 Read 'Evaluating your set design' carefully and complete Task 3.12.
2 Complete Task 3.13 with examples from the live performance. Remember that you are evaluating someone else's set design, not your own.

DESIGN TIP

Consider including one or two of your sketches in your notes for the exam.

Set design evaluation

The exam question will ask you about a specific design element in two moments or scenes of the production, but it will not specify which moments to write about. So, evaluate moments that stood out as examples of how the set was used to good effect.

Ideally, they will be contrasting moments to give you the opportunity to write about a greater range and avoid repetition.

TASK 7.41

1 If you can, find a copy of the script for the performance. Look for a moment where you remember the set having an impact.
2 Try to remember what the set looked like and why it had impact.
3 Write at least two paragraphs of critical judgement, which include:
   - subject-specific language, such as *flats*, *gauze*, *trucks* and so on
   - how the set contributed to the style of the production
   - how lighting changed the look of the set and the effect that had
   - the way the set was used by the actors and the effect of that
   - atmosphere or meaning that was enhanced for the audience
   - evaluations supported by detailed examples, such as, *The use of... was powerful because... and I was impressed by... because...*
4 Swap your writing with someone else's for feedback. You could use the bullet points above as a checklist.
5 Repeat for a second key moment.

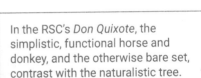

In the RSC's *Don Quixote*, the simplistic, functional horse and donkey, and the otherwise bare set, contrast with the naturalistic tree.

Working with an example answer

The mark scheme is a valuable tool when you are preparing for the exam. In the following tasks, you can use it to assess a sample answer and then practise one of your own.

TASK 7.42

1 Highlight the key words in the following example question:

> Analyse and evaluate how set was used in two key scenes to communicate meaning to the audience. In your answer, refer to:
> - the production style
> - how set was used to add atmosphere and communicate meaning
> - your response to the performance as an audience member. [15 marks]

2 Now check your understanding of these key words, using a glossary if necessary.

3 Annotate the following example response, about *Blood Brothers*, with:

F – Focus on all of the points in the question

Ex – Example to support argument or point

T – Appropriate technical language

U – Understanding and knowledge of set design in relation to the performance

E – Evaluation in terms of how successful the set was.

4 Use the AO4 mark scheme to decide on a band and then a mark out of 15.

I saw Blood Brothers at the Belgrade in Coventry on an end-on stage. The designer, Andy Walmsley, created a set which, as for many musicals, needed a production style that could shift easily in terms of multiple locations.

The set had composite elements, such as the two lines of house fronts that cleverly represented the different lifestyles of the Johnstones and the Lyons. There were many non-composite elements too, which could be quickly employed to change location and communicate meaning, such as the washing line. This suited the naturalistic aspect of the production style.

During the first part of Act I, we are introduced to the life of Mrs Johnstone and her children. The neutral dark-grey flooring, that was slightly reflective vinyl, seemed carefully designed. It was good at reflecting the colours of the lights during the song 'Marilyn Monroe', which helped me feel that Mrs Johnstone was in her own dream world.

The colour palette was largely naturalistic and combined well with the textures (of the deep red bricks for example) to create the council housing. The brickwork was painted onto large flats to create the house fronts and a wall upstage centre. Monochrome graffiti was painted onto it. The black and white letters looked harsh against the red brickwork and gave the impression of a run-down area. The house fronts were subtly different on either side of the street. The window shapes were different and a balcony outside the posh houses' first-floor windows provided other spaces where characters could overlook the action.

Levels were important in this scene, right down to the Johnstone's front step which offered an intimate space for Mrs Johnson to cradle Mickey. Something as seemingly unimportant as a front step also added realism to the whole set at moments such as when the creditors enter and leave the house with items from the house. It was details like these that made the largely naturalistic set so powerful.